Fierce Conversations

"Your book, *Fierce Conversations, Achieving Success at Work & in Life, One Conversation at a Time,* is a key component of our Leadership Alchemy Program."

—GAIL S. WILLIAMS,
NASA Goddard Space Flight Center

"Those whose conversations with coworkers or family members aren't producing the results they want will find plenty of helpful tools and assignments in this succinct guide."

—*Publishers Weekly*

"The results are . . . powerful, and Scott's workbook exercises will allow readers to have effective, life-changing fierce conversations of their own."

—*Booklist*

"Susan Scott is the master teacher of positive change through powerful communication."

—PETER NEILL,
executive director, AT&T Wireless

"If conversations are the lifeblood of our most important relationships, this book is a transfusion of ideas and inspiration. Susan Scott has written a life-affirming primer for moving us toward the conversations we need to have most."

—DOUG STONE,
coauthor of *Difficult Conversations*

continued . . .

"Practical and pragmatic. I can do something with this tomorrow."
—LINDA DUNN, Chief Torts Division,
Attorney General's Office, Washington, D.C.

"Susan Scott's emphasis on authentic communications, like all good therapy, directs readers to become conscious of their inner conflicts. She encourages readers to reach for their more authentic growth tendencies and ultimately to seek the rewards of self-actualization. She quite accurately directs readers to recognize that life's distress is often the result of inauthenticity. She builds a strong case and provides helpful tools for becoming more authentic."
—STEPHEN M. PFEIFFER, Ph.D.,
clinical psychologist and executive director,
Association for the Advancement of Psychology

"A rare and delightful blend of stimulating ideas and practical advice."
—SHELDON BOWLES, coauthor of *Gung Ho!*
Turn On the People in Any Organization

"The path to a fierce conversation is lined with the velvet words of wisdom of Susan Scott. Her deep insights artfully show us how most life problems can be solved or dissolved with a fierce conversation."
—ARIELLE FORD, president, Ford Group;
author of *Magical Souvenirs*

"A fierce conversation propels you from your mind into your guts, giving you the strength and confidence to make rapid and insightful decisions."
—VICTOR VILLASEÑOR, author of *Rain of Gold*

"When the authentic conversations so clearly described in the book catch on everywhere, it will be the end of gossip, corporate politics, bad marriages, and 360-degree feedback. *Fierce Conversations* is today's primer for success as well as for survival in our ever-changing world."
—STEPHEN C. LUNDIN, Ph.D., HARRY PAUL, and
JOHN CHRISTENSEN, coauthors of *Fish!* and *Fish! Tales*

"Susan Scott delivers a wealth of uncommon common sense . . . Her warmth and skill as a coach and counselor provide the healthy nudges we all need from time to time to jump in, get engaged, and manage ourselves and the world around us more directly, positively, and productively. It's a reminder that 'the way out is through,' and she provides great techniques for navigating the passage."

—DAVID ALLEN, author of *Getting Things Done*

"I love this book. What a refreshing departure from typical management superficialities! Susan Scott zeros in brilliantly, and charmingly, on the single most important activity of management and leadership—engagement through conversation—and she does it not by offering simplistic techniques, but by fostering what people appreciate most in their managers: genuineness. A must-read for managers certainly—and for anyone who cares about improving relationships."

—RICHARD FARSON, president, Western Behavioral Sciences Institute; coauthor of *Whoever Makes the Most Mistakes Wins: The Paradox of Innovation*

"I was captivated by this magnificent book right from the start. *Fierce Conversations* insightfully captures and clearly interrogates the heart of 'real' conversation. Spending time with Susan Scott's principles has the potential to make a significant difference in our work, our relationships, and in our understanding of ourselves."

—RICHARD CARR, president and CEO, TEC International

Susan Scott

FIERCE CONVERSATIONS

**Achieving Success
at Work & in Life,
One Conversation
at a Time**

**FIERCE, INC.
SPECIAL EDITION**

B

A Berkley Book
Published by The Berkley Publishing Group
A division of Penguin Group (USA) Inc.
375 Hudson Street
New York, New York 10014

PRINTING HISTORY
Viking hardcover edition / September 2002
Berkley trade paperback edition / January 2004
Fierce Inc. Special Edition / May 2011

Berkley trade paperback ISBN: 978-0-425-19337-2
Special Markets ISBN: 978-0-425-24632-0

The Library of Congress has catalogued the Viking hardcover edition as follows:

Scott, Susan, 1944–
    Fierce conversations : achieving success at work and in life, one conversation
at a time / Susan Scott.
      p.   cm.
    Includes index.
    ISBN 0-670-03124-0
        1. Conversation.   2. Success.   I. Title.
    BJ2121 .S42   2002
    302.3'46—dc21   2002024003

PRINTED IN THE UNITED STATES OF AMERICA

20   19   18

This book is dedicated

to the men and women of TEC International

and to my mother, Beverly Eaves Carr,

whose conversations are simply the best

Acknowledgments

My long-term association with TEC Worldwide has felt to me like an ongoing gift exchange, netting me friends and colleagues internationally, as well as tremendous personal growth. If it were not for TEC, I would not have had a lively conversation over mead in a Yorkshire castle, a late-night conversation in a conservatory overlooking the Sydney Opera House, and another watching fireflies from a porch in North Carolina. I would not have received unexpected aid regarding a personal decision during a banquet in San Diego. You can't get those conversations on any street corner. You know who you are. Blessings, every one.

I owe a huge debt to David Whyte for putting the words *fierce* and *conversation* together when he spoke to the TEC community in January 1999. Those words and much else that David said that day went through me like a current, both electric and oceanic, placing me directly in the stream of what has become a great adventure.

I am also indebted to the many colleagues from whom I have learned over the years. Pat Murray stimulated my thinking with ideas like "The problem named is the problem solved. Deliver the message without the load." This man is a great teacher. Lew Haskell brought me one terrific idea, resource, and opportunity after another. His generosity has been marvelous to receive.

I salute friends, family, and clients who have been game enough to put on their seat belts and go deep. Conversations with my daughters, Halley and Jennifer, take my breath away. I want to be just like them when I grow up. My friend Michelle Twohig interrogates reality with a truly stunning dedication. We've had some wonderfully fierce conversations over the years.

I would have come unhinged more than once if it weren't for my friend, neighbor, and TEC chair Steve Buckmaster, who walked across the street at countless inconvenient hours to kick the tires on my jerry-built laptop. All praise to my personal alpha geek.

I owe additional peace of mind to Stephen Singular, a marvelous writer and calm presence who took charge of the editing process when my schedule buckled my knees. Without Stephen's considerable skill, this book might still be in its original, somewhat incoherent form.

Janet Goldstein, my editor at Viking, kept a firm but gentle hand on the tiller. Few know how to lead so surely, with such a light touch. Janet championed and shaped this book from beginning to end, and for that, I will be eternally grateful.

To my agent, Margret McBride, whose instantaneous enthusiasm upon receiving the book proposal provided a bedrock of confidence, I happily send hugs and checks.

Finally, I apologize to all those with whom I learned a thousand and one ways *not* to have a fierce conversation. To you, I raise my glass. Thank you for all you taught me.

Contents

Foreword

by Ken Blanchard

The notion that our lives succeed or fail one conversation at a time is at once commonsensical and revolutionary. It is commonsensical because all of us have had conversations that, for better or worse, profoundly altered our professional or personal lives. It is revolutionary because a course on conversations won't be found in an MBA curriculum. Yet who among us hasn't spent time and energy cleaning up the aftermath of a significant but failed conversation? Who among us hasn't recognized, perhaps too late, that a client was frustrated or a loved one wounded because we failed to engage in the conversations that were needed? By the same token, most of us have left a successful conversation clicking our heels at the outcome, eagerly anticipating the next one.

While success is often measured by an accumulation of titles, acquisitions, and the financial bottom line, little or no attention is paid to the power of each conversation to move us toward or away from our stated business and life goals. No longer. Susan Scott set out to help us change our lives—one conversation at a time.

If you don't have time to read the whole book, it's a mistake. But since God didn't make junk and you are unconditionally loved, I will hold back on a One Minute Reprimand. And as a humanist, I will go one step further and give you the essence of this powerful book. Here's what it says:

Our lives succeed or fail gradually, then suddenly, one conversation at a time. While no single conversation is guaranteed to change the trajectory of a career, a business, a marriage, or a life, any single conversation can. The conversation is the relationship.

This book will help you gain the insight and skills to make every conversation count. Are you ready?

The Seven Principles
of Fierce Conversations

Principle 1: Master the courage to interrogate reality.

No plan survives its collision with reality, and reality has a habit of shifting, at work and at home. Markets and economies change, requiring shifts in strategy. People change and forget to tell each other—colleagues, customers, spouses, friends. We are all changing all the time. Not only do we neglect to share this with others, we are skilled at masking it even to ourselves.

**Principle 2: Come out from behind yourself into the
conversation and make it real.**

While many fear "real," it is the unreal conversation that should scare us to death. Unreal conversations are expensive, for the individual and the organization. No one has to change, but everyone has to have the conversation. When the conversation is real, the change occurs before the conversation is over. You will accomplish your goals in large part by making every conversation you have as real as possible.

Principle 3: Be here, prepared to be nowhere else.

Our work, our relationships, and our lives succeed or fail one conversation at a time. While no single conversation is guaranteed to transform a company, a relationship, or a life, any single conversation can. Speak and listen as if this is the most important conversation you will ever have with this person. It could be. Participate as if it matters. It does.

Principle 4: Tackle your toughest challenge today.

Burnout doesn't occur because we're solving problems; it occurs because we've been trying to solve the same problem over and over. The problem named is the problem solved. Identify and then confront the real obstacles in your path. Stay current with the people important to your success and happiness. Travel light, agenda-free.

Principle 5: Obey your instincts.

Don't just trust your instincts—obey them. Your radar screen works perfectly. It's the operator who is in question. An intelligence agent is sending you messages every day, all day. Tune in. Pay attention. Share these thoughts with others. What we label as illusion is the scent of something real coming close.

Principle 6: Take responsibility for your emotional wake.

For a leader, there is no trivial comment. Something you don't remember saying may have had a devastating impact on someone who looked to you for guidance and approval. The conversation is not about the relationship; the conversation *is* the relationship. Learning to deliver the message without the load allows you to speak with clarity, conviction, and compassion.

Principle 7: Let silence do the heavy lifting.

When there is simply a whole lot of talking going on, conversations can be so empty of meaning they crackle. Memorable conversations include breathing space. Slow down the conversation, so that insight can occur in the space between words and you can discover what the conversation really wants and needs to be about.

Preface

When you think of a fierce conversation, think passion, integrity, authenticity, collaboration. Think cultural transformation.

Think of leadership.

The success of this book since its first publication underscored a genuine hunger for conversations which build our world of meaning. Conversations during which we connect on a human level. Speak in a human voice. Our own voice. Conversations during which we touch one another in some way.

A client widely respected for its legendary, international business-consulting services failed to win new engagements because prospective clients liked the competition better. Not the competition's power point presentations. They liked the people. They enjoyed the relationships. It became clear that this client's greatest opportunity lay in extending their relationships with their clients beyond price, beyond brilliant proposals, and engaging them on an emotional level. This became their next frontier, where significant gains in market share could be made.

For many Fierce clients, the last frontier for exponential growth, the place where they have found a new and sustainable competitive edge, resides in improving human connectivity.

We resent being talked to. We'd rather be talked with. So will all of the experts and the terminally self-absorbed please leave the room and close the door behind you? Thanks.

Have You Met "The Man"?

Transformation. It's a big word.

Recently, Jennifer Brewer (our Operations Manager) and I went to Dixie's BBQ for lunch. Dixie's has the best BBQ in western Washington. Ask anyone. It's official. The proprietor visits each table and asks, "Have you met 'The Man'?" "The Man" is the hot sauce for which Dixie's is famous. Hot. Seriously.

"Lay it on us," we said. Within seconds, two businesswomen of reasonably professional demeanor were transformed into bleary-eyed, runny-nosed, red-blotched, mascara-streaked, ugly-faced, broken-down, beggin' for mercy, cryin' for Mama, fixin' to die, hiccupping lumps of humanity. Of humility. There was no way out but through. Sans dignity.

And if you've never heard your Operations Manager whisper, "Help me," it's unnerving, let me tell you. Particularly when you, yourself, expect your last vision to be the ceiling of a BBQ shack in Bellevue, Washington.

Outside in the parking lot, still gasping, there were three things for which I had a new appreciation.

1. The line, "I once was blind, but now I see."

2. If your mouth is on fire, do not attempt to quench it with soda pop.

3. Not all transformation is pleasant.

But enough about me. I have met "The Man," lived to tell about it and most of the lining of my mouth has regenerated. Now, let's talk about you. And the transformations you can reasonably expect when you and your team engage in Fierce Conversations.

A Basic Truth

Fierce, Inc.'s diverse and growing client list since the book's publication illuminates a basic truth. Business is fundamentally an extended conversation—with colleagues, customers, partners, and the unknown future emerging around us. Unfortunately, many conversations fail. Thus, in order to stay competitive, across the board, the best of the best are investing in becoming communications rich or, as one of our clients calls it—black-belt conversationalists.

Conversations are the work of a leader and the workhorses of an organization. While no single conversation is guaranteed to change the trajectory of a career, a company, a relationship or a life—any single conversation can.

Practicing and championing Fierce Conversations company-wide enhances employees' capacity to serve as effective agents for strategic success, structuring the basis for high levels of alignment, collaboration and partnership at all levels within the organization.

Whether it's coming up with a big idea, transforming a company into a great place to work, improving customer-renewal rates, enhancing cross-boundary collaboration or providing leadership development and the healthier financial performance that goes with it—success occurs one conversation at a time.

As you may have deduced, we are not neutral. We believe that, in order to execute initiatives and deliver goals, leaders must have conversations that interrogate reality, provoke learning, tackle tough challenges and enrich relationships. Consequently, our work with each client begins by putting into place a foundation—four conversational models that become workhorses for the organization.

❖ Team Conversations: Engage individuals and teams in frictionless debates that interrogate reality and ignite dialogue around clarifying goals, solving problems, evaluating opportunities and designing strategies, resulting in excellent decisions for the organization, impeccably implemented.

❖ Coaching Conversations: Engage individuals and teams in conversations which increase clarity, improve understanding and provide impetus for change, resulting in professional development, the advancement of projects and accelerated results.

❖ Delegation Conversations: Clarify responsibilities and raise the level of personal accountability, ensuring that each employee has a clear path of development, action plans are implemented, deadlines are met, goals are achieved and leaders are free to take on more complex responsibilities.

❖ Confrontation Conversations: Engage individuals and teams in conversations which successfully resolve attitudinal, performance or behavioral issues by naming and addressing tough challenges, provoking learning, and enriching relationships.

From X to Y: What Fierce Transforms

What transformations do fierce conversations achieve? Let's compare X (the "before" Fierce) and Y (the "after" or result of Fierce).

(X) Before Fierce	(Y) After Fierce
Focus on activities. On reasons why it is not possible to reach individual or collective goals. Stalled initiatives.	Focus on results. Deep-seated accountability. Initiatives executed.
Beating around the bush, dancing around the subject, skirting the issues. No one engages. Nothing changes.	Naming and addressing the issues truthfully and effectively. Impetus for change.

An "us versus them," "me versus you" culture. Politics, turf wars, competition for resources and attentions.	High levels of alignment, collaboration, partnership at all levels throughout the organization and the healthier financial performance that goes with it.
Leaders overwhelmed by the complexity of their tasks. Everything is a priority.	The timely resolution of periodic leadership challenges. Clear priorities.
Leaders micro-managing versus leading. No grassroots leadership development.	Improvement in leadership effectiveness, development of quality "bench" to fill future leadership positions.
A relationship with customers based solely on price. Difficulty maintaining margins.	A relationship with customers that extends beyond price. Customers are engaged on an emotional level.
Original thinking is happening elsewhere. Sleepwalking through the manual.	Shared enthusiasm for agility, continued learning and epiphanies; shared standard of performance.
A culture of terminal "niceness." Avoiding or working around problem employees. Tolerating mediocrity.	Effectively confronting attitudinal, performance or behavioral issues. Enhanced employee capacity to serve as effective agents for strategic success.

If you'd like some instant transformation, call 425-313-9850 and ask us for directions to Dixie's BBQ. Don't say we didn't warn you. A less painful, though no less difficult, step would be to transform how you bring yourself and others into a conversation. And out of a conversation. That's what "fierce" is about. That's what you'll explore in this book.

Meet Our "Man"—Mineral Rights

Mineral Rights is our version of "The Man." A form of leadership at its most powerful. This conversation breaks the mold and is not for the faint of heart. I think it's time you met.

You'll find a detailed description of this conversational model in chapter 2. You'll give yourself a secret rule. And if you follow the guidelines, you are likely to have conversations unlike any you've had before.

A Bonus Chapter

I hope you enjoy the new User's Guide at the end of the book. I have provided it to corporate teams, coaching organizations, faculty, and families. I am told that many of the conversations it has ignited have resulted in epiphanies. Makes me happy.

Fierce Conversations

The Idea of Fierce

How did you go bankrupt?
Gradually, then suddenly.

—Ernest Hemingway, *The Sun Also Rises*

I f you have opened this book, it may be because the conversations you've been having with your coworkers or with your family members often fail to produce the results you want.

Over ten thousand hours of one-to-one conversations with industry leaders, as well as workshops with men and women from all walks of life confronting issues of relationship and life direction, have convinced me that our work, our relationships, and, in fact, our very lives succeed or fail gradually, then suddenly, *one conversation at a time*.

Equally provocative has been my realization that while no single conversation is guaranteed to change the trajectory of a business, a career, a marriage, or a life, any single conversation *can*.

This book is a guide to tackling your toughest challenges and enriching relationships with everyone important to your success and happiness through principles, tools, and assignments designed to direct you through your first fierce conversations with yourself on to the most challenging and important conversations facing you. By the end of this book, you will have become highly skilled at crafting deeply rewarding professional and personal relationships—one conversation at a time.

Whether you intend to maintain positive results in your life or turn things around, considering all of the conversations you need to have could feel a bit discouraging, so let's take the curse off the somewhat daunting field of "communications." I'd like you to simply take it *one conversation at a time,* beginning with the person who next stands in front of you. Perhaps there are very few conversations in between you and what you desire.

We'll take it chapter by chapter, principle by principle. Once you get the hang of it, once you master the courage and the skills and, more important, enjoy the benefits of fierce conversations, there will be no going back. It could change the world. It will certainly change *your* world.

When *Here* Is Troubling

Be patient with yourself. You got here—wherever "here" is—one conversation at a time. Allow the changes needed at home or at work to reveal themselves one conversation at a time.

Sometimes *here* just happens. Following the high-tech carnage, crashing economies, corporate layoffs, and terrorist attacks of 2001, which altered our individual and collective realities in a heartbeat, it would be easy to conclude that life has grown too unpredictable, that there's nothing to do but hang on and muddle through as best you can.

Perhaps you received a major wake-up call. You lost your biggest customer—the one that counted for 40 percent of your net profit. Or you lost your most valued employee. Or you lost your job, and it wasn't due to a layoff. You lost the loyalty of your team. You lost your eighteen-year marriage, or the cohesiveness of your family.

Perhaps your company is experiencing turnover, turf wars, rumors, departments not cooperating with one another, long overdue reports and projects, strategic plans that still aren't off the ground, and lots of very good reasons and excuses why things can't be any different or better.

To experience what happens for many individuals and organizations facing challenges, put your right arm out and point your finger, then visualize pointing it at someone who is the bane of your professional or personal life right now. That's called the *accountability shuffle*. He did it, she did it, they did it to me.

Blame isn't the answer, nor is cocooning in the perceived safety of your home. Once you reflect on the path that led you to a disappointing or difficult point and place in time, you may remember, often in vivid detail, the conversation that set things in motion, ensuring that you would end up exactly where you find yourself today. It is very likely that you arrived at this destination one *failed* conversation at a time.

Ask yourself, "How did I get *here?* How is it that I find myself in a company, a role, a relationship, or a life from which I've absented my spirit? How did I lose my way?"

So many times I've heard people say, "We never addressed the real issue, never came to terms with reality." Or, "We never stated our needs. We never told each other what we were really thinking and feeling. In the end, there were so many things we needed to talk about, the wheels came off the cart."

In February 2002, Robert Kaiser and David Ottaway wrote an article for the *Washington Post* about the fragility of U.S.-Saudi ties. Brent Scowcroft, national security adviser to the first President Bush, is quoted as saying, "Have we [the United States and Saudi Arabia] understood each other particularly well? . . . Probably not. And I think, in a sense, we probably avoid talking about the things that are the real problems between us because it's a very polite relationship. We don't get all that much below the surface."

Take your finger and touch your nose. This is where the resolution begins. This is the accountable position. If you want to make progress toward a better "here" in your professional or personal life,

identify the conversations out there with your name on them and resolve to have them with all the courage, grace, and vulnerability they
require.

When *Here* Is Wonderful

And on the positive side, you finally landed that huge customer, the
one your competition would kill for. Or you successfully recruited a
valuable new employee. Or you discovered that your team is committed to you at the deepest level. Or you just received a promotion.
Or you enjoy a deeply fulfilling relationship. You are clear and passionate about your life.

You got to this good place in your life, this satisfying career path,
this terrific relationship, gradually, then suddenly, one *successful* conversation at a time. Perhaps one marvelously *fierce* conversation at a
time. And now you are determined to ensure the quality of your ongoing conversations with the people central to your success and happiness.

If you want better results at home or at work, you've come to the
right place. After reading this book, gathering your courage, and
working with the tools we'll explore together, you will return to your
colleagues at work, to your partner at home, and, most important, to
your *self,* prepared to engage in ongoing, groundbreaking conversations that will profoundly transform your life.

While it was tempting to give in to suggestions that I write two
books—*Fierce Conversations in the Workplace* and *Fierce Conversations
at Home*—breaking this material into two books would have been a
mistake. Perhaps you've bought into the premise that we respond differently depending on whom we are with, that our work and home
personas are really quite different. Perhaps you pay fierce attention to
conversations at work but slip into a conversational coma at home,
convinced there's nothing new, interesting, or energizing to discuss,
preferring the company of the remote control. Perhaps you leave your

warmth, playfulness, and authenticity at home and prop up an automaton at your desk at work, afraid to let your authentic self show up lest you be judged as poor fodder for the corporate feast. Perhaps you've told yourself that conversations at work are unavoidably and substantially different from conversations at home. That that's just the way it has to be. This is not true.

Each of us must discard the notion that we respond differently depending on whom we're with and that our work and home conversations are really quite different.

When you squeeze an orange, what comes out of it? Orange juice. Why? Because that's what's inside it. The orange doesn't care whether it's on a boardroom table or beside the kitchen sink. It doesn't leak orange juice at home and tomato juice at work.

When we get squeezed—*when things aren't going well for us*—what comes out of us? Whatever's inside us. To pretend that what's going on in our personal lives can be boxed, taped shut, and left in the garage while we are at work is hogwash. It seeps in everywhere. Who we are is who we are, all over the place. So if your conversations at work are yielding disappointing results, I'd be willing to bet you're getting similar results at home. The principles and skills needed to engage in conversations that produce mind-blowing, world-class results in the workplace are exactly the same principles and skills that produce mind-blowing, world-class results at home.

The Conversation Is the Relationship

Going hand in hand with the discovery that our lives succeed or fail one conversation at a time is a second insight, courtesy of poet and author David Whyte. During a keynote speech at TEC International's annual conference several years ago, David suggested that in the typical marriage, the young man, newly married, is often frustrated that this person with whom he intends to enjoy the rest of his life seemingly needs to talk, yet again, about the same thing they talked about last weekend. And it often has something to do with their relationship. He wonders, Why are we talking about this again? I thought we settled this. Couldn't we just have one huge conversation about our relationship and then coast for a year or two?

Apparently not, because here she is again. Eventually, if he is paying attention, it occurs to him, Whyte suggests, that "this ongoing, robust conversation he has been having with his wife is not about the relationship. The conversation *is* the relationship."

The conversation is the relationship. If the conversation stops, all of the possibilities for the relationship become smaller and all of the possibilities for the individuals in the relationship become smaller, until one day we overhear ourselves in midsentence, making *ourselves* smaller in every encounter, behaving as if we are just the space around our shoes, engaged in yet another three-minute conversation so empty of meaning it crackles.

Incremental degradation—if we compromise at work or at home; if we lower the standards about how often we talk, what we talk about, and, most important, what degree of authenticity we bring to our conversations—it's a slow and deadly slide. One company president has been known to stop candid input in its tracks with the pronouncement "Howard, I do not consider that a career-enhancing response."

Fortunately, few leaders exhibit such exaggerated violations of the general rules of communication. However, many work teams as well as couples have a list of undiscussables, issues they avoid broaching at all costs in order to preserve a modicum of peace, to preserve the relationship. In reality, the relationship steadily deteriorates for lack of the very conversations they so carefully avoid. It's difficult to raise the level if the slide has lasted over a period of years, and that's what keeps many of us stuck.

In our significant relationships, in the workplace, and in our conversations with ourselves, we'd like to tell the truth. We'd like to be able to successfully tackle the topic that's keeping us stuck or apart, but the task is too hard, we don't know how to avoid the all-too-familiar outcome of talks gone south, and besides, we've learned to live with it. Why wreck another meeting with our colleagues, another weekend with our life partner, trying to resolve the tough issues or answer the big questions? We're tired and we just want peace in the land.

The problem is, whether you are running an organization or your life, you are required to be responsive to your world. And that response often requires change. We effect change by engaging in robust conversations with ourselves and others.

Each conversation we have with our coworkers, customers, significant others, and children either enhances those relationships, flatlines them, or takes them down. Given this, what words and what level of attention do you wish to bring to your conversations with the people most important to you? Throughout the book we will explore principles and practices that will help you engage in conversations that enrich relationships, no matter how sensitive or challenging the topic.

What Is a "Fierce" Conversation?

But a "fierce" conversation? Doesn't "fierce" suggest menacing, cruel, barbarous, threatening? Sounds like raised voices, frowns, blood on the floor, no fun at all. In *Roget's Thesaurus,* however, the word *fierce* has the following synonyms: robust, intense, strong, powerful, passionate, eager, unbridled, uncurbed, untamed. In its simplest form, *a fierce conversation is one in which we come out from behind ourselves into the conversation and make it real.*

While many are afraid of "real," it is the unreal conversation that should scare us to death. Whoever said talk is cheap was mistaken. Unreal conversations are incredibly expensive for organizations and for individuals. Every organization wants to feel it's having a real conversation with its employees, its customers, its territory, and with the unknown future that is emerging around it. Each individual wants to have conversations that are somehow building his or her world of meaning.

If you are a leader, your job is to accomplish the goals of the organization. How will you do that in today's workplace? In large part, by making every conversation you have as real as possible. Today's employees consider themselves owners and investors. They own their time, their energy, and their expertise. They are willing to invest these things in support of the individuals, ideals, and goals in which they believe. Give them something real in which to believe.

What I've witnessed over and over is that when the conversation is real, the change occurs before the conversation has even ended.

Being real is not the risk. The real risk is that:

I will be known.

I will be seen.

I will be changed.

Think about it. What are the conversations you've been unable or unwilling to have—with your boss, colleague, employee, customer; with your husband, wife, parent, child; or with *yourself*—that, if you *were* able to have, might change everything?

My Own Journey

For thirteen years, I worked with corporate leaders through the auspices of TEC International, an organization dedicated to increasing the effectiveness and enhancing the lives of CEOs. Thousands of CEOs in eighteen countries meet for monthly one-to-one conversations with someone like myself to focus on their businesses and lives—from budgets, strategies, acquisitions, personnel, and profitability (or the lack thereof) to faltering marriages, health issues, or kids who are upside down.

Twelve conversations over the course of a year with each CEO. Since time is a CEO's most precious commodity, it seemed essential that our time together be qualitatively different from time spent with others. Each conversation needed to accomplish something useful. My success, and that of my peers, depended on our ability to engage leaders in conversations that provoked significant change.

In the beginning, a fair number of my conversations were less than fierce. They were somewhat useful, but we remained in relatively familiar, safe territory. Some, I confess, were pathetic. No guts, no glory. I wimped out. Either I didn't have it in me that day, or I looked at the expression on my TEC member's face and took pity. I don't remember those conversations. They had no lasting impact. And I am certain my TEC members would say the same.

The fierce conversations I remember. The topics, the emotions, the expressions on our faces. It was as if, together, we created a force field by asking the questions, by saying the words out loud. Things happened as a result of those conversations.

When people asked me what I did, I told them that I ran think tanks for corporate leaders and worked with them one-to-one. That was the elevator speech. What I really did was extend an intimate invitation to my clients, that of conversation. And my job was to make each conversation as real as possible.

As my practice of robust conversations became increasingly compelling to me, I imagined that I was turning into a conversational cartographer, mapping a way toward deepening authenticity for myself and for those who wanted to join me. The CEOs with whom I worked became increasingly candid, and with that candor came a growing sense of personal freedom, vitality, and effectiveness. The most successful leaders invariably determined to engage in an ongoing, robust conversation with themselves, paying fierce attention to their work and lives, resulting in a high level of personal authenticity, ferocious integrity, emotional honesty, and a greater capacity to hold true to their vision and enroll others in it.

My colleagues worldwide asked me to conduct workshops on what I was doing, to pass along the skills needed for these conversations about which I had become so passionate. This required me to articulate for myself the approach I was developing. I led my first workshop in 1990.

In January 1999, I ran a redesigned, incredibly "fierce" workshop attended by sixteen extraordinary individuals from seven countries. In my workshops there is no role-play. No one pretends to be someone else. No one works on imaginary issues. It's all *real* play. All the participants engage in conversations as themselves, using real, current, significant issues as the focus for our practice sessions. Following one of the exercises, a colleague from Newcastle on Tyne, England, had tears in his eyes.

"I've longed for conversations like this all my life," he said, "but I didn't know they were possible. I don't think I can settle for anything less going forward."

Attendees e-mailed others about the impact of the workshop, about how they were applying the principles and using the tools they had learned, and about the results they were enjoying with their colleagues and family members. Word spread and the demand grew. Each subsequent workshop had a waiting list and each workshop went deeper. Corporate clients invited me to work with their key executives to foster courageous dialogue within their companies.

In November 2001, I recognized that my travel schedule had gotten out of hand when I sat down in my seat at the Sydney Opera House and reached for my seat belt. But my work with clients has been worth it. Over time I recognized that we were exploring core principles, which, when embraced, dramatically changed lives . . . one conversation at a time. Fierce conversations are about moral courage, clear requests, and taking action. *Fierce* is an attitude. A way of conducting business. A way of leading. A way of life.

Many times I hear words to this effect: "Your work has profoundly improved our leadership team's ability to tackle and resolve tough challenges. The practical tools allow leaders to become fierce agents for positive change." Or this: "You've helped me engage my workforce in moving the company to a position of competitive superiority!" Or this: "A fierce conversation is like the first parachute jump from an airplane. In anticipation, you perspire and your mouth goes dry. Once you've left the plane, it's an adrenaline rush that is indescribable." Or this: "This weekend my wife and I had the best conversation we've had in ten years. It feels like falling in love all over again."

This book began as informal class notes mandated by workshop attendees. As the significance of what we were addressing became increasingly clear, people requested more material. As a result of constant urging from clients and colleagues—"Write it down. This is life-changing stuff"—I began to assemble my notes, to put on paper what I'd been practicing for more than a decade. The following pages emerged as a road map for each reader's highly individual journey.

Getting Started

Here is what I'd like you to do. Begin listening to yourself as you've never listened before.

Begin to overhear yourself avoiding the topic, changing the subject, holding back, telling little lies (and big ones), being imprecise in your language, being uninteresting even to yourself. And at least once *today*, when something inside you says, "This is an opportunity to be fierce," stop for a moment, take a deep breath, then come out from behind yourself into the conversation and make it real. Say something that is true for you. For example, my friend Ed Brown sometimes stops in midsentence and says, "What I just said isn't quite right. Let me see if I can get closer to what I really want to say." I listen intently to the next words he speaks.

When you come out from behind yourself into the conversation and make it real, whatever happens from there will happen. It could go well or it could be a little bumpy, but at least you will have taken the plunge. You will have said at least one real thing today, one thing that was real for you. And something will have been set in motion, and you will have grown from that moment.

I will support you chapter by chapter by telling you true stories about fierce conversations that caused shifts in tectonic plates, both personal and professional. I will tell you about a sixty-second fierce conversation that changed a friend's life. I will explain what fierce conversations are and what they aren't. Why they're so rare. Why you would want to have them. How to have them. Once you master the courage and the skills and begin to enjoy the benefits of fierce conversations, they will become a way of life. The way of your life.

Let's begin.

PRINCIPLE **1**

Master the Courage to Interrogate Reality

Life is curly. Don't try to straighten it out.

No plan survives its collision with reality. The problem is, reality has an irritating habit of shifting at work and at home, seriously complicating our favorite fantasies. And reality generally wins, whether it's the reality of the marketplace, the reality of a spouse's changing needs, or the reality of our own physical or emotional well-being.

Things change. The world changes. You and I change. Business colleagues, life partners, friends, customers. We are all changing all the time. As Lillian Hellman wrote, "People change and forget to tell one another." Not only do we neglect to share this with others, we are skilled at masking it to ourselves. It's no wonder relationships disintegrate.

The traditional practice of annual strategic planning sessions is a thing of the past. It no longer works for a company's executive team to spend two days on retreat, determine their goals, roll out an action plan, and call it a year. The team members must reconvene quarterly to address the question "What has changed since last we met?" As a company president recently admitted, "I'd like to get a firm grasp on reality, but somebody keeps moving it."

The best we can hope for, to quote business consultant Robert Bridges, is "the masterful administration of the unforeseen." Stuff happens. Internally. Externally. Some you can affect. Some you can't.

Life Is Curly

From working closely with corporate leaders, I know very well how quickly reality can change. The customer responsible for 50 percent of your business files for bankruptcy. Your most valuable employee is recruited away from you. Your competition comes out with a great, new whiz-bang product that you are not prepared to match or beat. New technology renders your product or service obsolete. The economy goes upside down. *You* go upside down, lost in the complexity of your organization's goals and challenges.

Perhaps you suddenly landed that huge customer you've been pursuing but never believed you'd get, whose expectations you are unequipped to meet. In the last quarter of 2001, the owner of a crab fishery in the Bering Sea scrambled to fulfill twice the normal orders for crabmeat from his customers in Japan. Why the demand? Following the September 11 terrorist attack, many Japanese canceled their travel plans and stayed home. And while they were home, they ate a lot of crab! Few of us would have foreseen a link between terrorism and the consumption of crab.

It would seem companies are stressed either because their sales are too low or because their sales are too high. As individuals, we are stressed either because we don't have enough of the things we want or because we have all of the things we want. We are either shedding or acquiring; either way, happiness eludes us.

Or perhaps you realize that you're operating at a new level of effectiveness in a particular area of your life. Life feels like your favorite class at school, with a rush of learning every day. You've received a

promotion or you've fallen in love with a wonderful person. Whatever it is, something spectacular has happened and you don't want to
blow it. It feels like acing a final exam and winning the lottery on the
same day—exhilarating and a touch frightening. You've been given a
valuable gift—a thrilling new reality—and you know it! And in some
corner of your heart, a loving voice suggests, "Listen up, bucko. You'd
better make some serious changes or you're gonna blow this deal!"

Let's face it. The world will not be managed. Life is curly. Don't
try to straighten it out.

Beach-Ball Reality

Whether you are running an organization or participating in a committed relationship, you will find yourself continually thwarted in
your best efforts to accomplish the goals of the "team" unless reality
is regularly and thoroughly examined. *You know this.* Describing reality, however, can get complicated. Let me show you what I mean.

Think of your company as a beach ball. Picture the beach ball as
having a red stripe, a green stripe, a yellow stripe, and a blue stripe.
Let's imagine that you are the president of the company. That's
you standing on the blue stripe. The blue stripe is where you live,
every day, day after day. If someone asks you what color your company is, you look down around your feet and say, "My company is
blue."

How do you know? You're surrounded by blue. You open a
drawer and it's full of blue. You pick up the phone and listen to blue.
You walk down the hall and smell blue. Every day you eat, drink, and
breathe blue. From where you stand, the company is as blue as it gets.
Cobalt blue, to be precise.

So here you are in a meeting, laying out your strategy to launch
an exciting new project. And, of course, you're explaining that this
strategy is brilliant because it takes into consideration the blueness of
the company.

Your CFO listens intently. Her brow is furrowed. She lives on the red stripe. All day she's up to her armpits in red. Cash flow is tight. She takes a deep breath and ventures, "I'm excited about this project, but when I hear you describe our company as blue, I wonder if you've studied the latest cash flow projection. I'm dealing with a lot of red these days. Can we talk about this?"

While many leaders do not welcome opposing views, you are highly evolved, so you respond, "Okay, put that red on the table and let's take a look at it." And the debate is on. Blue, red, blue, red, blue, red.

Meanwhile, your director of manufacturing is starting to squirm. He lives on the green stripe. He is thinking, "Man, oh man. The timing on this project couldn't be worse, but every time I share concerns I am viewed as a naysayer. Besides, it's nearly lunchtime and no one will thank me for complicating this conversation even further."

Win/win translates to I win. I win again.

Your VP of engineering, who lives on the yellow stripe, has a strongly held, differing opinion, but his experience has taught him that differences of opinion lead to raised voices and strong emotions, after which someone dies. In his experience, for some people *win/win* translates to *I win. I win again.* And the last time he stuck his toe over the line with a controversial idea, the most vocal member of the team shot it off. So this key executive, who is privy to useful information, pulls off an amazing feat. He shrinks his subatomic particles and disappears.

This *is* possible, you know. Think about all the times a meeting has ended and you found yourself trying to remember if your VP of engineering was present. He was; he just made himself invisible. Some people are extraordinarily talented at this. They may be brilliant, but disappointingly (and irritatingly), they neither fish nor cut bait, they are neither hot nor cold. They appear to be, at best, politely indifferent.

The Corporate Nod

The ability to hide out at meetings was so prevalent at one company that the behavior eventually got a name. Picture a leader holding forth from one end of the boardroom table. She is espousing the cleverness of the current strategy. Like all good leaders, at some point she offers an opportunity for others to respond. Something like, "So what do you think?"

It gets quiet around the table. Unnaturally quiet. Like the quiet before a tornado, when birds fall silent and not a leaf stirs and a bilious sky warns of an approaching storm. Around the table, eyes fall. Each individual practices the art of personal stealth technology, attempting to drop beneath the leader's radar screen. At one point the leader calls on some poor bloke who is less skilled at vanishing than his team members.

"Jim, what do you think of the plan?"

Jim gets that look on his face like a cat occupied in the litter box—sort of far away as if to indicate that he is not really here and neither are you. The leader waits Jim out. Jim has to do something.

Jim nods. His head moves up and down as he gazes fixedly at a spot on the boardroom table.

The leader smiles.

"And what about you, Elaine?" the leader persists.

Elaine steps into the litter box. Head down. Eyes averted. She nods.

And so forth around the table, as the leader scans the room.

The Corporate Nod.

Satisfied, the leader concludes, "Good. We launch on Monday."

In the funnies, characters' thought-bubbles float overhead, capturing the unfiltered notions bobbing about in their heads. We love the *Dilbert* comic strip because the characters actually say what they're thinking and it's often what we have thought ourselves. If we could read the thought-bubbles floating over the heads of people sitting around the boardroom table, the very people charged with implementing the strategy, we might see: "There's no way we can do that! This is crazy!" Or "This sucker is going down. Time to dust off my résumé." Or "Wonder if my family would notice if I bought a ticket to Barbados and disappeared."

Most people want to hear the truth, even if it is unpalatable.

We don't know what people are thinking unless they tell us. And even then, there's no guarantee they're telling us what they really think. Yet, if asked, most people avow that they want to hear the truth, even if it is unpalatable.

A friend who is a high-level executive, intimidating to many, recently promoted a courageous employee who walked into his office with a large bucket of sand and poured it on the rug. "What the hell are you doing?" demanded my friend.

The employee replied, "I just figured I'd make it easier for you to bury your head in the sand on the topic I keep bringing up and you keep avoiding."

You can be assured this employee would not have taken such a bold and risky step if he were not convinced that the company was about to embark on a road to ruin. After a sleepless night, he had determined that he owed it to himself, his colleagues, his customers,

There is something within us that responds deeply to people who level with us.

and his leader to either make himself heard or leave the organization. He told his boss, "Everyone's in-basket and out-basket are full, but I'm concerned we're avoiding the *too hard* basket."

The conversation following this outrageous act interrogated reality, provoked learning, tackled a tough challenge, and enriched the relationship. It is no small thing that, as a result, the company made the changes necessary to avoid a potential disaster.

If you're in a similar situation, I don't advise you to buy a bucket of sand. However, do recognize that there is something within us that responds deeply to people who level with us, who do not pamper us or offer compromises but, instead, describe reality so simply and compellingly that the truth seems inevitable, and we cannot help but recognize it.

And if you are the boss who deserves a bucket of sand, you may have been defending yourself with the complaint: "I pump out energy and it's unilateral. Nothing comes back." Perhaps you are not allowing it to come back.

Taking Stock

The Corporate Nod shows up in living rooms as well as boardrooms. Companies and marriages derail temporarily or permanently because people don't say what they are really thinking. No one really asks. No one really answers.

Ask yourself . . .

- What are my goals when I converse with people? What kinds of things do I usually discuss? Are there other topics that would be more interesting?

- How often do I find myself—just to be polite—saying things I don't mean?

- How many meetings have I sat in where I knew the real issues were not being discussed? And what about the conversations in my marriage? What issues are we avoiding?

> **Companies and marriages derail because people don't say what they are really thinking.**

- If I were guaranteed honest responses to any three questions, whom would I question and what would I ask?

- What has been the economical, emotional, and intellectual cost to the company of not identifying and tackling the real issues? What has been the cost to my marriage? What has been the cost to *me?*

- How often do I recall members of my team or staff putting their real concerns on the table in an attempt to make the conversation genuine? What about my conversations at home? How honest are my partner and I being with each other?

- When was the last time I said what I really thought and felt?

- How would I describe the level of collaboration, alignment, and accountability of my executive team? of my family members?

- What are the leaders in my organization pretending not to know? What are members of my family pretending not to know? What am I pretending not to know?

- How certain am I that my team members are deeply committed to the same vision? How certain am I that my life partner is deeply committed to the vision I hold for our future?

- When was the last time I confronted someone at work or at home about his or her behavior and ended the conversation having enriched the relationship?

- If nothing changes regarding the outcomes of the conversations within my organization, what are the implications for my own success and career? for my department? for key customers? for the organization's future? What about my marriage? If nothing changes, what are the implications for us as a couple? for me?

- What is the conversation I've been unable to have with senior executives, with my colleagues, with my direct reports, with my customers, with my life partner, and most important, with *myself*, with my own aspirations, that if I *were* able to have, might make the difference, might change everything?

- If all of my conversations with the most important people in my life, including my spouse and family members, successfully interrogated reality, provoked learning, tackled the tough challenges, and enriched relationships, what difference could that make to the quality of my life?

Are My *Truths* in the Way?

It would be a gross oversimplification to suggest that each of us simply needs to tell the truth. Will Schutz, who has taught seminars on honesty for decades, suggests that truth is the grand simplifier, that relationships and organizations are simplified, energized, and clarified when they exist in an atmosphere of truth. Yet Schutz acknowledges that *truth,* itself, is far from simple.

Pause for a moment and think about the truth. After all, what is the truth, and does anybody own it?

> **Perhaps what we thought was the truth is no longer the truth in today's environment.**

What each of us believes to be true simply reflects our views about reality. When reality changes (and when doesn't it?) and when we ignore competing realities (remember the beach ball?), if we dig in our heels regarding a familiar or favored reality, we may fail. Perhaps what we thought was the truth is no longer the truth in today's environment.

For example, most people believe that there are some people you just can't talk to. That, as Satchmo said, "some people, if they don't know, you can't tell them." After we've experienced countless failed conversations over the years, such a belief is understandable.

I've observed, however, that it is also possible that the *way* we've been talking with people isn't working. That our techniques for talking with "difficult" people haven't worked, but other techniques can and do work, without rattling sabers or giving ultimatums. That it is our beliefs about what we can say, as well as how and to whom we can say it, that are in the way, and that if we change our beliefs, productive conversations can easily occur.

Who Owns the Truth?

What about interrogating reality? Most of us find it easier to stick with the reality we've defined by operating, most of the time, from one color stripe on the beach ball. Yet our competitive advantage is to learn from our changing realities and respond quickly. If we entertain multiple realities, we create possibilities that did not exist for us before.

The question is: Who owns the truth about what color the company is?

The answer? *Every single person in the company,* including the entry-level file clerk, owns a piece of the truth about what color the company is. The operative word is *piece*. No one, not even the CEO, owns the entire truth, because no one can be in all places at all times.

Reality is unforgivingly complex.
—ANNE LAMOTT

And, of course, this applies to our personal relationships. Each of us owns a piece of the truth about what's going on in our marriage, and so does our spouse, so do our kids, and I wouldn't be surprised if the dog had a suggestion or two he'd like to offer.

Multiple, competing realities existing simultaneously: This is true *and* this is true *and* this is true. As Anne Lamott writes, "Reality is unforgivingly complex."

Since there is no *the truth* in any business, the question is "What is the best *a truth* for today?" We are more likely to discover the truth we most need to understand today by demonstrating that everyone has a place at the corporate table. That all voices are welcome. That no matter what our area of expertise, each of us has insights and ideas about other aspects of the organization, and, while each of us may know a better way for the company to do something, none of us knows more than the sum of everyone's ideas. I heard someone say, "We need to demolish the ensconced." I agree and offer fierce conversations as a marvelous cure for excessive certitude.

For example, what if we asked our teams, "What is impossible to do that if it *were* possible would change everything?" or "Imagine that we are a new competitor in town and that we have deep pockets. How would we put our company out of business?"

Later in this chapter I will introduce you to a powerful conversational model for interrogating reality with anybody on any topic, whether at home or in the workplace. But first, be reminded that one of the goals in a fierce conversation is to get everyone's reality out on the table, so it can be interrogated. *Everyone's!*

Fierce conversations are a marvelous cure for excessive certitude.

Many a corporate leader has groaned upon considering this point. "Taking the time to interrogate everyone's piece of the truth about what color the company is could take forever! I've got a business to run. Fierce conversations take too much time."

Not always. I've had fierce conversations that lasted only a few seconds (more about those later). But it's true, fierce conversations often do take time.

Fierce conversations often do take time. The problem is, anything else takes *longer*.

The problem is, anything else takes *longer*.

Most leaders have learned from experience that until the multiple—sometimes conflicting—realities of key individuals and constituents have been explored, implementing a plan can be a decidedly tentative endeavor. To the degree that you resist or disallow the exploration of differing realities in your workplace and at home, you will spend time, money, energy, and emotion cleaning up the aftermath of plans quietly but effectively torpedoed by individuals who resent the fact that their experience, opinions, and strongly held beliefs are apparently of little interest to the organization.

Getting Reality on the Table

There are three stages of interrogating reality. The first is to identify the issue on the table and, if you have a solution in mind, make a proposal. In other words, this is the area of the beach ball we are addressing today, and this is what it looks like from where I stand. Be clear and concise. "This is the issue. This is what I propose."

An alternative approach is to withhold your ideas until others have shared theirs; however, I find that conversations are best launched when there is a well-defined idea offered as a jumping-off place for everyone's thinking and discussion. If you don't have a proposal, simply identify the issue and proceed.

When you are in the presence of knowledgeable but cautious individuals, once you've made your proposal or described the issue, don't just ask, "What do you think?" Invite questions. Check for understanding. Say, "Before we go any further, please ask any clarifying questions you may have." If you notice someone who is silent but looks puzzled or concerned, ask, "Alison, what questions do you have?"

Note: I imagine some of you, over the course of your careers, have found yourselves with a team member who, like a character in Charles Baxter's *The Feast of Love,* adopted an attitude of "lethal neutrality and immobility." No matter how sincerely and graciously you invite such people to share their views, they decline the invitation. Yet, because of their position and power in the organization (or in the family), until they are onboard, they stand squarely in the way of progress, like the tree that a drunk driver swerves into: "It kills you just by standing there." In chapter 4, you will learn a model for confronting such behavior with courage and skill.

Once you are certain that everyone understands what you are proposing, check for agreement. For example: "I believe this is the right way to go, the right course of action. But I suspect some of you may see it differently. If you do, I'd like to hear it. I know that my enthusiasm may make it hard to challenge me, but my job is to make the best possible decisions for the organization, not to persuade you of my viewpoint. So please speak up." Then proceed to call on every individual at the table. "Sarah, what are your thoughts?" "Mike, what's your perspective on this? I invite you to push back on what I've said."

This kind of invitation will get people to open up because you publicly, openly, and actively encouraged them to share opposing views. You've shown that you are open to rational influence.

> **Tie a lure onto your line— a belief, an opinion, a provocative question—then chuck it into the stream and see what bites!**

Do the same thing following the sharing of others' ideas. "Jim, what is your perspective on Mike's idea?"

At times I've used other, more colorful words to encourage teams to challenge one another's thinking. "Tie a lure onto your line—a belief, an opinion, a provocative question—then chuck it into the stream and see what bites! If you are to build something other than unsatisfactory, loose-change relationships with one another, give your colleagues something to sink their teeth into and encourage them to challenge your thinking."

A caution: When someone takes you up on your invitation to challenge your strongly held opinion, resist the temptation to defend your idea immediately. So often I've observed teams respond to what appeared to be a sincere invitation, only to be shot down by a leader's knee-jerk attempt to build a stronger case. To everyone in the room, it feels as if the leader is saying, "Apparently you haven't grasped the brilliance of my idea. Let me explain it to you one more time." When we make this mistake, we teach all those in the room that when we encourage them to challenge our thinking, we don't really mean it.

Instead of trying to strengthen your own case, inquire into someone's position. "Tell us more, Mike. Help us understand your thinking."

Thus, the sequence in interrogating reality is:

1. Make a proposal

2. Check for understanding

3. Check for agreement

By the way, it isn't always helpful to look to the person with the most experience. Instead, look to the person with the best vantage point. Who is standing right at the juncture where things are happening? Who has the fifty-yard-line seat on the action? That person isn't always the designated leader. Also, who stands squarely downstream and, therefore, will be impacted by any decisions you make?

What's the payoff for interrogating multiple realities? People learn to think. Many so-called learning experiences don't provide opportunities for real thinking. Meetings are just thinly veiled attempts to persuade others (employees, family members) to agree with the teacher's (manager's, parent's, spouse's) conclusions. Real thinking occurs only when everyone is engaged in exploring differing viewpoints.

Who knows? You may shift your position as the conversation unfolds. When reality is thoroughly interrogated, participants often walk out of the meeting with ideas that no single individual had walking in. We sometimes discover that we have merely been operating out of the kitchen and living room of our organization, not noticing the highway out front.

Nothing is more dangerous than an idea, when it's the only one you have.

—ÉMILE CHARTIER

At times, mastering the courage to interrogate reality has allowed an organization to pull back from the brink of ruin. As Émile Chartier noted, "Nothing is more dangerous than an idea, when it's the only one you have."

Very importantly, interrogating reality allows you to generate internal commitment to a decision. People buy into it, even if they don't necessarily agree with it, because their perspective was sought out and valued and because they genuinely understand why the decision was made.

Avoid Laying Blame

If we can agree that reality is complex, we can probably also agree that the path by which we arrived at our current reality—all the *who, what, when, where,* and *why* that guaranteed we'd end up with the poor results on our plates today—is equally complicated. How do we talk about that? How do we talk about our mistakes and failures without shutting people down, without putting everyone on the defensive?

Here's a thought for your consideration: "In any situation, the person who can most accurately describe reality without laying blame will emerge as the leader, whether designated or not."

Author Edwin Friedman said that. Easy to say. Hard to do.

Most people point the finger. *He* did it. *She* did it. *They* did it. Or didn't do it. Such fault finding invariably provokes all of our defense mechanisms, thus slamming the door on the possibility of frictionless debate and resolution.

The person who can most accurately describe reality without laying blame will emerge the leader.

I witnessed the aftermath of such dynamics several years ago when a new CEO was appointed to lead a company out of a difficult period. I knew quite a few people who worked for the organization. The new CEO, Roger, had a tough job on his hands. Employees had become disillusioned by the behavior of his predecessor. Roger attempted to turn the tide with an ironfisted style of leadership. It seemed to many that Roger was unwilling to listen to advice and that, in fact, those who challenged his course were considered enemies. They were angry, frustrated, and fearful that the new regime would be just as noxious as the old.

The talk in the hallways and private offices was grim. Another failure of leadership seemed inevitable. Many withdrew their support from Roger, and he received the unfortunate nickname "dead man walking."

At an informal staff gathering in the lunchroom, as several employees recounted Roger's latest missteps, one employee, Elizabeth, said, "I am troubled at what we are doing here. I confess I've been guilty of bashing Roger, and I'm sitting here feeling ashamed. Guiding the organization at this time would be a thankless and difficult job for anyone. Morale is in the tank, revenues are sliding, customers are complaining, and our leader is doing his level best to lead us through this morass and out the other side. I wonder what we could do to support him in his endeavor."

Another employee responded, "Come on, Elizabeth. Nobody can talk to Roger. You can't tell him anything."

Elizabeth said, "Then how can we make ourselves the kind of people he *will* listen to? Maybe we need to change our approach. And how well do we understand the current strategy? Since change has to be the order of the day, perhaps we could learn a thing or two."

The mood shifted around the table as individuals contemplated the possibilities and began to offer suggestions. Elizabeth asked for a meeting with Roger the next day and began their conversation with these words: "I am here for two reasons. First, to apologize for my criticism of you behind your back and for my lack of support. I realize that my attitude has been a hindrance, and I want you to know that I've got a greatly improved attitude today. I'd like to help you in any way I can. Second, I'd like to suggest a meeting with the staff. As our leader, you need our support and I'd like you to receive it. Some potentially good ideas have been withheld from you because of fear of reprisal. I hope you'll entertain them and also share with the staff as many details as possible about your strategy for this coming year and the thinking behind it. I believe this could serve as a turning point for all of us and for the company."

Over the next few months, Elizabeth emerged as a highly respected agent for positive change in her organization.

And what about the home front? How do we describe reality without laying blame when someone we love behaves in ways that are damaging to the relationship?

A friend told me of an internal struggle she had recently when she attended a local festival with someone new in her life: "We were sitting at a table in the beer garden when this couple at the next table struck up a conversation with us. Before I knew it, Ben was engaged in an enthusiastic conversation with the woman. He had his back turned to me, and they were obviously enjoying talking about several experiences they discovered they had in common. The conversation went on and on. Finally, after about twenty minutes, Ben turned to me and asked, 'Am I ignoring you?' I answered with a rather sarcastic 'Yes.' Neither of us knew what to do after that. The rest of the afternoon was strained and I didn't like how I felt. I was upset and disappointed that Ben had ignored me for so long, but I didn't want to start a fight. I was afraid that if I said what I was thinking, it would come out all wrong."

As we talked, my friend pieced together what had happened for her.

"I'm still getting to know Ben; however, I believe he genuinely cares for me. I think he was just enjoying himself, not flirting, and that what I felt was about me, not about Ben. I have never wanted to feel I had to compete for the attention of the man in my life. I could have insinuated myself into the conversation, but I didn't. And I don't believe I ever would try to do that. If a similar situation occurs, I will let Ben know this about me. It might help him to understand this about me, and I might learn more about him."

What an elegant approach to a bump in the relationship road. No blame. Just, "This is what's going on for me. I thought you should know."

No More "Buts"

Throughout this book, you will gain many tools that will help you explore profound and provocative territory around reality in your workplace and in your life. To help you improve at describing reality without laying blame, a simple and effective shift you can make is to remove the word *but* from your vocabulary and substitute the word *and*. "I like what you've done here, but . . ." will be better received if you say, "I like what you've done here, and . . ."

Remove the word *but* from your vocabulary and substitute the word *and*.

For example, in a conversation with an employee, this is how things typically go:

I know you want more time to complete the project, but the deadline is looming. You want me to help out in Boston, but I only have a small window in which to make some critical things happen in Seattle. I'd like to help you, but I have no easy choices right now. You seem stressed, but I expect you to deliver this project on time with minimal involvement on my part.

In other words, this is true, *but* this is true too. Multiple realities are competing, and I've got to choose one or the other. Sorry, you lose.

At a recent workshop in Dallas, Rob Brown, a CEO whose company builds an astonishing quantity of pulpits and lecterns, suggested that "yes, but . . ." is an acronym for "your evaluation superlative; behold underlying truth."

If you substituted *and* every time you would ordinarily use the word *but,* the conversation might go like this:

Most people are shocked to discover how many times they use the word *but* during the course of a day.

I know you want more time to complete the project and the deadline is looming. You want me to help out in Boston, and I only have a small window in which to make some critical things happen in Seattle. I'd like to help you, and I have no easy choices right now. You seem stressed, and I expect you to deliver this project on time with minimal involvement on my part.

Feels better, doesn't it? To both parties. This is true *and* this is true. Multiple realities are not competing. They just exist. You own a piece of the truth, and so do I. Let's figure out what to do.

Most people are shocked to discover how many times they use the word *but* during the course of a day.

Assignment

Over the next twenty-four hours, practice describing reality accurately, without laying blame, at home and in your workplace.

To help with this assignment, catch yourself whenever you are about to say "but," and replace it with "and."

You may struggle with this assignment, and that's where the learning is—in the struggle. Get good at this and your career will gain momentum, aliveness. At home, well, things will gentle down. People will open up.

Participate fully in conversations. After all, your version of reality is as good as anybody's. Keep in mind that reality can never be absolute and that it isn't something that is handed to us. Clarity develops as we thoughtfully consider all aspects of a topic.

Your version of reality is as good as anybody's.

To encourage colleagues to voice their views candidly, you might explain the beachball analogy and say, "You can count on me to tell you what I think and feel and how I've arrived at my perception. I invite you to do the same, especially if you disagree with my view. Our differing perspectives are invaluable. After all, our goal is to make the best possible decisions for the company, not to be right about our individual points of view."

At a recent gathering of key employees from all points on the globe, a corporate client passed out beach balls with one of the four focuses for the year printed on each stripe: financial accountability, speed, new technology, innovation. He instructed everyone, "As we implement our action plan, we need to regularly interrogate reality from these perspectives. Sometimes they will compete; however, we must be advocates for each stripe on our corporate beach ball. Speak boldly on their behalf."

In a personal relationship, adapt the words to fit the situation: "This is what our relationship looks like and feels like to me. I truly want to know your thoughts, particularly if they differ from mine. The success of our relationship depends on our ability to understand each other and be truthful with each other, to stay current."

Above all, as you describe reality from your perspective, do not lay blame.

You may get some sideways glances. Don't let that concern you. Each time you describe reality accurately, *without laying blame,* you create a kind of force field around yourself—one that feels good to others.

When you practice describing reality without laying blame, notice the change in the tone and the outcome of your conversations as you make the subtle change of deleting the word *but* from your vocabulary.

The Fish Rots from the Head

John Tompkins, the CEO of a commercial fishing fleet, looks like a seawall against which many a ship has been wrecked. He is six foot six. He has girth. He looks solid. He smiles warmly as he greets me in the reception area of his company. I think I notice a slight limp and, like a fool, glance to see if he has a peg leg. As we shake hands, I think, if we were choosing sides, I'd want to be on his team.

John had called me in to help him prepare for a meeting with fifty-five key employees—forty Russian, Czech, Norwegian, Australian, and American vessel personnel, and fifteen land-based staff members in operations, sales, marketing, accounting, and human relations.

On the phone John had said they had a few challenges, some

things he hoped to resolve while everyone was in town during shipyard, the repair and refitting of ships. I'd been recommended. Could
I help?

A week later, I sink into the leather sofa in John's office, accept a
glass of water, and ask him what the issues are.

"There are two," John says. "The first is that there isn't enough
communication between the vessel personnel and the office staff."

John's nautical-themed office is beautifully appointed, and I
struggle not to be distracted by the weird and wonderful items on the
walls, shelves, and desk. A massive hunk of twisted metal that must
represent a bad day, an expensive trip. Maps of fishing waters. A Chi-
huly glass sculpture resembling an anemone.

"The vessel personnel catch and process fish. That's their job.
Here in the office it's our job to support the vessels. When something
breaks on one of the vessels, if they don't have the extra part they
need, we get it to them. If someone gets sick, we get them off the ship
and replace them. It's critical that vessel and office personnel stay current regarding performance—how much fish each vessel has caught,
how crew members are doing. Based on results, we move our vessels
to different fishing waters or replace crew members. The problem is,
nobody is talking to anybody else."

"Why?"

"The vessel staff doesn't feel supported by the office staff. The office staff doesn't feel appreciated by the vessel staff."

"Keep talking."

"The vessel crew are out there busting their butts to catch fish. If
they don't catch fish, none of us would have a job. They're frustrated
at the way the office staff treat them. They feel the people in the office don't value what they do or understand how hard the work is.
Meanwhile, the office staff are convinced the vessel personnel think
they just sit around smoking cigars."

"Okay. What's the second issue?"

John takes a deep breath and looks at the floor.

This one's closer to home, I imagine. *And close to the bone. Looks like this one hurts.*

"I've got two talented guys, Ken and Rick, handling operations. Rick helped me get the company started, so when I hired Ken and put him in charge, Rick was angry. I had my reasons. Rick is a hot-head. Ken's better at working through issues with people, thinking through how things should be handled. I thought Rick would get over it, but it's been a year and he's still angry and he's found a million ways to sabotage Ken. He's even been caught in some lies."

I raise my eyebrows. John shrugs. "I know. You're wondering why he's still here."

"I'm wondering if you have considered making him available to industry."

John chuckles. "That's good."

"The latest euphemism."

John shakes his head. "Rick's too good to lose."

"Now I'm thinking you get what you tolerate."

John nods, grimacing.

"Sounds like you've got an integrity outage here," I say, "unless, of course, lying is one of your corporate values."

John frowns and nods. "I need to talk to him. I *will* talk to him."

"Does the thought of that conversation nauseate you?"

John smiles wanly. "Yeah."

"Well, it's a serious issue, but we'll come back to it later. Anything else?"

"No. That's it. That's enough!"

I ask permission to talk with people in the office and on the vessels. Confidentially. "Sure," he says, "but most of them don't speak English."

I also ask to meet with several key customers and vendors.

We hire an interpreter, Vasily, who signs a confidentiality agreement and drives with me to the shipyard.

Gulls and oystercatchers cry overhead. This is December. A cool, erratic wind is blowing, but there is no musical pinging of lines against masts. The sounds here are different from those of a marina. These ships are huge, larger than the Parthenon. Heavy metal. The vessels sit solidly in the water, monoliths 345 feet long and 65 feet wide, built to house and sustain 165 people for as long as six months.

Vasily and I gaze up the sloped sides of the vessel on which we will have our first interview. I wonder what would happen to the water level if the vessels were magically lifted. We begin the climb up and up and up to the deck. Vasily is breathing hard. My imitation of Long John Silver—"Avast there, matey. Har, har, har"—does not amuse him. Perhaps he thinks I've choked on something and is turning away in consideration of my feminine dignity.

Let's Meet in the Field

One of my favorite quotes is from Rumi, a thirteenth-century Sufi poet: "Out beyond ideas of wrongdoing and rightdoing, there is a field. I'll meet you there."

This is the field in which I prefer to converse, a field where we do our best to suspend judgment, where we walk and talk with one another, where learning may be provoked.

The bread crumbs always lead to the CEO.

I didn't talk about Rumi's field on the fishing vessels. Hard to translate into Russian! However, because most of the time I imagine I'm conversing in the field where judgment is suspended, often about ten to fifteen minutes into a conversation, people will say, "I can't believe I'm telling you this." When this happens I often respond, "I am privileged to hear it."

With the vessel crew it was "I vas not goink to tell you nutting, but mebbe I trust." I learned a lot of great phrases. "The fish rots from the head." This is true. The bread crumbs always lead to the CEO. Or in this case, the fishmaster.

The stories rolled out. Here is some of what I learned.

- If you go fishing with a bunch of your buddies, what do you hope will happen? *You hope* you *catch the biggest fish, the most fish.* The captain and crew of fishing boats want bragging rights. After all, they have their reputations in the industry and significant personal income at stake.

- What if you go fishing with people you don't like? *You conceal your pleasure when they don't catch any fish at all, and you give them lousy advice.* All of the vessels were competing with one another. When they found good waters, the fishmasters on each vessel would withhold information about their location.

- Ken and Rick each favored a particular vessel—different ones— so they fought to make sure their favorite vessel got the best equipment, soonest, so it could catch the most fish. Ken and Rick's competition had spread to all vessel personnel on those two vessels. The two vessels and all hands were at war.

- The other vessels felt like ugly stepchildren, operationally adrift.

- During shipyard, when the crew was in town, an HR director debriefed the vessel crew, who felt she was actively trolling for gossip. When she heard dirt on someone, she would later let slip to the accused person what was said and who had said it. The crew dreaded their interviews with her at the end of the season. They called her names I won't repeat. They vowed not to tell her anything.

- There are rules about drinking and fraternization on factory trawlers, but all the vessels held impressive quantities of booze. One fishmaster drank and fraternized at a decidedly intimate level with several of the galley workers. HR knew it, but his vessel caught more fish than anyone anywhere, so everybody looked the other way.

- The vessel crew broke their backs to catch fish. And they were good at it. If they didn't catch fish, the office staff wouldn't have a "cushy" office to come to every day. Add to that the hardship of the work itself, plus being away from their families for months, cooped up in the bowels of a floating tin can. And there are no guarantees. If they caught fish, they made money. If they didn't catch fish, they didn't make money, at least not enough to compensate for the hardship. It is a tough life. Granted, they chose it, but they would be a lot happier if they felt as if the office staff appreciated what they did, what they endured. Just getting decent videos to watch on board seemed an impossibility.

- The office staff resented living on call day and night during fishing season to support vessel personnel who wouldn't send in reports or return calls. Meanwhile, they were trying to sell a product. If they didn't sell the product at a good price, the company didn't turn a profit. The office staff needed to know how the vessels were doing out there—the quantity and quality of the catch. They needed reports. Accurate reports. Because of the competition between Ken and Rick, some of the reports were greatly exaggerated.

These stories were familiar. I recalled working with a company that manufactured machinery used in commercial kitchens. Their machines kept breaking down. Customers were angry. Engineering was convinced no one in the organization appreciated the impossibility of fixing the problems with the machines in the time frame demanded. The engineers were frustrated with customers whom they described as demanding and unreasonable. The sales staff were demoralized over their failure to close lucrative deals with prospective customers who had heard about product problems. Customer service was burned out—angry, bordering on hostile: "What are you guys promising out there that we can't deliver?" The president was spending all his time visiting international customers and trying to keep them from canceling orders for new machines. He had no life. His wife was issuing ultimatums. His children missed him . . .

Did I mention that most of the crew did not speak English?

A day and a half in the office reveals the same stories told on the vessels. Everyone is aware of Ken and Rick's rivalry and its consequences, including Ken and Rick.

As I share my discoveries with John, he leans forward with his head in his hands and stares morosely at the carpet. When I describe a particularly colorful detail of what is happening and the outcomes, John groans softly.

We talk about the good things—the loyalty to John, the company's reputation in the industry, customer loyalty despite current frustrations, the talent of his staff in the office and on the vessels. We digest it all.

I finally say, "Some of this stuff is not pretty."

Deep sigh.

I venture, "Why do I have a feeling that none of this is news—that you've been pretending not to know a lot of stuff?"

Deeper sigh. Long silence. John addresses his first comment to the floor.

"I hate conflict." Another sigh. Then he looks me in the eye and says, "It's important to me to be liked."

I smile. "You're in excellent company."

As the facilitator, I will ensure that the scheduled meeting with employees takes place within important guidelines. However, tackling these issues will not be easy for John, so after I've gotten a picture of what is going on with him, I move to the conversation model I use more often than any other with clients. It is extraordinarily powerful and wonderfully fierce, and one with which you will become intimately familiar. I use it with John because it is essential that we review what is at stake for John and his company, what is to be gained or lost based on what he chooses to confront or ignore.

Mineral Rights

Years ago this model was named "Mineral Rights" by a workshop participant who suggested, "If you're drilling for water, it's better to drill one hundred-foot well than one hundred one-foot wells." This conversation interrogates reality by mining for increased clarity, improved understanding, and impetus for change.

Even during conversations that begin with a clear focus ("We need to talk about *this!*"), it's easy to get sidetracked onto rabbit trails. Typically, we begin on one topic, quickly veer off course, and end up somewhat lost and frustrated, having made little progress on the main issue. Our job is to juggle the frivolous with the significant. Our challenge is to tell them apart.

Mineral Rights will help you drill down deep on a topic by asking your col-

If you're drilling for water, it's better to drill one hundred-foot well than one hundred one-foot wells.

league, customer, boss, direct report, spouse, child, or friend a series of questions. This is not a dentist's painful drilling sans novocaine; it's a natural exploration that accomplishes all four purposes of a fierce conversation, which we'll explore throughout the book.

1. Interrogate reality

2. Provoke learning

3. Tackle tough challenges

4. Enrich relationships

The questions asked during a Mineral Rights conversation help individuals and teams interrogate reality in such a way that they are mobilized to take potent action on tough challenges.

My Mineral Rights conversation with John took about an hour. Following is an abbreviated version of the conversation.

ss: *Of the issues we've uncovered, which one, when resolved, will give you the greatest return on investment of whatever time, energy, dollars, you allocate to it?*

JOHN: *(unhesitating)* The competition between Ken and Rick.

ss: *Summarize for me the current impact of this competition.*

JOHN: The problems between Ken and Rick translate to competition between vessels and goes directly to the bottom line. When a favored vessel ends up with better equipment than the others, it performs better. The others are struggling to do their best with marginal equipment.

ss: *Keep talking.*

JOHN: Well, on top of some vessels having lousy equipment, the fishmasters are actually giving one another wrong information about where the fish are, all because of this competition thing. This makes me crazy.

ss: *Crazy . . .*

JOHN: It makes me nuts! We're all supposed to be working together—all our people, all the vessels—but because Rick and Ken have got this power struggle going on, I've got one ship doing great while the others are still trying to *find* the fish, much less catch them!

ss: *Who else is being impacted? What else?*

JOHN: Morale is the lowest it's ever been. Key personnel are threatening to leave. I've got some great talent here, and I don't want to lose them. I can't afford to.

ss: *How is it impacting the company?*

JOHN: We're not as profitable as we should be, as we could be. Frankly, I'm fed up.

ss: *You're fed up. Talk to me about what you're feeling, how this is impacting you . . .*

JOHN: When grown men, highly skilled . . . act like children, it's . . .

ss: *(I wait . . .)*

JOHN: . . . beyond frustrating. It's maddening. These are well-paid professionals. I take good care of them. When they dig in their heels over who's got the shiniest toys, who's got the most clout, when they sneak around pulling off all kinds of devious bullshit to see whose vessel can catch the most fish . . . *(John leans back, looks up at the ceiling, then slumps forward.)* We are one company. Many ships, one company. If they can't see that . . .

ss: *What are you feeling?*

JOHN: *(silence, then . . .)* Betrayed. I feel betrayed.

ss: *Imagine that it's six months from now, a year from now, and nothing has changed. What are the implications?*

JOHN: *(groans)* I'd have to fire myself, say to hell with it.

ss: *What's at stake for you to lose or gain?*

JOHN: Millions of dollars. Pleasure in the work. Self-esteem. Physical health. *(We explore specifics.)*

ss: *What are you pretending not to know about your contribution to this situation being exactly the way it is?*

JOHN: *(frowns)* I don't understand. I don't know.

ss: *What would it be if you did know?*

JOHN: *(Smiles, frowns, thinks. I wait. After a long silence, he sits up straight and looks directly at me.)* I haven't outlined clear consequences if Ken and Rick's rivalry continues.

SS: *Keep talking.*

JOHN: They probably feel safe. My guess is they doubt I'd pull the trigger on those consequences and fire one of them if they can't work together.

SS: *Are they right?*

JOHN: No. *(long silence)* No. *(another long silence)* If this doesn't stop, one of them will have to go.

SS: *John, let's shift gears. Let's imagine you have tackled this head on and the issue is resolved—completely, brilliantly. Ken and Rick are working together, rather than competing with each other. What difference will that make?*

JOHN: All the difference!

SS: *For example . . .*

JOHN: If Ken and Rick put their heads together and collaborated— they're both geniuses at this—all the vessels would be equally well equipped. Good fishing grounds would be shared. Everybody would catch more fish, which translates into better profitability for the company, better pay for the crew, better morale. Happier times for all of us.

SS: *What else?*

JOHN: Well, obviously, higher profits would allow us to upgrade equipment, expand the fleet. As they say, all ships would rise. And I'd sleep better. I wouldn't be thinking of selling the whole damn thing.

ss: *When you consider those outcomes—better profitability, improved morale, sleeping better—what do you feel?*

JOHN: Hope.

ss: *Say more.*

JOHN: I love this business. I'd love to stay in the game. Things would be a lot more fun around here. I wouldn't feel like the lone ranger.

ss: *Given everything we've talked about, what's the next most potent step you can take to improve this issue prior to the company meeting?*

JOHN: Talk to Ken and Rick individually and together. One more time.

ss: *What's going to differentiate this from previous conversations you've had with Ken and Rick?*

JOHN: That's where you come in. *(I agree to prepare him for that talk.)*

ss: *What's going to try to get in your way?*

JOHN: My need to be liked, which translates into rarely making clear requests—in this case, requirements, not requests. With consequences attached.

ss: *What about the other issues? Possible bribery in Vladivostock? Fraternization? Drinking? What difference will it make when those issues are resolved?* (We go through them one by one.) *What exactly are you committed to do and when?*

JOHN: Talk to Ken and Rick on Monday.

ss: *What's your ideal outcome?*

JOHN: They stop competing and work as a team. I don't lose either one of them.

ss: *If the competition continues, what action are you prepared to take?*

JOHN: Fire the sons of bitches! Sell the company. Move to Tahiti.

ss: *Let's craft a conversation that will lessen the possibility of those out-*
comes, at least in the near future. I feel strongly that our goal is to
retain both Ken and Rick. (It is Friday and John wants time to prepare. We agree to work over the weekend on the phone.)

On Monday John talks with Ken and Rick separately, then together. I meet with John and his six key executives on Tuesday to debrief them about the findings from my interviews with crew, office
staff, customers, and vendors. Although there are no surprises, it is
eerily quiet as the words float in the air above the boardroom table.

Ken and Rick apologize to the executive team for the damage
their rivalry has caused. I am impressed. It takes a big person. From my
talks with Rick, I suspect that he is in no immediate danger of over-
hauling his hardwired manipulative nature. He has a certain charm,
however, and is exceptional at his job. I see how valuable he is to the
company. John will circle back to issues with Rick later.

I remind the executive team that *fierce* does not mean barbarous,
menacing, or cruel. *Fierce* means powerful, strong, unbridled, un-
restrained, robust. It means coming out from behind ourselves into
the conversation and making it real. There will be no blood on the
floor. No violence. I talk about the principles

The answers are   and purposes of fierce conversations.
in the room.   I coach them regarding their role in our
upcoming session, especially John, Ken, and
Rick. I answer questions, turning most of the questions back to the
executives to answer for themselves. I tell them, "The answers are in
the room. If they aren't, we have the wrong people. You are the right
people. You have the answers."

A week later, John, two interpreters (they spell each other; we
wear them out), forty vessel personnel, fifteen office staffers, and I engage in two days of memorable conversation. There are skid marks

across the floor from heels dug in. The seats fill in from the back. Arms are tightly crossed against massive chests.

I lay out the issues without mincing words. They are stunned as John and I describe what is really going on, naming each of the issues without putting pillows around them. I remind myself to breathe.

The interpreters struggle to find the words in Russian. I hope they are close to what I want to convey. I say that we will confront real issues, that *confront* does not mean argue or beat up. *Confront* means search for the truth. *Honesty* means full disclosure to myself and others, with good intent.

I tell them that we are going to take on the biggest, smelliest, ugliest, nastiest issue first so we will find out what we are made of, and go from there.

We begin by addressing the rivalry between Ken and Rick. We experience our first moment of truth when Ken stands, faces everyone, and says, "I *have* shown favorites among our vessels. I admit it. It's unacceptable and I apologize. It's stopping now."

Ken waits quietly as fifty-four people digest what he has said. The turning point comes when Richard, a highly regarded engineer whose vessel, *Clearwater*, is the one Ken has favored with equipment and supplies, stands and admits, "It's put some of us in a difficult position, Ken. On the one hand, I appreciate what you've done for the *Clearwater*, but it's made it hard to help out the guys on the other vessels and that's what we're supposed to do."

Honesty means full disclosure to myself and others, with good intent.

Ken looks as if he's been kicked in the gut. Richard is one of Ken's most valuable employees. Ken shakes his head. This is not easy. The interpreters trade places. It's been only one hour and the first interpreter looks pale.

Rick stands. "Some of you know I've been . . . I haven't felt good about . . . hell, you all know I wanted Ken's job. I've made no bones about that. But that wasn't your problem. I made it your problem. Shouldn't have happened. Gonna fix it."

The attendees, whom John and I have invited to come out from behind themselves, begin to show up authentically, honestly. Some defend; others reveal the amazing grace of those who engage without defense. They set the bar for the rest of us.

Chris, a deckhand from Australia, shows us the way. He is passionate about fishing and about his love for the work, for his mates. He is angry that so much damage has been done to morale. We ask for suggestions as to how to begin to turn this around. Chris offers ideas, then faces John and says, "Good on ya for having this meetin'."

Through it all, John is impeccable. He asks questions and when he asks, he's really asking. He listens thoughtfully, offers the perspective that only he can offer, answers questions. And when he answers questions, he really answers them, doesn't duck them. No shuck and jive. I see why they respect him and watch their respect deepen.

Things happened as a result of the session. The fishmaster who was drinking and fraternizing was made available to industry. The vessel he had captained continued to catch the most fish. Rick wasn't sure he could accept the changes he'd have to make. He resigned to take another job, was gone for one week, and asked to return. John took him back. Rick returned *slightly* humbled. Ken and Rick still engaged in minor power struggles, but the struggles were less visible to the larger community. Vessel favoritism was stopped dead in its tracks. Communication among vessels became timely and accurate. All vessels caught fish. Reports were accurate. The HR director still had a fatal attraction to gossip, but she stopped leaking it to crew members. Morale turned around.

Following the meeting with fifty-five employees, John and I met monthly to continue our fierce conversations about his work and what was next for him. When I asked John if I could use his company as a case study, he said, "I'd be honored. I'm proud of my company and what we've accomplished." He has a right to be.

Though John's story concerns a unique industry, the issues are similar to those in many organizations—high-tech, low-tech, no-tech. Competition for titles and bragging rights among individuals and teams. Lack of appreciation for others' realities. Competition for scarce resources. Tolerance of the ineffective or harmful behavior of a high performer. Or of entrenched victims, who feel, *He did it to me. She did it to me. They did it to me. It's not my fault. Not my problem.*

Ground Truth

Several years ago I was introduced to the military term *ground truth,* which refers to what's actually happening on the ground versus the official tactics. One of the challenges worth going after in any organization—be it a company or a marriage—is getting to ground truth.

Seems to me you have to get at ground truth before you can turn anything around. John Tompkins mastered the courage to interrogate reality in his organization, to get at ground truth. Publicly. No hidden agenda.

What is ground truth in your organization? Every day companies falter and fail because the difference between ground truth and the "official truth" is significant. The official truth is available for general circulation and is viewed by most team members as propaganda.

> **You have to get at ground truth before you can turn anything around.**

Ground truth is discussed around the watercooler, in the bathrooms, and in the parking lot, but it is seldom offered for public consumption and rarely shows up when you need it most—when the entire team is assembled to discuss how to introduce a new product or to analyze the loss of a valuable customer and figure out how to prevent it from happening again.

I recently talked with a friend who attends the kinds of high-level political meetings you read about in thrillers. He reminded me that politicians are adept at navigating within the sizable gap between ground truth and official truth. Everyone is careful, guarded. No one admits to vulnerability, to failure, that they are not the center of the universe, that they are not in control.

My friend went on to say that the China policy is referred to as "the China policy of ambiguity." All communications on the topic are oblique and soft. Nothing anyone says has any meat on the bones. Trying to enforce anything would be like trying to nail Jell-O to the wall.

Trying to enforce anything would be like trying to nail Jell-O to the wall.

In June 2001, when President Bush attended a meeting with European leaders to discuss global warming, Jacques Beltran, a military affairs expert at the French Institute for International Relations in Paris, was widely quoted, describing the talks as full of backslapping bonhomie, yet on matters of substance, they were "the polite dialogue of the deaf."

I recall my attempt to have a meaningful conversation with a local politician during a dinner party. Trying to engage him was like trying to sculpt air. There was nothing there, no discernible human being with whom to converse. It may sound harsh, but this individual seemed, frankly, a waste of skin.

Following the September 11 attack on America, dialogue got real in a hurry. It had to. Buildings had literally come to the ground, and now we had to come to the ground as well. To ground truths. Individuals all over the world began to understand that, in a very real sense, the progress of the world depends on the progress of each individual human being now. Leadership must be for the world, rather than being an appeasement of individuals with special interests. None of us can afford to operate in that mode. Certainly companies can't. There's this little matter called profitability. Profitability requires an ongoing interrogation of reality, of ground truth.

Leadership must be for the world.

John Tompkins's *official* truth had been that the competition between his two highly capable operations executives was invisible to the rest of the organization. He had convinced himself that a little creative tension between top executives could be tolerated, could perhaps even be healthy for his company. Meanwhile, *ground* truth was inflicting significant harm on a daily basis.

What conversation can we have with one another to help our collective understanding of ground truth?

Let's examine current reality. What has changed since last we met? Where are we succeeding? Where are we failing? What have we learned in the last few months? What is required of us now?

Each of us needs honest answers to these questions, in the workplace and at home. We can begin by identifying the official truths in our companies and in our relationships that conflict with ground truth.

Assignment

Before you read further, stop for a moment and have a quiet conversation with yourself. Are there differences between official truths and ground truths in your workplace? in your personal relationships? in your life? If so, write them down. The following examples may help you get started:

- My company's official truth is that our goal is to be world-class in everything we do. Ground truth is that many of us are embarrassed by frequent blunders which have not been acknowledged or addressed.

- The official truth in my marriage is that we are happy, that everything is fine. Ground truth is that we've been avoiding significant issues. If we fail to we resolve them, our marriage could fail.

- The official truth in my life is that I am on track to be successful. Ground truth is that my job is unfulfilling. I am just going through the motions.

Fierce conversations with yourself, such as these, are not for the faint of heart. They require courage, from the French word *coeur,* meaning "heart." They are conversations during which you're likely to overhear yourself saying things you didn't know you knew, or didn't want to know.

Return to me when you are empty. We each have our own sense of the reality of any situation, our own truths. These "truths" can be far removed from reality and often cause our conversations to travel the same ground over and over and over again.

I am reminded of the story of the man who visits a Zen master. The man asks, "What truths can you teach me?" The master replies, "Do you like tea?" The man nods his head, and the master pours him a cup of tea. The cup fills and the tea spills. Still the master pours. The man, of course, protests, and the master responds, "Return to me when you are empty." The lesson here is that we need to empty ourselves of our preconceived beliefs in order to be open to a broader, more complex reality.

During fierce conversations we are more likely to get all our answers questioned than the other way around. Before we can learn, we must unlearn. Empty the cup!

Official truths in my workplace:

-
-
-

Ground truths in my workplace:
-
-
-

Official truths in my personal relationships:
-
-
-

Ground truths in my personal relationships:
-
-
-

Official truths in my life:
-
-
-

Ground truths in my life:
-
-
-

Psycho-neuro-immunology

When it comes to profitability, keeping our businesses healthy and growing, we must determine whether the assumptions on which our organization was built and is being run match current reality.

What kind of assumptions? Assumptions about markets, about customers and competitors, about values, beliefs, and behavior, about technology and its dynamics, about the organization's strengths and weaknesses—even assumptions about what the company gets paid to do.

These assumptions are what Peter Drucker would call the company's "theory of the business," and they need to be regularly and rigorously interrogated. To test these assumptions, organizations must interrogate two realities at once . . . engage in two ongoing fierce conversations. The first has to do with the organization's values. The question posed is "What values do we stand for, and are there gaps

The corporate soul reflects shared values.

between these values and how we actually behave?" When I asked John Tompkins, the CEO of the fishing company, to share with me the core values on which his organization was founded, he paused, then admitted, "We've never declared them."

No wonder John's organization was floundering. The corporate soul reflects shared values. Embedded in the reasons we get out of bed every day and in every action that we take as individuals are *our* values.

A value is a tightly held belief (as opposed to a vague notion) upon which a person or organization acts by choice. It is an enduring belief that one way of behaving is personally, professionally, spiritually, or socially preferable to an opposing way of behaving.

In considering your values and any gaps that might exist between those values and your behavior, there is more at stake in interrogating this particular reality than most of us realize.

Psycho-neuro-immunology is a field in which medical physicians and quantum physicists have met, shaken hands, and engaged in a startling conversation. It seems that you and I have the ability to strengthen or weaken our own immune systems. The surprising news is that it has less to do with a healthy diet or an exercise regimen, and more to do with the degree of integrity with which we live our lives.

Does psycho-neuro-immunology suggest that if you get sick, you're a bad person? No. Bad things happen to good people. Maybe you just caught a bug. Maybe you inherited a troublesome gene. However, if you feel a creeping, deadening depression, a malaise, as if you are merely drifting, bumping into the bank in a rudderless boat, held in the current of the particular river you are in, if you are tired and listless much of the time, if you sense something's off . . . then do an integrity scan.

Ask yourself, "What values do I stand for, and are there gaps between these values and how I actually behave?" In fact, if you are depressed, it may be because you have repressed some important truths from yourself. Truths *about* yourself.

Integrity requires alignment of our values—the core beliefs and behaviors that we have claimed as important to us—and our actions. So if, for example, you say that you value time with your family members yet haven't spent much time with them lately, you are, by your own definition, out of integrity. If you have taken the stand that fidelity in a marriage is essential, and you're cheating on your spouse, you're out of integrity. If you tell yourself that honesty is important, yet you frequently bend the truth in an attempt to stay out of trouble or get what you want, you are out of integrity.

Remember ground truth? All too often there is quite a difference between stated values and ground truth.

Most of us don't go around consciously violating our values, nor do we spend our days obsessively checking: "Okay, am I in or out of integrity?" However, if your behavior contradicts your values, *your body knows,* and you pay a price at a cellular level. Over time, depending on the severity of the integrity outage and how long it's been going on, your immune system will weaken, leaving you increasingly vulnerable to illness.

If your behavior contradicts your values, *your body knows.*

Each individual has an immune system. Each marriage has an immune system. So does every organization. What happens when promises to customers are broken? When employees are feuding? When lack of profitability is camouflaged as a onetime write-off? When there are conflicts of interest involving large sums of money?

If behaviors within an organization are not in alignment with the values described so prettily in the mission statement, the company's immune system is weak, rendering it vulnerable when opportunities to get sick come along.

Bad things happen to good companies. When a company takes a blow, if the corporate immune system is weak, things can go south in a heartbeat.

And what happens in your marriage during a tough time? What integrity outages are causing or contributing to a bad patch? Do you support each other through the difficult times, or do the wheels come off the cart?

Pay attention here. When bad things happen at work or at home, if our corporate or personal immune systems are weak, it's likely that things will worsen. On the other hand, when bad things happen and our immune systems are strong, our defense system can kick in and return us to health.

Bad things happen to good companies. What if we know we're out of integrity and do nothing about it? If we continue to ignore the part of us that says, *This is wrong. This is not right for me,* we're playing Russian roulette with our physical, emotional, spiritual, and financial health. Sadly for many, we have only to hear the name Enron to recognize a spectacular example of corporate psycho-neuro-immunology at its most devastating.

Assignment

Conduct an integrity scan. In preparation for your integrity scan, you must first clarify your values. It won't do to spout the values that have been suggested to you by others, even by those whom you admire. The question is "What are *your* values?"

A value I have identified for myself is *passionate engagement.* Looking back on personal and professional peaks and valleys, I find that I do the best work and enjoy my life most when my passions are thoroughly engaged. *Authenticity* is another core value for me. Just the sound of the word creates a thrumming in my bones.

When I work with clients, there is often a sense of personal discovery when the right words spring to mind. One woman in a workshop regained her fierce resolve to take a class in writing once she realized her life had fallen into a routine that had dulled her sense of aliveness. "I am too comfortable. I haven't learned anything new in a long time. I've always said that a lifetime of learning is one of my core values, yet I'm in a rut in just about every area of my life. No wonder I'm so bored."

Look for the words that speak to you, that wake you up. Don't worry about what anyone thinks of your list of values. This is *your* life. You and only you decide.

The conversation that follows is one of the most important conversations you will ever have with yourself and deserves annual revisits.

Personal Integrity Scan

Clarify and write down your core values. Pay attention to each word you consider. Maybe there's only one word or phrase that rings true for you. That's fine. Write it down.

MY CORE VALUES

Now run an integrity scan.

Is my behavior out of alignment with my values in the workplace? in my personal relationship? in my life? Are there integrity outages? If so, where and what are they?

Integrity outage in my workplace:

What must I do to clean it up?

When am I going to do this?

Integrity outage in my personal relationship:

What must I do to clean it up?

When am I going to do this?

Integrity outage in my life:

What must I do to clean it up?

When am I going to do this?

Corporate Integrity Scan

If you are a leader in an organization, invite your team to conduct a corporate integrity scan. In preparation, review your company's vision or mission statement. Does it include clearly stated values? Is it compelling? Most mission statements sound the same, containing such sentiments as . . .

We will be the premier provider of [insert your product or service here] *in* [geographic territory]. *We will exceed our customers' expectations, provide growth opportunities for our employees, and ensure a reasonable return for our shareholders.*

Boring! There is no vitality in such statements, and unless *I'm* a shareholder, who cares? The language doesn't provide us with anything we can sink our emotional teeth into; it doesn't compel us to take action, doesn't motivate us to get out of our warm beds on cold, rainy days and go into the office to tackle a job, some parts of which are not fun.

I subscribe to the idea that you want your convictions to come up out of the work and out of the people doing the work, not have them imposed on people by upper management. That you have to trust the act of involving all your employees in scanning their brains and hearts and guts to represent whatever beliefs and values they have. You cannot impose those beliefs and values on people by twisting and banging and rewarding and sanctioning and inspiring and motivating and hanging your imposition on the wall, no matter how noble a statement you have conceived, because if you do, you become a propagandist and you spend your corporate life's energy attempting to push, pull, and persuade rather than get on with the business of your business, whatever it may be.

People yearn to be connected to something of substance. They are oriented to values. *How shall I live my life so that it means something more than a brief flash of biological existence soon to disappear forever?*

This is especially true for all those who assess their lives and are not satisfied. Few employees are content with a merely contractual relationship in which they exchange their time and skills for a paycheck, then go home to spend their paychecks on what their lives are really about. Most care deeply about the reputation and values of the companies they work for and would like to feel that their ability to live up to those values in their organization matters.

A compelling vision, including shared values, is not just an idea.

It is, rather, a force in people's hearts, a force of impressive power. It may be inspired by an idea, but once it goes further, if it is compelling enough to acquire the support of more than one person, then it is no longer an abstraction. It is palpable. People begin to see it as if it exists. Few, if any, forces in human affairs are as powerful as shared vision.

Few, if any, forces in human affairs are as powerful as shared vision.

The best kind of vision statement is written during a four-hour fierce conversation with as many employees as possible (and a few customers). It answers four important questions:

1. "Why are we here?" (The answer to this question must get beyond identifying the product you manufacture or the service you provide; it must answer the challenge "So what?" In other words, what do we do for our customers that matters to them? Consider the compelling response of a telecommunications company: "Our work brings the human family closer together.")

2. "What is our ideal relationship with one another?" (How would we describe the best possible relationship we could envision with everyone inside the organization? More compelling than "trust and respect" are specific, actionable values such as: "We want consistency between our plans and our actions. To disagree without fear. Each person to be connected with the final product. Freedom to fail; people are shot only for not trying.")

3. "What is our ideal relationship with our customers?" (This is the same as question 2, only applied to customers. Consider such responses as: "We act as partners with our customers. We encourage them to teach us how to do business with them.

Our customers leave us feeling understood. We understand the impact of our actions on our customers.")

4. "What contribution do we wish to make to the global community?" (What impact do we wish to make in the larger community in which we are visible, beyond our customers? What do we want to be known for? Examples: "We give our unconditional commitment to enhance the quality of life and human growth," and "We are committed to fulfilling our ethical and social responsibilities.")

If your vision statement needs rewriting, involve as many employees, customers, and strategic partners as possible in doing so. Periodically review it with your coworkers and ask, "Where are we off?" If an integrity outage becomes clear, discuss what needs to be done to correct it. Develop a plan that includes specific actions and dates by which they will be taken. Thank the team for their candid responses. Conclude your integrity scan by identifying where the company's behavior is in alignment with its values. Ask the team, "Where are we on . . . ?" Thank them for their contributions to the company's alignment of values and behaviors, and let them know what it means personally to you, their leader.

You Get What You Tolerate

Now let's take a look at a second reality every organization must regularly examine: "What are the skills and talents of our employees, and are there gaps between those resources and what the market demands?"

Several years ago, I sat in on a meeting of managing directors in Edinburgh, Scotland. Once I got past my enchantment with the brogue and could pay attention to the issues being discussed, my thought was: "They have the same issues as the CEOs in Seattle. And London. And Indianapolis. And Sydney. And Chicago. And Vancouver." The common thread—*people.*

When solving problems, producing results, or addressing strategy, we invariably turn to the performance of individual employees.

I have not yet witnessed a spontaneous recovery from incompetence.

Do we have the talented people we need to successfully deliver our product or service to our customers? It's been interesting to note that the vast majority of leaders with whom I have worked—who for the most part are fairly well grounded in reality—tend to hold out hope that marginal employees will magically transform themselves overnight into high performers. I'm reminded of a client who told an employee, "I'm not here to evaluate your performance. I'm here to locate it."

I don't know about you, but I have not yet witnessed a spontaneous recovery from incompetence.

What's needed is a fierce conversation, perhaps a series of them, followed by relentless follow-through and ongoing support. While some people can't be saved, many can. Most people will comply with clear requests. Perhaps the fierce question leaders need to ask themselves is: "Were my employees dead when I hired them, or did I kill them?"

As a leader, you get what you tolerate. People do not repeat behavior unless it is rewarded. *The same goes for our families, our marriages, our friendships.* For example, what are

As a leader, you get what you tolerate.

your children doing? How are they spending their time? And what are the results?

Have you communicated clearly not only the results but also the behavior that you want? What about attitude? I appreciate the comments of Herb Kelleher, the chairman of the board of Southwest Airlines, who said, "We are prepared, including legally, to fire you for a bad attitude."

Southwest Airlines employees are rarely accused of sleepwalking through the manual; instead, they bring a playfulness and individuality to their work. How does an airline get this behavior out of its employees? By clearly communicating what is expected.

During all of my conversations with Peter Schutz, former president of Porsche, his message was consistent: "Hire attitude. Train skill." Peter was successful in large part because he was clear about the attitude he was looking for at Porsche. The key question is "What attitudes will lead to success in our company?" The follow-up question is "To what degree do our employees exhibit these attitudes?"

Getting Real with Yourself

How do the two realities we've explored for companies apply to you as an individual? You've already interrogated the first reality by conducting a personal integrity scan: *"What values do I stand for, and are there gaps between these values and how I actually behave?"*

We need only to modify the second reality slightly to make it deeply personal, as well: *"What are my skills and talents, and are there gaps between those talents and what I am bringing to the job market, to my career, and to my personal relationships?"*

In Studs Terkel's book *Working,* a young woman named Nora describes her excitement when she landed her first real job after college. It was for a large, well-known company, and she was intent on bringing everything she was and everything she had learned to the task at hand. The problem was, her coworkers made it clear in subtle and not so subtle ways that if she brought everything she had to the task, she would wreck the curve for everyone else.

Nora said—and this is the part I remember so vividly, the part that went through me like a chill—"Within a few weeks, as I was driving to work I psyched myself down for a job that was too small for me. Within a month, I had absented my spirit from my work."

Absented my spirit.

What a price to pay, both for Nora and for her company. No one does herself (or her company) any favors by staying in a job in which there is very little of her alive. Perhaps your current job isn't the right place for you and you know it. Perhaps it is asking only a small fraction of what you are capable of delivering, and every attempt to deliver more has been denied. Perhaps your job requires you to deliver results that hold little interest for you or that are beyond your capabilities.

Maybe you've been telling yourself that it's not so bad where you are. That while it may not be your dream job, you've gotten used to it. That it's actually kind of comfortable here. You've got a salary and benefits and a place to go five days a week. After all, you've got only fifteen years until retirement. You can hang on until then, for the sake of keeping a roof over your family's heads.

What happens in your gut when you hear yourself thinking this way?

Meanwhile, you have dreams of breaking free, of a different career altogether. In fact, there are days when you'd rather write, read, walk, sculpt, teach, work in a paint store, drive a forklift, sell seashells on the seashore—do anything except the job to which you are currently attached.

If you want to see someone in real pain, watch someone who knows who he is and defaults on it on a regular basis.
—PAT MURRAY

One of my colleagues, Pat Murray, suggests, "If you want to see someone in real pain, watch someone who knows who he is and defaults on it on a regular basis."

If there is no joy in Mudville when you contemplate your job, if you live only for weekends, you are in real pain. Yet often the companies we work for are the right companies, and the problem is that we are in the wrong place in the company or underutilized in our job. Perhaps a fierce conversation with coworkers can open doors to new, more satisfying challenges.

However, if your job is no longer appropriate or sufficient for you and the situation cannot be remedied unless you were to become a different human being entirely, it's time to leave. You can't afford to sit there like a possum in the headlights, or you may end up as the critter *du jour* at a roadside tavern.

Make yourself available to whatever is out there with your name on it.

It may be time to screw your courage to the sticking-place and *fire yourself.* Make yourself available to industry. Make yourself available to whatever is out there with your name on it. Ask yourself:

What activities do I have my heart in?

What am I called to do?

And if you're still hesitating, ask yourself:

Is the personal cost I'm paying really worth it?

As we've seen, one of the rules of engagement for companies, couples, and individuals who are practicing the principles of fierce conversations is that while no one has to change, everyone has to have the conversation.

When we are real with ourselves and others, the change occurs before the conversation has ended. Insights about who we are and what we really want and need are already at work, rearranging our interior furniture, cleaning our internal closet of unnecessary clutter, revealing the way we must go.

When we are real with ourselves and others, the change occurs before the conversation has ended.

And what if the path with your name on it requires a radical upheaval of life as you know it? What if you recognize that, to step into a more pleasing life, you must change career direction entirely? You may be thinking, "If I do what I really want to do, I will make less money. How would my family feel about simplifying our lifestyle, cutting back on expenditures? What would people think? After all, everyone thinks I'm successful where I am."

My response to such concerns is addressed by a definition of success that has served me well for many years: I am successful to the degree that who I am and what I live are in alignment.

In getting to this place of alignment, one thing is clear: The quality of our lives is largely determined by the quality of the questions we ask—and the quality of our answers.

> **There are certain individuals who, in the process of resolving their own inner conflicts, become paradigms for broader groups.**
> —ERIK ERIKSON

Answered thoughtfully and candidly, the right questions offer the possibility of a life that is much more than a satisfactory compromise. As a leader or as a lover, you must answer the right questions for yourself first, and then for the company. Erik Erikson wrote, "There are certain individuals who, in the process of resolving their own inner conflicts, become paradigms for broader groups."

What are the right questions? They are the big questions that define your ideal future:

Where am I going?

Why am I going there?

Who is going with me?

How am I going to get there?

Am I realizing my full potential?

Am I fully extended in my capabilities?

Is there value and fulfillment in my work today?

What unmet needs am I moved and positioned to meet?

The biggest barrier to addressing such questions is fear of the journey—fear of discovering who we are or the impermanence of who we are. Yet these questions are compelling because they lead to an eminently desirable outcome: They enable deep, positive personal change. They open up possibilities not previously accessible.

Companies, teams, families, and communities have been changed by individuals who have arrived at compelling clarity about the trajectories of their corporate and individual lives, having personally wrestled these questions to the ground. Our answers provide the context through which we experience the content of our lives. How do you build this internal context? Articulate the highest and best contribution your company, your family, and your life can make.

We'll take a closer look at several of these questions in chapter 2. In this chapter, you've begun to focus on *your* reality, on what color the beach ball is from your perspective. You've clarified your core values and engaged in a fierce conversation with yourself about your life's focus and that of your company and your career.

In subsequent chapters, you will gain skills in drawing out your colleagues', customers', and life partner's view of reality. You will learn how to really ask—in such a way that people really respond. You'll learn how to engage others in conversations resulting in greater clarity, intimacy, understanding, and impetus for change, bringing you closer together no matter how far apart your current realities and hopes for the future seem today.

❖ A Refresher . . .

- ❖ Regularly interrogate reality in your workplace and in your personal life. What has changed? Does the plan still make sense? If not, what is required of you? of others?

- ❖ Since everyone owns a piece of the truth about reality, consider whose realities should be explored before important decisions are made.

❖ Avoid blame by modifying your language. Replace the word *but* with *and.*

❖ Ensure that your personal and corporate immune systems are healthy by conducting an integrity scan and correcting any outages.

PRINCIPLE **2**

Come Out from Behind Yourself into the Conversation and Make It Real

No one has to change, but everyone has to have the conversation.

—David Whyte

Y ou are an original, an utterly unique human being. You cannot have the life you want, make the decisions you want, or be the leader you are capable of being until your actions represent an authentic expression of who you really are, or who you wish to become.

In the context of fierce conversations, authenticity requires that you pay attention to Woody Allen's first rule of enlightenment: "SHOW UP!"

You must deliberately, purposely come out from behind yourself into the conversation and make it real—at least *your* part of it.

But aren't most people pretty real during a conversation?

I wish I could answer with a resounding "Yes!" but even when you are committed to authenticity, it can be surprisingly difficult. If you listened in on my conversations with employees, learned their

views of their organization's strategy, and then watched them reverse
their positions in the presence of higher-ups, or if you tuned in to the
internal anguish of someone in a troubled marriage and heard him or
her respond "Nothing's wrong" to an inquiring
spouse, you might conclude, as did Martin
Amis, that "we are out there on the cutting
edge of the uncontroversial."

**Authenticity
is not something
you have; it is
something you
*choose.***

In news reports, we often read that someone was "speaking on condition of anonymity."

A near-pathological anonymity and inauthen-
ticity are the stuff of many lives. A friend whose mother had recently
died said, "My mother never shared her dark days, her troubles with
me. I don't feel I really knew her." How real are any of us if we do not
share our dark days with those closest to us, if we do not claim our
failures as well as our successes?

Authenticity is not something you have; it is something you
choose.

Alice and Gary

A sixty-second fierce conversation startled a friend into *showing up*
and changing her life.

After graduating from college, Alice married a fine person. Gary
was in law school, and Alice taught in a high school. Halfway through
law school, Gary realized he had gotten into law for all the wrong reasons—recognition, status, income, his parents' approval. His roman-
ticized version of what it would be like to attend law school did not
match the reality. In fact, he found that he didn't enjoy his classes and
had no real calling for law, so he dropped out and joined Alice in
teaching. At the time, Alice defended Gary to his disappointed parents and particularly to his mother, who pulled Alice aside and said,
"You'll see. He's never finished anything he started."

When the military draft was about to intervene in their lives,

Gary joined the air force. Alice stopped teaching to follow him from base to base and begin a family. After a few years, however, a yearning to farm possessed Gary, so when his stint in the military ended, he and Alice moved to the Midwest, where Gary helped his parents with their small farm, intending to do more as his parents aged.

As the reality of what it took to run a farm became increasingly clear, Gary became restless once again. His idealized, Norman Rockwellian view of farming did not match up with the reality of endless chores, long days, and meager income. Gary began to toy with the notion of teaching college, envisioning himself on a campus, happily immersed in academia. So the family, which now included two young boys, moved to Oregon, where Gary had been offered a scholarship to complete the degrees necessary to launch his new endeavor.

Three years into the program, Alice discovered that Gary had not attended classes for over a year. Instead, he had been slipping back into the house after their sons had gone to school and Alice had left for work. Gary had derailed professionally again. He was, by this time, understandably embarrassed. He suggested that the best plan for the foreseeable future was for him to remain at home, handling the cooking and cleaning, running the endless errands required of a busy family, and most important, being there when the boys got home from school. He had discovered that he was very happy being a househusband.

At the time, Gary and Alice attended a Sunday school for couples in their thirties. About a year into their new arrangement, the topic in Sunday school was the role of the woman in a marriage. The discussion leader read passages from the Bible that suggested women should be at home filling jars with oil, weaving cloth, and putting up olives. Alice stood up and gave an impassioned speech about how, while that may have made sense when the Bible was written, things were different now. Women had many options available to them, and, as everyone knew, though Gary and Alice had reversed the traditional roles, they were deeply happy. Alice got a standing ovation and sat down feeling pleased with others' response to what she had said.

As Alice walked out of the room on her way to the eleven o'clock service, a man she barely knew came up, put his arm around her shoulders, and whispered, "I love you a bunch, but with all due respect, you are full of shit!"

Alice stared, openmouthed, as he continued, "This isn't working for you, Alice. You hate the whole arrangement, and you have lost respect for Gary. What are you pretending not to know?"

What are you pretending not to know?

In that instant, and not a moment before, Alice knew that he was right.

Had Alice really not known what she was feeling? Some people might find that difficult to believe. But until that moment, Alice had been unconscious of her true feelings. She had successfully swept them under the rug. In the movie *The Madness of King George,* a character says to the king, "You seem yourself, Majesty." King George responds, "I have always been myself, even when I was sick, but now it seems I've developed a talent for seeming to be myself."

Both Alice and Gary had seemed to be themselves. But now, as Alice thought about it, she imagined that Gary was probably as unaware and as unhappy as she was. They were both suppressing emotions too painful to examine. Talking about their feelings might force an outcome for which they were not prepared. It took one comment from a virtual stranger who must have been paying fierce attention to the intent beneath Alice's words, to her body language—the slant of her back, held too proudly perhaps—to put her in touch with reality.

Six months later, after many impassioned conversations, Alice and Gary realized that it is possible to love someone and not love your life together.

Gary returned to the Midwest, while Alice and her sons remained in Oregon. Gary has since remarried and is enjoying a satisfying career as a high school teacher and football coach. Alice's career continues to thrive, and she is dating someone with whom she feels deeply compatible.

To this day, Alice wonders how long she and Gary might have trudged along, pretending not to know how deeply off-kilter their marriage was. She is grateful to the man who took the risk to deliver a badly needed message to her—unfiltered and to the point.

Healthy Selfishness

Perhaps you've had an experience similar to Alice's, when a new understanding reared up like a tsunami, startling and disturbing—and undeniable. Perhaps in time you discovered the gift in the message and wondered how you managed to suppress your real feelings from yourself and others for so long

Even individuals who wield significant power at times withhold their real thoughts and feelings from those central to their success and happiness. It has much to do with an underlying impulse to survive by gaining the approval and support of others (boss, customer, coworker, family member, significant other) who we imagine hold the keys to the warehouse wherein is kept everything we want and need. To ensure that such power brokers are on our team, we aim to please. While the desire to please is not a flaw, at crucial crossroads we sometimes go too far. *Way* too far. When faced with a so-called moment of truth, we find ourselves chucking the truth over the fence or tucking it behind the drapes in exchange for a trinket of approval.

What's that behind the curtain, you ask? Oh, nothing important (just my entire identity). May I refill your glass?

Some fear that becoming authentic is a form of selfishness, and unknowingly limit the possibilities within their relationships, feeling it's inappropriate to put their own interests first. After all, what would people think?

During a workshop, Lauren, a delightful woman in her forties, described the unsettling experience of awaking one morning *unrecognizable to herself.* Having spent a lifetime accommodating the needs and desires of so many others, both at work and at home, she had developed amnesia about who she was and what it was she had wanted to do with her life when she was younger and all the possibilities seemed so vast.

At another workshop, a participant said, "I always drive carefully when there's someone important with me in the car." It took her a moment to understand why everyone in the room was gasping.

Do you think you shouldn't need the help, support, or experiences that make you happy?

"I shouldn't need to be told that I am loved."

"It's not fair to insist on quality time with my partner; after all, he is so busy with work."

"I really need to talk this issue through with my boss, but she has different priorities."

Consider this: Successful relationships require that all parties view getting their core needs met as being legitimate. You won't articulate your needs to yourself, much less to your work team or life partner, until and unless you see getting your needs met as a reasonable expectation. So pry the permission door open just far enough to consider that you have a right to clarify your position, state your view of reality, and ask for what you want.

Successful relationships require that all parties view getting their core needs met as being legitimate.

Coming out from behind yourself is part of the search, whether born of panic or courage, for that highly personalized rapture of feeling completely yourself, happy in your own skin. It is a reach for authenticity—a process of individuation—when you cease to compare yourself with others and choose, instead, to live *your* life. It is an opportunity to raise the bar on the experience of your life. It is a deepening of integrity—when who you are and what you live are brought into alignment. No more damping down your soul's deepest longings in order to get approval from others. As André Gide wrote, "It is better to fail at your own life than succeed at someone else's."

Authenticity is a powerful attractor. When we free our true selves and release the energy, others recognize it and respond. It is as if we have set ourselves ablaze. Others are attracted to the warmth and add their logs to the fire.

> **It is better to fail at your own life than succeed at someone else's.**
> —ANDRÉ GIDE

The principal job at hand is to intertwine addressing your current business and personal issues with self-exploration and personal development, building a bridge between yourself as a person and yourself as a professional. The assignments in this chapter are designed to help you ground yourself in original thought and potent action, in work that breaks you open and devastates your habitual self. Parts of your habitual self serve you wonderfully, while others stand squarely in the way of your happiness and success. Do you know which are which?

The Good News and the Bad News

All the bread crumbs lead to the CEO's office. My colleagues at TEC often say, "We advertise for CEOs, and human beings show up." For example, the visionary who founded the company often lacks the attention to detail needed to run the business on a daily basis. The parent who always kisses a child's hurt to make it better may fail when it's time to teach the child to identify and solve the source of the pain.

> **We advertise for CEOs, and human beings show up.**

The good news and the bad news are the same news. The news is: Our companies, our relationships, and our lives are mirrors accurately reflecting us back to ourselves. The results with which we are pleased reflect parts of ourselves that are working well. The results that disappoint and displease us reflect aspects of ourselves—beliefs, behaviors—that simply aren't working.

Doug Stone, author of *Difficult Conversations,* suggests "To say of someone 'He died with his identity intact' is not a compliment." When our idealized views of ourselves are set in stone, despite evidence that there's an imperfection or two (or three), the people in our lives have little recourse other than to work around our flaws or to leave. We can see an organization or a department or a relationship with clarity only when we look ourselves full in the face.

> **To say of someone "He died with his identity intact" is not a compliment.**

Following Doug's example, in my workshops, I ask participants, "Barring all else, what is one word or phrase that absolutely describes you?" Before you read on, take a moment and do this for yourself. What is a word or phrase that unfailingly describes *you?*

Write it down: _____

Stephen, a workshop participant, recently declared with great conviction, "The word is *focus*. Everyone who knows me will tell you that I'm focused on what's important and getting it done."

After all the participants have shared their words, I suggest, "Think of times and situations when you are exactly the opposite of this." Some insist, "I'm never the opposite."

When pressed to identify a time when he is not focused, Stephen realized that, while he is extraordinarily focused in his job, many weekends are given over to aimless activities. "I'm just hanging out, slumped in a chair, watching TV, eating chips. I'm not focused on quality time with my wife or achieving personal goals. I told myself I was going to pick up a guitar I haven't touched in years. It's still in the closet missing two strings."

My accountant recently asked me to sign a paper that would allow her to act on my behalf when I am "in absentia." I laughed. After all, a word that describes me is *present*. But it got me thinking.

When am I not present? With whom? When I am tired. When something else is pressing on my thoughts. At times like these, I have to forcibly reel myself back to the present. I'm not always successful.

The purpose of this exercise is to help us recognize the multiple realities about how each of us shows up in the world, not just when we're at our best.

If we are to develop as leaders, as human beings, our very identities (primal things) must become fluid. For example, is it a fact that you are fair-minded, good-hearted, and generous of spirit? Okay. Have you ever wished, just for a moment, that something bad would happen to someone who has wronged you? Well, that's true about you too. It's neither good nor bad. It's just what is.

Our very identities must become fluid.

One of the most painful realizations upon reaching forty or fifty or sixty can be that you have *no* discernible identity, that somehow your identity has been compromised. It's not that your credit card or social security number was stolen. It's that an internal voice is whispering, insisting, "This isn't you. This isn't enough of you. Parts of you are failing to show up."

In Steve Tesich's novel *Karoo*, Saul Karoo admits, "It occurred to me that I wasn't a human being anymore. Probably hadn't been for some time. I was a loose cannon, whose spin and charge and direction could be reversed at any moment by forces outside myself."

The truth will set you free—but first it may thoroughly irritate you!

It is through such humbling insights into ourselves that we come to know, reshape, and trust the self we may then offer to others. It takes courage to look at ourselves unflinchingly in the mirror called our lives. Sometimes what we see isn't particularly attractive. It has been said that the truth will set you free—but first it may thoroughly irritate you!

You'd Like Thom

Everyone likes Thom Porro, a member of a group of key executives that I chaired in Seattle for many years. He is funny, good-natured, candid, authentic, and skilled at putting his finger on the source of any issue under discussion. Thom's metabolism is the envy of everyone. He appears not to have one ounce of fat on him. *Yes, we hate him for that.* His mind is equally lean and mean.

A few years ago, Don Aubrey, another member of the group, introduced Thom to mountain climbing. Don was all grins as Thom made trip after trip to REI, Seattle's famous everything-you-could-ever-need-to-do-anything-outdoors store, eventually buying every piece of climbing gear known to man and spending as much time as his wife would tolerate learning the sport. In fact, just before his and Don's planned climb of Mount Rainier, Thom had spent thirteen days climbing in Alaska.

The four-person climbing party had purposefully split up. Don and J.J., an experienced female climber, got a four-hour head start. They planned to reach base camp, recuperate, and greet Thom and Mike, the climb leader, with a hot meal. At about ten o'clock in the morning, halfway to base camp, Don and J.J. came to a glacier where bamboo poles marked the recommended route around a crevasse.

A snow bridge offered an enticingly direct, shorter route to base camp. The snow bridge seemed solid. However, after Don carefully examined the dark crevasse, the path marked by the poles was clearly the wiser choice. He and J.J. took the longer route. When they arrived at base camp it was sunny and clear. A gorgeous day.

Thom and the leader arrived at the glacier at about two in the afternoon. They sat in the snow and retrieved sandwiches from their packs. Thom glanced toward the crevasse, then at the bamboo poles. Thom and Mike had discussed route options, and Thom was to take the lead on this section of the climb. He gulped down the last of his meal, turned to Mike, and said, "I vote for the snow bridge."

Thom moved quickly, without roping up. As Mike stood to shoulder his pack, he was horrified to see the top of Thom's head disappearing as the snow bridge collapsed beneath him.

As Thom fell, he glanced off the ice walls, breaking something with each hit. A rib. The cheekbone supporting his left eye. Another rib. An ankle. Another rib. With each collision with the icy walls of the crevasse, Thom wondered, "Is this the one that's going to break my neck? Is this my last moment of consciousness?"

Thom fell the equivalent of seven stories. If he had not landed on a three-foot-wide ledge of ice, he would still be down there. It took hours to get him out of the deep, narrow icebox. Each pull on the rope sent showers of snow down the crevasse. It was feared that a large chunk would dislodge and finish Thom off.

When Don and J.J. heard about the accident on their radio, it was too late to get back down the mountain, so it was the next day before they could retrace their steps. On the way down the mountain, Don photographed the crevasse. He and J.J. stopped at a one-hour photo developing shop and got the film developed. When they walked into Thom's hospital room, the first thing Thom said was, "That crevasse came out of nowhere!"

This was your basic moment of truth. The executives in Don and Thom's group have had many a fierce conversation over the years, and this seemed like a prime candidate for another one. Don took a deep breath and said, "You look like hell, buddy. I'm awful glad you're alive. But that crevasse didn't come out of nowhere. It was risky enough at ten in the morning. Look at this photo. You got there four hours later. Four more hours of melting in full sun. What the hell were you pretending not to know?"

Thom did look awful. Since one of his eyeballs was hanging disconcertingly low in its socket, he could barely see the photos. He squinted and moved the photos farther from and closer to his face, attempting to focus. After about a minute Thom became abnormally still. Not at all like our familiar, attention-deficited friend. After a long silence, he murmured, "God almighty. What *was* I pretending not to know?"

At a meeting two months later, Thom hobbled in for a session with the group. We insisted on a blow-by-blow account of the entire misadventure, which was sobering and graphic to the point of inducing nausea and a keen desire to rush home and kiss our children. After Thom had answered all of our questions, he shared his insight. "Well, now I know what a fierce conversation is. I had the fiercest one of my life while plummeting seven stories into a crevasse. It was brief—but memorable!"

We all laughed, as Thom continued, "Lying in the hospital forced me to lie still and think about some things. I saw that the way I approached that crevasse is pretty much the way I live my life. One foot after the other. Head down. Don't look up. No time. Just move. Now, now, now. What's coming next? Sorry, too busy. Got things to do."

We nodded. We knew Thom and we knew ourselves. Most of us weren't much different.

Then Thom added quietly, "It almost cost me my life."

While most of us don't behave in ways that put our lives at risk, without realizing it we often put our careers and our marriages at risk at the conference table or the kitchen table, by operating much of the time like Thom. By not paying attention to what others are really saying or asking. Not even to our own words. Instead, we string meaningless words together, all the while complaining that today seems an awful lot like yesterday.

A Nervous Breakthrough

I remember Beth, a woman who attended one of my workshops several years ago. It was January. The class was held in the visitors' center of the Washington Park Arboretum. The wintry view out the windows put us all in a reflective mood. Beth had been quiet, lost in thought for the better part of the day. At one point I said, "Beth, will you let us in on your thoughts?"

She answered quietly, in a soft Southern accent, "I've been thinking about my life." We waited. Beth barely took a breath during the following stream of consciousness:

When I was first married, I was right on time with the biological clock, which set the pattern of correctness and timely dutifulness and the predictability of a marriage that lasted fourteen years, kids, two of them, of course, divorce, a second marriage which was a disaster because, like everyone who divorces after fourteen or eighteen or twenty-two years, you're crazy as a loon, only you don't know it and you think you've learned so much and now you know what you really want or at least what you don't want, and then this man shows up who tells you you're the one he's been looking for forever, and your body wakes up and you feel attractive and valued and excited about life again, and so what if he's a lot younger than you and even though all your friends and all the books and articles warn you that it's too soon, that you need at least a year or two to figure things out and date several people, what's the rush, et cetera, you're so caught up in the look in his eyes and, besides, he seems to know what he's doing and it just feels so good to be in love or in lust again that you go ahead and marry him and then it takes a week or two, maybe a month, to figure out that you blew it, all your friends and books and articles were right, I mean, he doesn't even know the words to your favorite songs, but then it takes a year or two to finally give up and get out and then you finally meet someone right for you and you marry him and you don't see it coming one morning two weeks before Christmas when you're reading the newspaper over a cup of coffee and you are in your nice home with your nice husband and you are suddenly terrified that your life will continue exactly as it is until the day you die and you realize you better put your seat belt on because lunacy is sitting in the corner behind the Christmas tree, and it just irritates the hell

out of me that all this is part of the schedule, you know, all that midlife
crisis stuff, and I'm right on time as usual. I'm a compulsive punctual.

There was a stunned silence and then Beth chuckled. "Y'all can
laugh. I think I'm having a nervous breakthrough." We roared with
appreciation for an authentic, kindred spirit. What Beth did was
show up to herself.

The following four assignments will help you show up to yourself, as boldly as Beth and Thom. They will require you to be daring,
but, let's face it, you've tried prudent planning long enough. It's time
to show up in 3-D, Technicolor, wide-screen, Dolby surround sound,
to yourself. Even, perhaps, to overhear yourself saying things *you
didn't know you knew.* It is highly likely that your own learning will be
provoked.

First, you will do a gut check on how you feel about your life today. Next, you'll describe key aspects of the future you desire. Third,
given the gap between your current reality and your ideal future,
you'll identify the conversations you need to have with others. Finally, before you have conversations with anyone else, you'll have one
with yourself about an issue that is troubling you.

What are the rewards for coming out from behind yourself into
the following conversations and making them real? You will find
yourself abandoning the safety of confusion (confusion and safety are
illusions, anyway) for the juice and motivation of clarity. You will nurture your own deepening dissolution and the emergence of healthier, more effective qualities and behaviors. Your desire to control others will be balanced with the willingness to surrender. As a result, you will move toward what you desire—a happier marriage, personal freedom, professional accomplishment, a life that simply fits you better. A lot better. The experience of being awake, alive, and free.

> **How we spend
> our days
> is how we spend
> our lives.**
> —ANNIE DILLARD

Assignment 1

Annie Dillard wrote, "How we spend our days is how we spend our lives." How are you spending your days, your life? Write down how you feel about yourself, your life, and your work—several words or phrases that capture your thoughts and emotions.

MYSELF

MY LIFE

MY WORK

Assignment 2

Write your personal stump speech. There are several forms of stump speeches. One of my favorites is Kevin Costner's memorable "I believe" speech to Susan Sarandon in the movie *Bull Durham*. Most women recall the line: "I believe in long, slow, deep, soft, wet kisses that last three days . . ." *Ahem. Moving right along . . .*

In chapter 6, if you are a leader, you will write your corporate stump speech. For *your* stump speech, I suggest you take a broad perspective. You'll answer four questions: *Where am I going? Why am I going there? Who is going with me? How will I get there?*

It helps to pull back from your life and look at it as if you're the screenwriter, director, producer, and star. What's the plot? What's the story? What's the arc? What's the ending? You can't always foresee the interesting side trips you may take, but where are you headed? A trajectory and destination are essential for clarity, even though you will likely make course corrections throughout your life, as wisdom and maturity broaden your perspective and scrub that last shred of inauthenticity off you. But for now, where you are today, take a stand for the ideal future you envision.

This exercise requires and deserves time. Ideally, a one- or two-day personal retreat. At a minimum, several hours. Your living room will work just fine—though, if possible, I suggest that you get out of your everyday environment. A change in your literal horizon will boost your ability to see new horizons for your life and career.

This fierce conversation with oneself during which we revisit our personal stump speech has become so valuable to me through the years that I go to considerable lengths to ensure the quality of that conversation. Each September, I take a long walk—typically five to seven days—*alone*. The purpose of my September walks is to revisit, reclarify, and recommit to what my soul desires.

Revisit, reclarify, and recommit to what your soul desires.

In September 1999, I walked the Yorkshire Dales in England. It was late afternoon of the first day before the chatter in my head began to quiet down. By day two, I felt completely alive, overcome by the beauty of the territory. Most of day three was spent on the high moors. My only companions were sheep, rabbits, and curlews. Midafternoon, I climbed atop a stone outcropping to enjoy my lunch and to drink in the view.

Before continuing the walk that would take me down into a village for the evening, I opened up to a fierce conversation with myself: "Am I on the right path? Is the life I'm living an authentic expression of who I am, of who I wish to become? Is there anything I am pretending not to know? What is next for me?" I got answers.

That evening, on my bedside table in the cozy inn, I found the book *Watership Down,* which I had read to my daughters years ago. It was delightful to reread parts of this favorite book, reacquainting myself with Hazel and Fiver and the peculiar language of rabbits. I was deeply happy. On this night, outside my window, three stars soaking up twilight lit the way forward. And I was certain of the path.

> **All conversations are with myself, and sometimes they involve other people.**

Why is it so important to spend time conversing with ourselves? Because *all conversations are with myself, and sometimes they involve other people.* This is incredibly important to understand. Embracing this insight changes the way we relate to and interact with everyone in our lives. I may think I see you as you are, but in truth, I see you as *I am.* The implications are staggering, and not the least of them is this: *The issues in my life are rarely about you. They are almost always about me.*

This means that I cannot come out from behind myself into conversations with others and make them real until I know who *I am* and what I intend to do with my life. Each of us must first answer the question "Where am I going?" before we can address the question "Who is going with me?" It is essential not to get those out of order.

This September will find me in the Swiss Alps. When I am alone, in nature, my life automatically properly reprioritizes itself. I return—to my family, to my company, and to myself—refreshed. Clear and clean.

> **Our bodies manifest the pictures our minds send to them.**

Whether you end up spending four hours at home or manage to get away for a day or two, I assure you that your work, your relationships, and your life will begin to be transformed as a result of addressing these questions. You will bring into your life whatever it is that you have the most clarity about. The trouble is, most people have a great deal of clarity about what it is they *don't* want. So guess what they get!

Our bodies manifest the pictures our minds send to them. Clarify what you want. See it on the movie screen of your mind in 3-D, Technicolor, wide-screen, with Dolby surround sound.

Don't allow your inner critic to edit your answers to the following questions. Set reality considerations aside. Just write whatever comes to mind. If you hear yourself answering "I don't know" to any of the questions, ask yourself, "What would it be if I *did* know?"

Stump Speech

- Where am I going?

- Why am I going there?

- Who is going with me?

- How will I get there?

Assignment 3

Now that you've written your personal stump speech, you're ready to list the fierce conversations you need to have with others. They may be the conversations you've been assiduously avoiding for months or years. Some of them may be about the undiscussables in your life—the topics that you and others have been avoiding at home or at work, the topics that need to be addressed and resolved in order for you to move forward. You won't address them quite yet, but it's time to identify them.

Write down the name of each person and a sentence or two about the topic for the conversation. For example:

- Bob (my boss): My career ambitions; in particular, my desire to prove myself a worthy candidate for the position of VP of operations.

- Jane (my wife): We're both so busy. We haven't spent much time together or had many laughs lately. I'm worried that our relationship is becoming stale. How do we resolve the challenges of our busy lives and create quality time together?

- Alison (my direct report): Her performance has really slipped. I no longer feel I can rely on her to get things done. The stakes are high for her, for me, for our department. I'd like to resolve this.

- Jeff (my son): I don't think he knows how proud I am of him, how much I love him. I want to tell him and schedule something special to do together.

Fierce Conversations I Need to Have . . .

PERSON	TOPIC
■	■
■	■
■	■

Assignment 4

In chapter 1, you were introduced to the Mineral Rights conversation that I had with John Tompkins. Now I'd like you to have it with yourself. I'm asking you to take on the issue that is troubling you the most, perhaps the one that you least want to face, the one you sense may require courage you're not sure you have. You will need an hour. Alone. Uninterrupted.

In preparation, identify your single most pressing issue, something that is currently going on in your professional or personal life that you want and need to resolve. In workshops, participants' issues cover a wide range . . .

- Our strategic plan looks good on paper, but it's not being implemented. We're headed for a bad day.

- I'm failing in my job. I'm afraid I'm going to be fired.

- My marriage is stagnant. My wife and I are housemates, not lovers.

- I'm overweight. If I don't make a change, my health will suffer.

- I think my spouse is having an affair. I encountered more evidence last week. It's driving me crazy.

- I suspect our sales manager has a drinking problem. I hear stories about what happens on the road. I've asked him about them, but he makes light of them. I just heard another story—from a customer.

- My daughter may be doing drugs. I know she'll deny it.

- My job pays well, but when I imagine myself doing this for another ten years, well, just take me out back and shoot me now.

- I'm successful in my work, but my personal relationships keep failing. I don't want to end up alone, but it looks like that's where I'm headed.

To the degree that you are fierce with yourself—passionate, real, unbridled, uncensored—a Mineral Rights conversation will help you explore issues by mining for greater clarity, improved understanding, and impetus for change. It will shine a bright light on that issue of yours, the one growling in the dungeon, and you'll live to tell about it.

So now it's time to begin. Write down your response to each of the following questions. Do not edit your responses. Just write. In the appendix, you'll find a blank copy of Mineral Rights to use on additional or future issues.

Step 1: **Identify your most pressing issue.**
The issue that I most need to resolve is:

Step 2: **Clarify the issue.**
What is going on?

How long has this been going on?

How bad are things?

Step 3: **Determine the current impact.**
How is this issue currently impacting me?

What results are currently being produced for me by this situation?

How is this issue currently impacting others?

What results are currently being produced for them by this situation?

When I consider the impact on myself and others, what are my emotions?

Step 4: **Determine the future implications.**
If nothing changes, what's likely to happen?

What's at stake for me relative to this issue?

What's at stake for others?

When I consider these possible outcomes, what are my emotions?

Step 5: **Examine your personal contribution to this issue.**
What is my contribution to this issue? (How have I contributed to the problem?)

Step 6: **Describe the ideal outcome.**
When this issue is resolved, what difference will that make?

What results will I enjoy?

When this issue is resolved, what results will others enjoy?

When I imagine this resolution, what are my emotions?

Step 7: **Commit to action.**
What is the most potent step I could take to move this issue toward resolution?

What's going to attempt to get in my way, and how will I get past it?

When will I take this step?

Contract with Yourself . . .

During this fierce conversation with myself, I've identified a potent step to take to begin to resolve this issue. I have chosen the date by which I will take this step. There will be other steps, perhaps many of them. This is the first. I commit to taking it.

_____   _____

action   *today's date*

Now take a break. Walk around. Breathe. Breathing is good.

Take It Personally

A final note: The phrases "Don't take this personally" and "Don't take yourself so seriously" are misguided suggestions. Do take it personally; do take yourself seriously. The opposite of "So what?" is to take it personally! Work is deeply personal. Leading is intensely personal. Ultimately, everything is personal, assuming you've addressed the questions . . .

Who am I?

What price am I willing to pay to be that?

This is your life. I hope it has its hilarious moments; however, this is serious business—or what's the point? If you don't take it seriously, there won't be enough of *you* here. The results you're experiencing and the emotions roiling within you are direct results of how you are showing up to yourself and others. All day. Every day.

What about making it personal at home but keeping a politically strategic distance at work? If that is the model, we ultimately absent our spirit from our work. Then we come home and complain about it all. *My boss is an idiot. Our customers are unreasonable. My colleagues aren't pulling their weight.* Whoever awaits our arrival at home receives the brunt of all our angst and anger.

There is no workable separation of selves at work and at home. We are ourselves all over the place, and it is this real self that is felt and experienced at a deeply personal level by ourselves and everyone on the receiving end of us, whether we acknowledge it or not. In *Traveling Mercies*, Anne Lamott writes, "Everything is usually so masked or perfumed or disguised in the world, and it's so touching when you get to see something real and human . . . no matter how neurotic the members [of the group], how deeply annoying or dull . . . when people have seen you at your worst, you don't have to put on the mask as much. And that gives us license to try on that radical hat of liberation, the hat of self-acceptance."

❖ A Refresher . . .

❖ Free your true self and release the energy. Others will recognize it and respond.

❖ Your body will manifest the pictures your mind sends to it, so clarify where you want to go with your life in 3-D, Technicolor, wide-screen, with Dolby surround sound.

❖ If you overhear yourself saying, "I don't know," ask yourself, "What would it be if I did know?"

❖ Take yourself seriously. Take your life personally. Otherwise, there won't be enough of *you* here.

PRINCIPLE **3**

Be Here, Prepared to Be Nowhere Else

The experience of being understood, versus interpreted, is so compelling, you can charge admission.

—B. Joseph Pine II, *The Experience Economy*

There is a profound difference between having a title, a job description, or a marriage license and being someone to whom people commit at the deepest level. If we wish to accomplish great things in our organizations and in our lives, then we must come to terms with a basic human need: We must recognize that humans share a universal longing to be known and, being known, to be loved.

When our conversations with others disregard this core need, our lives can seem like an ongoing, exhausting struggle to influence others to do what we want them to do, to rise to their potential, to accomplish the goals of the organization or of the relationship. We persuade, cajole, manipulate, and issue directives. Nothing changes. Deadlines are missed. The scenery is boring. People and relationships are on automatic pilot.

Consider this passage in *The Fifth Discipline Fieldbook*, edited by Peter Senge:

Among the tribes of northern Natal in South Africa, the most common greeting, equivalent to "hello" in English, is the expression: "sawu bona." It literally means, "I see you." If you are a member of the tribe, you might reply by saying "sikhona" or "I am here." The order of the exchange is important: until you see me, I do not exist. It's as if, when you see me, you bring me into existence.

Only when we genuinely *see* the people who are important to us can we hope to succeed as agents for positive change.

Having misread many individuals throughout our lifetime, however, we often find that discovering someone else's authentic self can be complicated by our increasing cynicism. In Philip Roth's *The Human Stain,* a character suggests, "By a certain age, one's mistrust is so exquisitely refined that one is unwilling to believe anybody." Or to *know* anyone. Or to get too close.

Discovering someone else's authentic self can be complicated by our increasing cynicism.

Yet we must learn to rebuild the links that connect people and that provide an effective antidote to cynicism and disaffection. We must transform the way we speak, the way we ask, the way we listen. How do we get to know another person? How do we get past "How are you? I'm fine."

By really asking and really listening. By being with someone, even if only for a brief moment, prepared to be nowhere else.

Fred Timberlake

When I was sixteen, I got a summer job as an assistant to Fred Timberlake, head of sales and marketing at Cook Paint and Varnish in Kansas City, Missouri. I could type a hundred words a minute and, as this was long before computers in every cubicle, I sat at an IBM Selectric, the metal ball of type twirling furiously. During my second week on the job, the Selectric suddenly froze, and I looked up, shocked to see Mr. Timberlake holding the cord after having pulled the plug from the outlet. He was smiling. He handed me a sheet of paper.

"What do you think of this advertising layout, Susan?"

I glanced at the layout, then looked behind me, certain that there must be another Susan on the payroll, one who could provide intelligent input. But there was no one there, and Mr. Timberlake was still standing in front of me, waiting for a response. The expression on his face, his posture, and the full-stop silence encompassing my desk and seemingly everything within miles persuaded me that he was really asking. I studied the advertising layout. It featured a stack of paint cans with colorful graphics.

My impulse was to shrug and say, "I don't know. I don't have any experience in advertising." However, I had the impression that Mr. Timberlake anticipated my response with genuine interest. I didn't want to disappoint my boss, so I thought hard.

"Well, my mom thought about painting our living room for a long time, but she couldn't make up her mind what color to use. Then she saw a photograph in a magazine of a really pretty room with walls painted a color she liked and she went right out that day and bought paint. I think the picture helped her imagine what our living room could look like. Maybe if you showed a pretty room with walls painted a great color, it would give people the courage to go buy some paint."

Mr. Timberlake listened as I spoke. When I stopped, he stood quietly for a moment, then said, "Remarkable. Thank you, Susan. I'm sending this back to the drawing board."

Throughout that summer, whenever my Selectric froze, I would smile and prepare to answer another of Mr. Timberlake's questions. In his presence, I became a bigger human being. Every person who worked for Fred Timberlake would have followed him anywhere.

It's amazing how this seemingly small thing—simply paying

fierce attention to another, really asking, really listening, even during a brief conversation—can evoke such a wholehearted response. A Chinese proverb says, "When a question is posed ceremoniously, the universe responds." When someone *really* asks, we really answer. And, somehow, both of us are validated.

When a question is posed ceremoniously, the universe responds.

Think for a moment about the kind of attention you bring to your conversations. While someone is talking, where are your thoughts? When you are face-to-face, do you look at the individual in front of you or do your eyes roam the room in a sort of perpetual surveillance? While you're talking with someone on the telephone, do you scan your e-mail? And can you tell when someone else is scanning his?

The assignment in this chapter will help you learn to be with someone, prepared to be nowhere else. You've done important work in the first two chapters. You've conducted an integrity scan, written your stump speech, and listed others with whom you need to have important conversations. You've had a fierce conversation with yourself using the Mineral Rights model.

The first question you answered in your stump speech was "Where am I going?" You can't answer the second question—"Who is going with me?"—until you know who that someone is.

Do I want this person as a member of my team? As a client? Is it time to commit to this relationship? Do I really know this person?

By the end of this chapter you'll be ready to have a fierce conversation with someone else, a conversation that will be significantly differentiated from others you have had. You'll explore an important issue by asking questions and listening carefully to your partner's response. Anyone with whom you have this conversation will go away from it having enjoyed your complete attention and feeling known by you—a rare and wonderful thing.

The One-to-One

One of the most difficult decisions I've ever made was to stop chairing my group of Seattle CEOs in order to free up more time for writing and speaking. For thirteen years I had a fifty-yard-line seat on some of the most interesting lives in town.

Each month, sixteen noncompeting CEOs spent a day together. At times I would bring in an outside expert for the morning, someone who would engage the group in an intimate dialogue guaranteed to provoke learning. In the afternoons we focused on the most pressing issues of three or four of the members.

- In this tough economy, should I lay people off or keep them on?

- What customer-relationship management system is the best fit for my company?

- What is your evaluation of this potential acquisition?

- How can we build our brand?

I loved those days and looked forward to the interaction of the group. They were genuinely glad to be together, focused on their businesses in the company of peers with no agenda other than to help one another succeed. Once an issue was introduced, we mined for the group gold and struck rich veins by posing hard questions.

But the other interaction each month—the one-to-one—was in some ways more satisfying to me. I've talked about these conversations already. This was a member's time alone with me and mine with him or her.

I knew, because my clients had told me in ways I could not discount, that these fierce conversations meant as much to them as to me. Reality was interrogated, learning was provoked, the tough issues were tackled, and our relationship was enhanced.

During the gorgeous days of summer and fall, several members preferred to get out of their offices and meet me at Green Lake. It took an hour to walk around the lake. Two strolls around Green Lake provided just enough time to cover everything going on in the CEO's corporate and personal life. I once made the mistake of scheduling three Green Lake sessions on the same day. During six trips around the lake, the conversations were so riveting that I didn't feel a thing until the next morning, when I leapt out of bed and my legs buckled beneath me.

Here's the thing I most want you to understand: I had little or no experience in such diverse businesses as rapid prototyping, software development, fine art supplies, public accounting, telecommunications, and commercial construction. What I *did* have was fierce affection for each of my clients, genuine curiosity about the topic of the moment, an insatiable appetite for learning, and a fierce resolve to be with each individual, prepared to be nowhere else.

This set of characteristics translates to personal relationships as well. For those relationships to move forward and upward, you must have fierce affection for the other person. You must have genuine curiosity about what is going on with that person at any given time. You must have an insatiable appetite for learning more every day about who he or she is and where he or she wants to go and how this does or does not mesh with who you are and where you want to go. And all of this is helped significantly by your willingness to occasionally set aside all of the topics ping-ponging inside your own head and simply be with this other person, here and now.

Perhaps you have a creeping foreboding that, in some instances, all this getting to know someone, all this *being present* stuff, involves listening endlessly to someone telling you more than you ever wanted to know about a series of boring topics. All the gory details about who did what to whom.

This would not work for me or for most people I know. Few of us are blessed with unending patience or the ability to demonstrate genuine interest in every individual or issue that crosses our paths. This is certainly true of anyone heading up an organization, or a team within an organization tasked to pull off miracles in a short time frame—which is what the business world requires of us daily. Time that busy people have set aside to talk with anybody about anything is time not to be taken lightly. Something needs to be set in motion as a result of their time with others. Every conversation has to count.

If this sounds like you, or like you in certain situations, then be comforted by the following. . . .

Yes, the conversation *is* the relationship. One conversation at a time, you are building, destroying, or flatlining your relationships. It is possible, however, to create high-intimacy, low-maintenance relationships—one relatively *brief* conversation at a time. If that sounds good to you, read on.

Getting Past "How Are You?"

Somewhere in our histories, most of us have come across an individual who remains a cipher to us. A coworker who seems to be wrapped in Teflon, carrying a shield. A relative with whom you always end up in some kind of misunderstanding. No matter how much you try, you don't seem to be able to connect with that person in any meaningful way. You're not sure where he or she is coming from, and the feeling is probably mutual. You've been tempted to say, "I've been hanging out with you for years, and I still don't know who you are or what you want."

The problem does not always lie in a lack of time together. Almost every busy parent has felt guilty about not spending enough time with his or her child. Most couples express concern that they have not been spending as much time with their mates as they feel they should. Most leaders suspect that things would go more smoothly if they spent more time with the individuals on their leadership team and that they, in turn, should do the same with the people who report to them. So we carve out the time, sometimes grudgingly.

A parent sits down to talk with a child. A couple gets a babysitter and goes out to dinner. A leader schedules a meeting with a direct report. What happens? Not much. Just space, uncomfortable space, stretching out in front of you. Many do not make it past "How are you?" "I'm fine."

Many of us have imagined saying, "By the way, I only have three days to live," or "I robbed a bank and I'm running away with the bartender at Trudy's Tavern," just to see if anyone would notice.

Kathleen de Burca, the central character in *My Dream of You* by Nuala O'Faolain, describes a missed conversation with a companion escorting her to an awards ceremony, who tells her not to be nervous. Kathleen replies, "I'm not nervous in public." She then shares her interior dialogue with the reader.

> **Unconsciously, we end our conversations as soon as we initiate them, too afraid of what we might say or hear.**

"This was an invitation to ask me what I meant, and for me to tell him about being afraid of the people I knew, not the people I didn't know, and for him to tell me what he felt, and so on. But he didn't know how to talk that kind of talk."

When people are not paying attention, not really engaged, there are many missed opportunities to clamber out of the usual conversational box and talk about something interesting and memorable. However, while most people think the problem lies with others, what if there is something else at work here? What if *you're* the problem? What if you're so unengaged or unengaging that nobody hears you, nobody really listens to you, nobody really responds to you?

Perhaps you're too polite. Or too self-conscious. Or too self-absorbed. Or too politically correct. Or too cautious. The net result? Unconsciously, we end our conversations as soon as we initiate them, too afraid of what we might say or hear.

In the workplace, this translates into the typical exchange:

"How's the project going?"

"Great."

"Everything working out?"

"You bet."

"Good. That's what I like to hear."

No one's really asking. No one's really listening.

"Have a good day?"

"Yeah. You?"

"Sure."

"Hmmm."

No one engages; nothing changes.

So what do we do about this? For starters, being with someone prepared to be nowhere else takes courage. It's unlikely any of us will really ask, unless and until we are prepared to really hear the response and respond in turn, addressing a potentially difficult or complex topic authentically with someone, here and now.

Where do we get the courage? In part, simply by recognizing that if you chicken out now, you'll pay the price later. Recognizing that if you or someone else feels a conversation is needed, it is. If a sensitive or significant topic comes up unbidden, seize the moment. Those conversations you listed in chapter 2 need to take place. They're important to your success and happiness and, I would venture to guess, to other people's success and happiness as well. Avoiding or postponing a conversation, downplaying its importance, or trying to bluff your way through it only delays, or may even accelerate, a very bad day.

If you or someone else feels that a conversation is needed, it is.

A reminder here: So often people forget that one of the fiercest conversations any of us can have is to tell someone how important he or she is in our lives, how much we value and love that person. For many people, that is more difficult than bringing up a concern. If none of the conversations you listed in chapter 2 involves letting someone know what he or she means to you or to your organization, go back and add a conversation.

Now let's focus on one of the basics of being present—eye contact. So simple, and yet so difficult.

Soft Eyes and Ears

Many people make little contact during a conversation. Not even eye contact. A vivid experience I had of this was with Mark, a high-level leader of a global organization. Mark had invited me to talk about fierce conversations with his executive staff during a two-day retreat. When I arrived at the site, I met with Mark to review the ideal outcomes from my time with his team and to find out how things were going so far.

Mark didn't look at me. During my conversation with Mark, no matter who was talking, he simply did not look at me. Eventually I said, "While we've been talking, I've noticed you haven't looked at me."

Mark smiled, glanced at me, then looked away and responded, "I haven't decided if I like you yet."

"So until you've made up your mind whether or not you like me, you will withhold eye contact?"

He smiled again. "That's what I do."

"Do you do this with members of your executive team? For whatever period of time it takes you to decide whether or not you like them . . . you withhold eye contact?"

"That's right."

"Well, I feel it acutely, this withholding of yourself, of your approval, and I'm puzzled. You invited me here to produce a result you say you want. It seems we should be collaborating. I'd like to feel you are joining me in this conversation, and it would help if you'd look at me while we talk."

Mark was looking at me now. Not smiling. I wondered if he would stand up and say, "We're done. You're outta here." But instead, he thought for a moment and then said, "Okay, let's work."

"One more thing," I offered. "If you are not looking at the people on your team when you're talking with them, be aware that they may feel they're invisible to you. Devalued. I don't imagine that's what you want."

Half an hour later, as Mark introduced me, he said, "Susan practices what she preaches. I know. She told me I had lousy eye contact and that it didn't feel very good. So I'm going to work on that."

Fifty people smiled and nodded.

I do not, however, recommend maintaining *maniacal* eye contact during your conversations. Many of us have wanted to back away from an avid individual whose eyes seemed to drill through us and out the other side. What I do recommend are "soft eyes."

Years ago, I lived near Tokyo and studied karate. During the last half hour of each session, everyone formed a circle around one individual and could attack the person in the center of the circle from any direction at any time, with no warning. When I was the vulnerable individual in the center, I initially strained to see everyone, my eyes darting from person to person, whirling and turning so that I wouldn't miss anything. I often ended up felled, not by someone behind me but by someone right in front of me. It seemed that the harder I tried to see, the more I missed.

The sensei taught us that if instead of trying to focus on any one thing we softened our eyes and allowed the world to come to us, we would see a great deal more. We would catch subtle motion. Our peripheral vision would become acute. This was true. Over time, we developed the proverbial eyes in the backs of our heads. And it was effortless.

The same thing happens with our listening. We may succeed in hearing every word yet miss the message altogether.

At a business meeting in Tokyo, I noticed a young woman writing continuously. Following the meeting, I commented that it was good to have someone capturing everything that was said.

We may succeed in hearing every word yet miss the message altogether.

"Oh, she wasn't writing down what was said," a friend explained. "She was writing down what was *not* said."

"But she never stopped writing the entire time!"

My companion simply smiled.

In conversations, soft eyes and soft ears allow a partner to come to you, to communicate to you. It is not about being clever or having degrees in a particular field. It's about being genuinely interested, really asking, and paying fierce attention to the response. To the whole person responding.

Years later, when I worked for a search firm, someone asked me how I could bear to interview people all day. It was as if this person felt that interviews with job candidates couldn't be interesting, that somehow they must all be alike. The question astounded me. I almost always lost myself in those interviews.

Sometimes a colleague would later ask, "Was she the one with the pink piping around the collar of her jacket?" Or, "He wore glasses and had a beard, right?" I could never remember.

Who cares if the guy has a beard! He is a delightful, interesting human being who raises basil as a hobby, makes incredible pesto. I don't remember what color his eyes are, but I do know that he has an eye for detail, incredible organization skills, and a wonderfully wry sense of humor. I think he'd be successful with several of our clients. And who notices piping, for God's sake?

More recently, I worked with a woman who had incredible hands. I could listen to her through isolated hand movements. At first I felt self-conscious focusing on her hands, but they had so much to say. At one point, I told her that her hands were wonderfully expressive. She looked at her hands a moment and said, "This morning I put on my coat and my mother's hand came out the sleeve."

There is so much more to listen to than words. Listen to the whole person.

How Aren't You?

For many people, the answer to the question "What's the opposite of talking?" is "Waiting to talk." Many think that not speaking when someone is talking is the same as listening. Hearing people's words is only the beginning. Do you also hear their fears? their intentions? their aspirations? In the words of the thirteenth-century Sufi poet Rumi:

> *Reach your long hand out*
> *to another door, beyond where*
> *you go on the street, the street*
> *where everyone says, "how are you?"*
> *And no one says how aren't you?*

At a recent workshop in Florida, I asked a participant, David, to come to the front of the room and talk about a problem he'd like to solve. I asked a third of the participants to listen for content, a third for emotion, and a third for intent. David spoke about his ongoing struggle with his weight. He discussed his concerns about how his health might suffer if he didn't get on top of this issue, how he didn't feel good in his clothes, how important it was for him to start eating better and exercising, how long he had been struggling with this issue.

Hearing people's words is only the beginning.

After a few minutes I stopped David and asked each group to tell him what they had "heard." The content group fed his words back to him almost verbatim. David nodded. The emotion group picked up on his frustration, embarrassment, and helplessness. David acknowledged all of this. The group listening for intent delivered the blow: "You aren't going to do anything about this. Right now, it's all just words." David blanched and disagreed with their assessment. On the very next break, he helped himself to brownies.

David had given us the usual rhetoric that most of us hear and even say ourselves when trying to lose weight: "I've got to get a handle on this. I'm going to watch what I eat and start exercising."

When we listen beyond words for intent, for the scaffolding on which a story hangs, clarity and character emerge. We need to listen this way to ourselves, not just to others.

The Samurai Game

I got a unique perspective on being present years ago when I did some training for an organization called Sports Mind. It was marvelous preparation for the work I would soon be doing with leaders. Three facilitators took work teams out into the boonies for four days of weird and wonderful stuff. We climbed poles and leapt for trapeze swings, zip-lined across rivers, and walked beams fifty feet off the ground. The most controversial activity was the Samurai Game, played on the third night. Before I became a trainer, I remember being prepared for the Samurai Game as a participant.

We were told, "Go spend an hour alone, in silence. When you return to this room, enter it as a samurai—in silence."

An hour later, as about sixty other participants and I sat on the floor, ready to learn the rules of the game, I sensed an intense, impassioned spirit in myself and others. It was as if each of us had experienced a "walk-in" by the ghost of a samurai from long ago. The facilitator, who had adopted the unnervingly stern visage of a Fate of War, gave us plenty to think about.

"How would a samurai sit?" he asked in a deep voice.

We straightened our spines.

"How would a samurai listen?"

Every synapse and neuron went on alert.

For the next five hours, we were caught up body and soul in the game, which was not so much a game as a vivid and utterly compelling reality. While we were never in danger of physical harm, many battles such as rock, paper, scissors, or holding one's arms up until the point of exhaustion, or standing on one leg in the "crane" position, were won or lost on the battlefield. Many samurai were "killed" and the battlefield became littered with bodies. Occasionally, the Fate of War would halt the battle long enough for the two armies to drag off their "dead."

My army's daimyo, the equivalent of a CEO, repeatedly chose me to fight challenging battles. I brought to the game everything I had learned about centering and focus. While other battles raged around me, I fought with fierce attention. Silently, I read the mind of each opponent and communicated my will to defeat him or her. In one particularly arduous battle, compassion for my opponent caused me to will her to endure. In my head and heart, I upheld both of us. The battle was a draw.

Amazed, I remained standing until the end, humbled and inspired by the power of being completely present and attentive to everything that was happening. The concept of changing my life by merely paying fierce attention to it had become entirely real to me. I was paying attention not as a means to an end—to be liked or to make another person feel liked or understood—but as a new way of experiencing myself and others. I felt utterly calm, clear, and alive. I felt like, as my colleague James Newton, founder of Newton Learning, would say, "an unanxious presence in an anxious world."

How would you approach a conversation if you were a samurai?

Preparing for Your Assignment

Now you're ready to have a wonderfully fierce conversation with someone at work and someone at home. A powerful aid to being here, prepared to be nowhere else, is your old friend Mineral Rights. Before you take the leap, I want to provide answers to some frequently asked questions.

FAQ

How should I frame these kinds of one-to-ones and set expectations with my direct reports or family members? This is your uninterrupted time with the people you've said are important to the success of your company or the success of your relationship. People will rise or fall according to your expectations. If you always create and drive the agenda, that will become everyone's expectation. Additionally, if you always drive the agenda, you may be missing something important. Set the stage by telling the individual ahead of time:

> *When we meet tomorrow, I want to explore with you whatever you feel most deserves our attention, so I will begin our conversation by asking, "What is the most important thing you and I should be talking about?" I will rely on you to tell me. If the thought of bringing up an issue makes you anxious, that's a signal you need to bring it up. I am not going to preempt your agenda with my own. If I need to talk with you about something else, I'll tag it onto the end or plan another conversation with you.*

Won't some people be suspicious? Might some people get the deer-in-the-headlights look? You bet. That's okay. If they press you for reasons why you should meet, just say: "You're important to me, to the team, to this project. We owe it to ourselves to stay current on where we're going, what's happening, and what's needed." If someone protests, possibly insecure lest he or she overlooks what *you* want to talk about, stand your ground: "I hold you able to identify the most important thing we should be focusing on together."

What if someone doesn't put his or her finger on the topic I feel is most important? If someone wants to discuss what to you seems like an organizational or familial hangnail, bite your tongue and explore the topic. Why? Because if you asked that person what he or she deemed most important and that person told you and you then disregard it and place your own agenda on the table instead, you have essentially just said that when you ask, you aren't really asking. That nothing has changed. That this was just an exercise of smoke and mirrors. *If it's important to that person, then it's important.* So go there. Observe an individual whose pressing topic is overridden or dismissed by others, and you will likely see that person explode or disappear. If you're the boss, it's unlikely he or she will explode in front of you; instead, the explosion will be saved for colleagues at the watercooler or a poor, unsuspecting spouse later that night. With you, the individual will smile and nod and endure the conversation, and little that's useful will have occurred. If over time an individual persists in avoiding the topics that need to be addressed, you have a different issue. Then it will be up to you to put an issue on the table for exploration.

What are some reasonable goals and outcomes for such one-to-ones? Each Mineral Rights conversation will be productive and memorable. Each will move important issues down the field. Each will develop leadership capabilities of your team members, maturity in your children, closeness with your lover. Each will accomplish the goals of any and all fierce conversations:

- *Reality will be interrogated.* You'll stay current regarding ground truth. You won't be blindsided by surprises down the road. Using Mineral Rights will help both of you peel off the proverbial layers of the onion and get to the heart of the issue.

- *Learning will be provoked.* Yours and others'. In fact, you and your partner are likely to learn much more during a Mineral Rights conversation than you've learned in other meetings.

- *People will be mobilized to tackle the tough challenges.* People solve the problems and seize the opportunities that they themselves have named. They will leave this conversation with a sense of accountability for their understanding of the conversation, for their ownership of the outcomes, and for any action that has their name on it.

- *The relationship will be enriched.* One of the greatest gifts you can give another is the purity of your attention. Not your advice! Mineral Rights will require that you hold your ideas about what needs to be done until your partner has had an opportunity to formulate his or her own solutions.

How often should the one-to-ones be held? How long should they last? That depends. In the workplace, if someone is new, more often. If someone is experienced and proven, less often. Flexibility is important, but I recommend that the optimum schedule is once a month for one to two hours. If that thought buckles your knees, you may have too many direct reports. Twelve times a year, ask each of your key people to explore his or her most important issues with you. In a personal relationship, you may want to do this once a week.

What are some process tips and techniques that will make the one-to-ones more effective? Mineral Rights is a seven-step process that will guide you through a scintillating conversation from beginning to end. Just as important as following the process, however, is checking your belief system. What you believe to be true about people absolutely affects how you lead and how you partner with someone personally. For example, I worked with a client, Mike, who continually complained about the incompetence of his executive staff, "They wait for me to come up with the answers." On the rare occasions when they did have answers, it seemed the answers were inadequate. Mike unconsciously broadcast his beliefs—*I am the only one here who is capable of intelligent thought*—to everyone who worked for him. So Mike got to be right about his belief. What do you expect of the people on your team? from the members of your family? How are your expectations affecting their behavior?

Why is it essential during Mineral Rights to ask about someone's emotions? If you don't ask what someone is feeling, it's as if you leave that person sitting in an exquisite car—one that he or she could take apart and put together blindfolded—with no gasoline in the tank, which means this car is in no danger of going anywhere. Emotions serve as the gasoline that propels us into action. I have listened to executives, friends, and relatives describe in detail the current ghastly results and future implications if an issue doesn't get resolved . . . even though they clearly have no intention of doing anything about it in this lifetime. Not until they explore emotions do they get in touch with the price they are paying. Then, and only then, does the lit match have something to ignite.

What are the most common mistakes made during one-to-ones?

1. *Doing most of the talking.* Don't. It's that simple. Really ask, and then really listen. What happens if it gets really quiet? Take a deep breath and wait. As long as you're talking, you're not learning anything you didn't know already.

2. *Taking the problem away from someone.* No matter how skilled someone is at giving the problem back to you, don't take it. If someone asks for your opinion, say, "I'll share my thoughts with you before we end our conversation, but right now, let's keep exploring yours."

3. *Not inquiring about feelings.* For some people, asking what someone is feeling is an unnatural act. If this is true for you, do it anyway and learn from the experience. If you fail to inquire about emotions, you'll notice that nothing much changes as a result of your conversations.

4. *Delivering unclear messages, unclear coaching, and unclear instructions.* Ideally, you will deliver few or no messages, coaching, or instructions; however, if you do have something to add, do it clearly and succinctly. If you have a request, make sure your partner hears and understands it. Don't leave it open for interpretation.

5. *Canceling the meeting.* Don't do it, unless someone dies—like you. You said these meetings were important. Are they or aren't they? Your actions will tell the story. This meeting with you should be considered inviolate.

6. *Allowing interruptions.* Turn off your cell phone and your e-mail alert, and hit the "do not disturb" button on your telephone. You cannot be here, prepared to be nowhere else, when you are interrupted by beeps, buzzes, and bells. If you're talking on the telephone, don't put someone on hold to take another call. Not only is it disrespectful, but when you return to the conversation something will have been lost and may or may not be regained. The tone, the sound, the timbre, the welling emotion. If you want to engage in fierce conversations, if you don't want to waste your conversational time or that of the person on the other end of the line, do not allow interruptions of any kind.

> **You cannot be here, prepared to be nowhere else, when you are interrupted by beeps, buzzes, and bells.**

7. *Running out of time.* Every Mineral Rights conversation concludes with clarity about the next most important step. If that next step needs to be another conversation, schedule it; however, in many cases you won't need to because of a wonderful phenomenon that's part of Mineral Rights conversations: The conversation hasn't ended just because the *conversation* has ended. During a Mineral Rights conversation, things are set in motion. The conversation is

> **The conversation hasn't ended just because the *conversation* has ended.**

ongoing. What we set in motion deserves and receives fierce attention.

8. *Assuming your one-to-ones are effective.* I know someone who periodically opens a one-to-one by giving his clients a form. He says, "When you looked at today's schedule and noticed our meeting, what was your immediate reaction? Pick one." The form has seven choices:

- Okay, no big deal.

- Oh no, two hours wasted!

- Should I cancel and reschedule?

- Maybe I can shorten this today.

- Great! I need to talk about _____.

- Great, a few moments of sanity.

- Other _____

Is he guaranteed a candid response? That depends on how he has handled feedback in the past.

Assignment

Schedule a one-to-one with someone at work *and* someone at home. Choose a person who you sense is struggling with an issue. Speak and think of it as a conversation rather than a meeting. Use Mineral Rights as your model. Before you begin, ask yourself, "What do I need to do to be fully present? What are all the things I am thinking about that could interfere with my being here, prepared to be nowhere else?"

You'll begin by asking, "What is the most important thing you and I should talk about today?" Give your colleague or partner some time to check in and consider what you've asked. Don't help the person out. Don't get itchy during the silence and try to help with, "For

When you can do nothing, what can you do?

example, you said you weren't sure if John is going to work out. Maybe we should talk about that." Or, "Last weekend we didn't have much time together and you seemed upset. Do you want to talk about that?"

Let them decide! And if anyone ever responds with "I don't know," your reply should be, "What would it be if you did know?" This question was inspired by the Zen koan "When you can do nothing, what can you do?"

Ask the question. And wait.

Below, take a moment to revisit the Mineral Rights model. Before having your conversations, however, I recommend that you read the rest of this chapter.

Mineral Rights: A Simplified Version

1. What is the most important thing you and I should be talking about?

2. Describe the issue. What's going on relative to _____?

3. How is this currently impacting you? Who or what else is being impacted? *The emphasis is on the word* current, *so keep your partner focused on current impact and results. Ask, "What else?" at least three times. Probe feelings.* When you consider these impacts, what do you feel?

4. If nothing changes, what are the implications? *Say, "Imagine it is a year later and nothing has changed. What is likely to happen?" Ask, "What else?" Probe feelings.* When you consider those possible outcomes, what do you feel?

5. How have you helped create this issue or situation? *If someone says, "I don't know," then ask, "What would it be if you did know?" Don't comment on the response other than to say, "That's useful to recognize." Move on.*

6. What is the ideal outcome? When this is resolved, what difference will that make? *Ask, "What else?" Probe feelings.* When you contemplate these possibilities, what do you feel?

7. What's the most potent step you can take to begin to resolve this issue? What exactly are you committed to do and when? When should I follow up with you?

Debrief

As you practice Mineral Rights and Principle 3—*be here, prepared to be nowhere else*—it is helpful to debrief yourself after each conversation. Ask yourself:

- Was I genuinely curious about this person and his or her reality?

- Did I work to understand what color the corporate or relationship beach ball is from where he or she stands?

- Did feelings get expressed, as well as issues and solutions?

- What parts of me failed to show up?

- Who did the most talking? "Me" is the wrong answer.

Over the last fifteen years that I've taught and worked with Mineral Rights, I've seen amazing results and conversations that have unfailingly delved into rich territory. The following list of additional questions has also provided useful openings to memorable conversations. As you deepen your understanding of the seven principles of fierce conversations, you will gain considerable skill in asking these questions and in responding to the answers. But no harm will come from beginning to try them on. The risk is that you will hear things you have been pretending not to know. *The risk is that you will be changed.*

Additional Good Questions

You will rarely need to ask anything other than the first question of Mineral Rights to launch a highly useful conversation. It is always comforting, however, to have a few other questions in your back pocket. Here are some of my favorites.

1. What has become clear since we last met?

2. What is the area that, if you made an improvement, would give you and others the greatest return on time, energy, and dollars invested?

3. What is currently impossible to do that, if it were possible, would change everything?

4. What are you trying to make happen in the next three months?

5. What's the most important decision you're facing? What's keeping you from making it?

6. What topic are you hoping I won't bring up?

7. What area under your responsibility are you most satisfied with? least satisfied with?

8. What part of your responsibilities are you avoiding right now?

9. Who are your strongest employees? What are you doing to ensure that they're happy and motivated?

10. Who are your weakest employees? What is your plan for them?

11. What conversations are you avoiding right now?

12. What do you wish you had more time to do?

13. What things are you doing that you would like to stop doing or delegate to someone else?

14. If you were hired to consult with our company, what would you advise?

15. If you were competing against our company, what would you do?

16. What threatens your peace? What threatens the business? your health? your personal fulfillment?

How would *you* answer these questions? How might your teammates answer them? Questions 14 and 15 are particularly effective in inviting a reluctant individual to open up and share his or her ideas.

A Secret Rule

I give myself a secret rule during all Mineral Rights conversations. In workshops, I demonstrate the use of the secret rule and see who can guess what it is. As a volunteer engages in a conversation with me in front of the room, I give the following instructions to those observing:

During this conversation, please write down two things:

First, see if you can identify the secret rule I give myself in order to accomplish the goals of the conversation, which are to . . .

- Interrogate reality

- Provoke learning

- Tackle tough issues

- Enrich relationships

Second, note any questions you would have wanted to ask our volunteer if you were having this conversation with him or her.

Throughout the conversation, observers write pages of questions, all of which could have been useful. In trying to identify my secret rule, they note "techniques" (I put the word *techniques* in quotation marks because when you master the courage and skill required for fierce conversations, you no longer consider any part of your behavior to be a technique; everything you do is natural and vital) such as these:

- You identified and focused on the real issue.

- You didn't get sidetracked by rabbit trails.

- You took him deeper and deeper into the issue until you found the core.

- You maintained eye contact; your eyes never left his face.

- You weren't distracted by anything else going on in the room.

- You mirrored his body language. *(While I don't do this deliberately, sometimes it just happens.)*

- When he got emotional, you didn't rescue him.

- You nodded and made sympathetic sounds indicating empathy.

- You didn't offer advice, even when the solution seemed obvious.

- You used silence powerfully.

All of these are accurate observations; however, rarely does anyone recognize that my secret rule is . . . *questions only.*

Until the person I am with has answered the question in Step 7— *What do you see as the next most potent step you need to take?*—I do not allow myself to make a declarative statement. No cheating. No leading questions such as "Have you considered trying . . . ?"

You will be mightily tested. Most people don't do well here. What most of us do when someone says, "I have this issue, or I have this problem," is jump in with, "I have this solution, or I have this point of view about your issue."

Many of us are eager to show what we know, to demonstrate our value to our coworkers, clients, and family members. So as soon as someone says, "This is my issue," we leap in with suggestions, stories about our experience, quotes from the latest journals. And we don't notice that our companion's eyes have glazed over.

A common experience you no doubt have had is the conversation that begins with your telling someone about something you are grappling with and before you've even finished the story, the other person says, "I know exactly what you mean. About three years ago . . ." And he's off and running. In a matter of seconds, this conversation shifted from being about you to being about *him.*

When that occurs, what happens to your interest level? How do you feel about the person who is now regaling you with his story? Not good, right? And let's face it, you've done this yourself. Almost everyone has.

If you want to have conversations that further individuals and organizations, then don't do what I just described. Don't take the conversation away from the other person and fill the air with your stories.

If my "voice" seems to have taken on a bit of an edge here, you're not imagining it. This practice of taking the conversation away from other people and making it about ourselves goes on all day, every day, and is a huge relationship killer and a waste of time. Nothing useful happens here. Even if your story is riveting, don't tell it until your companion has answered question 7, by which time you may conclude that the story you wanted to tell is not relevant.

The point here is to draw others out with good questions and incredible listening on your part. If you can't do this, you may fail to build deep relationships. So leave your expert, storyteller, fix-it hat at the door. Come into the conversation with empty hands. Bring nothing but yourself.

It is likely that your boss, valued customer, prospective customer, husband, wife, teenage daughter, or next-door neighbor will come away from this conversation feeling furthered in his or her life somehow, sensing that his or her world of meaning has been expanded, and most decidedly looking forward to another conversation with you.

Come into the conversation with empty hands. Bring nothing but yourself.

Not bad for a single conversation.

A fierce conversation is not about holding forth on your point of view, but about provoking learning by sitting with someone side by side and jointly interrogating reality. The goal is to expand the conversation rather than narrow it. Questions are much more effective than answers in provoking learning.

And even when you're not using Mineral Rights, at least once a day, let a conversation truly be about someone else.

The Decision Tree

I'd like to conclude this chapter with the Decision Tree, a marvelously useful method of delegation and professional development.

The president of the company I worked for in my late twenties took me through this exercise when I was promoted to my first management role. She drew a rough sketch of a tree and said:

Think of our company as a green and growing tree that bears fruit. In order to ensure its ongoing health, countless decisions are made daily, weekly, monthly. Right now in your development, you have a good history of making decisions in these areas [we reviewed those areas]. So let's think of these areas as leaf-level decisions. Make them, act on them, don't tell me what you did. Let's make it our goal to move more decisions out to the leaf level. That's how you and I will both know you're developing as a leader.

She pointed to her sketch of the tree and explained four categories of decisions.

Leaf Decisions:
Make the decision. Act on it. Do not report the action you took.

Branch Decisions:
Make the decision. Act on it. Report the action you took daily, weekly, or monthly.

Trunk Decisions:
Make the decision. Report your decision before you take action.

Root Decisions:
Make the decision jointly, with input from many people. These are the decisions that, if poorly made and implemented, could cause major harm to the organization.

The analogy of root, trunk, branch, and leaf decisions indicates the degree of potential harm or good to the organization as action is taken at each level. A trunk decision isn't necessarily more important than a leaf decision. Poor decisions at any level can hurt an organization, but if you unwittingly yank a leaf off a tree, the tree won't die. A leaf decision will not kill the tree if it is poorly made and executed. A wrong action at the root level, however, can cause tremendous damage.

As an independent person who does not enjoy having someone

looking over my shoulder, I thought I had died and gone to heaven when the Decision Tree clarified my professional development path. I knew I was progressing when I found myself making more and more decisions without the president's input.

The goal of the Decision Tree is threefold:

1. To identify clearly which categories decisions and actions fall into, so that an employee knows exactly where he or she has the authority to make decisions and take action.

2. To provide employees with a clear upward path of professional development. Progress is made when decisions are moved from root to trunk to branch to leaf. As an employee demonstrates a track record of making good decisions in the trunk category, for example, it will be satisfying to both the employee and the person to whom she reports when those decisions can be moved to the branch category.

3. To assist companies in consciously developing grassroots leadership within their organizations, freeing up executives to take on more challenging responsibilities themselves. A direct outcome of using the Decision Tree is that learning is provoked—one of the purposes of a fierce conversation.

This is a great way to tell people where they are free to play and how they can grow. Best of all, if you follow the Decision Tree model, members of your team will take on more responsibilities and your own to-do list will shrink. And in case you haven't noticed, she who has the shortest to-do list wins. At a GE plant, managers were told, "You have six months to teach everyone who reports to you to get along without you." Marvelous. Give people information and a goal; let them figure it out. The Decision Tree will help you do this.

She who has the shortest to-do list wins.

Additionally, the Decision Tree raises the level of personal accountability. Whenever we work diligently, and possibly brilliantly, to advise others concerning decisions in which they are involved, their internal reaction may well be "This is great. She's doing the work, coming up with all the ideas. I'm off the hook. And if her idea bombs, well, it wasn't mine, so I'll still look good. And the bonus is, I'm not putting myself or my own ideas at risk. I get to stay hidden."

This conscious or unconscious internal response is incredibly expensive both for the organization and for the individual. Trying to build leaders by regularly exposing them to your brilliance guarantees a lack of development. You will not have allowed anyone around you to show up with solutions outside the reach of your own personal headlights. If your employees believe their job is to do what you tell them, you're sunk.

If your employees believe their job is to do what you tell them, you're sunk.

Engaging others in Mineral Rights conversations and providing a clear direction with the Decision Tree develops leaders by providing frequent opportunities for them to bring their own brilliance to the fore.

Assignment

Put the Decision Tree to work as a delegation and leadership development tool for your team. If you have a teenager at home, use it with him or her as well.

Explain the Decision Tree to your direct reports. Ask each of them to pay attention over the next thirty days to all of the decisions that fall within their responsibilities and to categorize them as leaf, branch, trunk, or root. Review their conclusions and reach consensus about where each kind of decision falls on the Decision Tree. Remind everyone that the goal is to move more and more decisions out to the leaf level. This is the leadership-development path. Following this agreement, adhere to the boundaries and agreements required. For example, if someone comes to you for help in making a decision that falls within the trunk category, say, "Come back to me when you've made your decision. Then we'll talk."

Additional Assignments

During the coming week, focus on one conversation at a time. Just one at a time. And be there, in each of those conversations, prepared to be nowhere else.

If you create the space, if you offer the invitation, what happens will be new and fresh, and if you are not attached to the result, it cannot be a disappointment. You will learn much more about the value of nonattachment in chapter 5.

The rare and valuable gift you can give to others this week, and I hope for many weeks and years to come, is to be fully present in the moment. It helps me to remember a cartoon I once saw that shows a wizard sitting behind his desk. A big clock is behind him and each hour says NOW. NOW. NOW. NOW. NOW.

What are you dragging into your conversations on your back? Put it down. It will wait for you.

What time is it? Now. Even your memories are experienced *now.* Now is the only time you have. What are you dragging into your conversations on your back? Put it down. It will wait for you. When you are present in the moment, allowing each conversation to be brand-new, you will be surprised. You will find more of the other person. You will find more of yourself. It's all a matter of choice.

❖ A Refresher . . .

❖ Whether at home or at work, whether for five minutes or for an hour, give your partner the purity of your attention.

❖ Take the pulse of the relationship by really asking and really listening.

❖ Come into the conversation with a beginner's mind. Bring nothing but yourself.

❖ Use the secret rule: No advice or declarative statements. Questions only.

❖ Use the Decision Tree to provide your direct reports with clear decision-making boundaries and thresholds.

PRINCIPLE 4

Tackle Your Toughest Challenge Today

The need for change bulldozed a road down the center of my mind.

—Maya Angelou

Burnout happens, not because we're trying to solve problems but because we've been trying to solve the same problem over and over and over. Hand in hand with the courage to interrogate reality comes the courage to bring to the surface and confront your toughest, most often recurring personal and professional issues.

It is possible that the emperor is, indeed, sans clothing, that a sacred cow must be shot, that identities will unravel, that forms will break down, that there will be a period of free fall. It is also possible that a conversational free fall is what is most needed to help you turn the corner.

"Tell me again," I hear you ask, "exactly why I would put myself through this. Why would I subject myself and my organization to discomfort?"

Because what's on the other side of your toughest issue is worth it: relief, success, health, freedom from stress, happiness, a high-performing team, a fulfilling personal relationship.

And because of what's in store for you if you continue to avoid addressing and resolving the tough issues. Think confronting an executive about his or her behavior could be costly? Consider the cost of a good headhunter. Think confronting an emotional issue with a life partner is too risky? Ask your divorced friends how long it took for them to regain their sanity. Think this glitch in the organization is too complex to solve? Ask someone whose company failed which of its competitors is still standing and why.

Up to this point you've worked hard to engage yourself and others in conversations that interrogate reality, provoke learning, and enrich relationships. In this chapter, you will gain the courage and skills needed to confront and resolve the issues that stand between you and success, between you and happiness.

Mole Whacking

As an introduction to tackling tough challenges, let me tell you about my brother, Sam. In our teens Sam and I had Saturday chores to attend to before we could do as we pleased. Sam's responsibility was to tackle the mole problem in our yard. Each Saturday morning Sam would look out the window and heave a sigh. Our yard was mole central. Dozens of trails ended in large mounds of freshly turned dirt.

Resolute, Sam would head out the door to do battle. Sometimes he would use the hose, shoving it as far down into the burrows as possible. There would soon be rivulets of water running throughout the yard. Another approach was to stuff foul-smelling smoke bombs into the burrows, after which our yard resembled a fantastic galactic landscape riddled with active volcanoes spewing toxic fumes. And then there were traps. In one battle plan, a mole would trigger the trap, whereupon it would be skewered. I didn't like to think about that one.

Sam devoted many Saturday mornings to mole whacking. He took his job seriously. However, when the day came for him to move out on his own, Sam admitted that the only dead mole he ever saw had clearly died of old age.

Many years later, Sam called me and said, "Suze, you won't believe it. I was at the hardware store standing in line behind a guy with a big bag of something that had a skull and crossbones on it. I asked him what it was for and he said, 'The mole problem.' So I asked him, 'How do you get that stuff down into the burrows?' And he said, 'Oh, it's not for the moles. You sprinkle it on the grass and it kills the grubs that the moles eat.'"

There was a moment of silence on the line, and then I overheard a faint "Damn!"

As I chuckled, Sam continued, "If I had gone after the grubs, I could have spent Saturdays riding my bicycle. The thing is, I'm still whacking moles. It's what I do all day at work. And I'm good at it, an enthusiastic and capable mole whacker. Almost every morning I wake up weighed down with the items on my to-do list. So I get up and come to work early, determined to make progress, to get that one thing that's nagging me handled, only to find someone leaning in the doorway of my office. Holding a mole. Saying, 'We've got a problem, boss.'

"'Okay,' I say. 'Put that problem on my desk and let me take a whack at it.' Half an hour or an hour later, when that person drags the mole out of the office, just when I think, 'Now I'll focus on my top priority,' the phone rings and it's somebody else who essentially says, 'Boss, I got a mole here I need to run by you.' By four in the afternoon, when the last sorry mole has been carted out of my office, I'm running on fumes. I couldn't have an original thought if my life depended on it, and I still haven't tackled item number one on my own to-do list. This is the stuff of my days. And this, I recognize, is a problem!"

Sound familiar? Behind one mole is another one. For many of us, mole whacking seems to be the stuff of our professional lives. And let's face it, in a way, mole whacking is kind of fun. It's satisfying when people turn to you to whack moles for them. After all, you've gotten this far in your career because you're known for your mole-whacking skills. Besides, if you are no longer a mole whacker, who would you be? What would you do?

Make it your job as a leader to give up mole whacking and take up grub hunting.

So we continue whacking moles and by mid-afternoon we are exhausted, having expended precious energy flailing around on the periphery, in the margins, rather than identifying and tackling core issues, the grubs that attract the moles.

Leaders devoted to mole whacking are frozen in place professionally, as are the people who report to them. Make it your job as a leader to give up mole whacking and take up grub hunting. Implementing the Decision Tree in chapter 3 will help you accomplish this important transition.

How Many T-shirts Does One Person Need?

Early in my tenure of working with top executives, I experienced a stunning end to a meeting with Jim, the owner and president of a company that manufactured T-shirts.

Jim and I had filled almost two hours reviewing his progress on his to-do list from our previous session and identifying his priorities for the upcoming month. We had talked about the purchase of a new screen-printing machine, strategies to increase sales, improvements in communications among top executives, Jim's negotiations with a talented but difficult designer. We had talked about a recurring theme: Jim's struggles to balance work and family. And, as often happened, we spoke briefly about a shared love—fly fishing—and Jim's latest fly-fishing jaunt with his best friend.

It had been easy to fill two hours with agenda items, and I was about to walk out Jim's door thinking I had done my job. In reality, we had merely been whacking moles. With ten minutes left in our session, Jim fell silent and leaned back in his chair. Finally, he said, "What if everyone who buys T-shirts has all the T-shirts they need?"

I got a chill.

Jim continued, "I mean, think about it. How many T-shirts do you have?"

"A drawerful. Around ten, fifteen, maybe twenty. You gave me most of them."

"How many of those did you buy?"

I thought about it. "Probably seven or eight."

"When did you last buy a T-shirt?"

"Maybe two years ago."

"Where?"

"On vacation in Maui."

"But you've taken vacations since then, haven't you?"

"Sure."

"And you didn't buy T-shirts the last couple of places you went. Why not?"

"Hmmmm. Well, I don't wear them that often. Mostly I wear them on vacation." Jim waited while I thought some more. "I just pack the ones I already have. I prefer to spend my vacation dollars on other items, gifts for the family, et cetera."

"Have you bought T-shirts as gifts for the family?"

"Yes, sometimes."

"But not lately? Why is that?"

"Well, everyone has a drawerful of T-shirts, just like I do. They don't need any more."

"Exactly."

I felt the air being sucked out of the room. This was what we should have been talking about for the last two hours and now it was time for me to leave. Another client was expecting me.

Jim said quietly, "I suspect I may be in a declining business."

"Jim, why haven't we been talking about this since I walked in the door?"

Jim sighed. "It's not something I want to think about, much less talk about, but avoiding it is no longer an option. I suspect our flat sales aren't just a short-term dip. I think we've got trouble."

In the remaining minutes, I assured Jim that I would carve out time on the agenda for him to put this in front of his peers at the group meeting the next week. I handed him a copy of the form we used in presenting issues to the group. I had been introduced to a variety of issue discussion forms when I became a TEC chair. Over time, every chair developed his or her own form. This was my version.

Presenting the Issue

THE ISSUE IS:

(Be concise. In one or two sentences, get to the heart of the problem. Is it a concern, challenge, opportunity, or recurring problem that is becoming more troublesome?)

IT IS SIGNIFICANT BECAUSE:

(What's at stake? How does this affect dollars, income, people, products, services, customers, family, timing, the future, or other relevant factors? What is the future impact if the issue is not resolved?)

MY IDEAL OUTCOME IS:

What specific results do I want?

RELEVANT BACKGROUND INFORMATION:

Summarize with bulleted points: How, when, why, and where did the issue start? Who are the key players? Which forces are at work? What is the issue's current status?

WHAT I HAVE DONE UP TO THIS POINT:

What have I done so far? What options am I considering?

THE HELP I WANT FROM THE GROUP IS:

What result do I want from the group? For example, alternative solutions, confidence regarding the right decision, identification of consequences, where to find more information, critique of the current plan.

I asked Jim to complete this form in advance of the meeting and send it to his peers to prepare them for our discussion.

Naming the Problem

Whenever a member of a team has an issue on which he or she would like input, preparing the issue presentation before the meeting helps to prevent incoherent or incomplete explanations of the problem. Additionally, the team appreciates good use of its time. At the top of the appreciation list is the accurate identification of the problem.

> **The problem named is the problem solved.**
> —PAT MURRAY

Pat Murray suggests, "The problem named is the problem solved."

It is crucial to spend time in the problem-naming part of the exercise. If that takes a while, it takes a while. Unfortunately, after half an hour or so of sincerely attempting to help someone who has misnamed the issue, most people find it difficult to muster the energy and attention needed to shift gears and stay engaged.

I know from experience that high-performing teams get frustrated when they feel they are doing the work a colleague should have done beforehand. They like it short and simple. They like to hit the ground running. This preparation form helps team members grasp the issue and its importance, and quickly provides the group with the relevant information and context needed for good work.

What is the recurring problem in the organization? How does the system reward this? Where does the problem originate? What is the "grub"?

This is the question on the table. This is why it's important. This is what I want to achieve. This is what you need to know. These are the options I'm considering. This is what I need from you today.

Hold the Advice

Once the issue is on the table, what is the role of the team? Unfortunately, what most people do the minute someone says, "I have a problem," is to say, "I have a solution." We dive into answers before our companion has finished describing the issue. Preventing this behavior is one of the reasons for the secret rule in chapter 3. Yes, each of us may have a solution. Could be a darn good one. Yet our solution is only one solution.

If our job is to make the best possible decisions for the company, or the team, or the family, or to help others do this, we need access to all available options. Often I've witnessed someone bring an issue to the team and say, "I am considering options A, B, and C. Which one do you think is best?"—only to discover that there is an option Q out there that he or she didn't even know existed. And option Q is exquisite and complete.

By jumping in too quickly, team members often offer solutions to a mole-level problem, missing the grub altogether. No matter how much work someone has done to correctly name the problem, that person may not have hit the nail on the head. Before jumping in with solutions, it is essential to spend some time asking clarifying questions.

When a facilitator leads this kind of conversation, his or her most important role is to create spaciousness throughout the conversation, which helps individuals and teams discover what the conversation really wants and needs to be about. If you are leading the discussion, encourage your peers to ask questions for quite a while. And remember, no cheating with leading questions. Your ideas may be wonderful and absolutely appropriate, but don't be too quick to interject them.

Facilitating a Team Issue Discussion

To improve the quality and results of issue discussions with any team of which you are a member or for which you serve as facilitator, I offer the following process.

- Require that an issue be as well prepared as possible before bringing it to the team.

- To help with this, create and use an issue preparation form that fits your organization.

- Help new team members fill out the form and prepare for the meeting the first time or two. You want them to name the issue correctly, present it clearly and succinctly, and put the team's time to good use. New team members appreciate a facilitator who helps them succeed and gain the respect of their peers.

As you read the following suggestions for facilitators, think about applying these guidelines to a conversation you might have with someone whose counsel and support you seek. In addition, these guidelines can help couples and children engage in helpful, courageous dialogues that identify possible solutions to problems.

Facilitator Guidelines

1. Ensure that team members are provided with a written copy of the issue form prior to the meeting or at the beginning of the issue presentation.

2. Once the team member with the issue has presented it to the team, allow ample time for clarifying questions. You will undoubtedly need to intervene when eager solution providers jump in with ideas too early in the process.

3. Once the team members are satisfied that the real issue has been identified and they have all of the relevant information, move to ideas for solutions. Let this be relatively free-flowing. Make sure you call on anyone who hasn't spoken: "Mary, what's your take on this?"

4. Begin wrapping up the discussion by asking everyone to formulate a one-sentence recommendation: "Okay, no more discussion. I'd like each of you to distill your thoughts into a one-sentence recommendation. I'll give you a minute to write it down. The question is 'If you were Joe, what would you do?'" After one minute, go around the table and have each team member give his or her recommendation. The person with the issue may not respond, only listen. When people know they will always be asked to provide focused advice, to put a personal stake into the ground, no one tunes out. Just as important is that everyone's voice is heard; thus everyone has an equal place at the table.

5. Ask the member with the issue, "What did you hear?" When the issue presenter knows this is coming, he or she will pay fierce attention to everything said during the meeting, particularly to everyone's final recommendation in Step 4.

6. Close the discussion by asking the member with the issue, "What actions are you committed to taking and when will you take them?" This is a satisfying end to an issue discussion. Nothing is left in the air, unclear. Everyone knows what is going to happen next regarding this issue. Occasionally, someone may respond, "I need time to digest these ideas. I will let you know what action I'll take by next Monday."

7. Follow up! Make sure that the member with the issue lets the team know what has been done so far, the results, and the intended next steps. When a team has worked hard to help a peer, it deserves to know what happened next.

If the issue to be explored is complex and the thoughts are likely to be complicated, consider taping the issue discussion. Following the meeting, give the tape to the person who brought the issue to the table. That way, the individual won't feel he or she must take notes during the discussion. Knowing that everything is captured on tape allows the issue presenter to be fully present, maintain eye contact, and really listen throughout the discussion. Many times I've heard people say, "When I listened to the tape, I heard some useful thoughts and ideas that I missed in the meeting."

The Undiscussables

Some things are much more difficult to talk about than others. Many business groups and family members operate with an unspoken rule book, including a list of undiscussables, topics that are too risky to bring up. *After all, your last attempt netted you two weeks as the corporate pariah. Or you ended up sleeping on the couch.*

Some topics on the undiscussables list are in the form of quid pro quo agreements. Without discussing it, everyone instinctively understands the deal that has been struck.

- I won't mention your bungling of the Ross account if you won't bring up how many people have left my team.

- I won't yell at you about the credit card bill if you won't go ballistic when I buy a Harley.

- I won't mention your drinking if you don't talk about my weight.

Sometimes we avoid saying what needs to be said because we're sure there will be consequences.

- Are you crazy? Say that to him and he'll hand you your head on a platter!

- She's on a rampage, disappointed with the team. The team's fine. She's the problem. But if anybody tries to tell her that, there will be hell to pay.

- I think my husband is having an affair, but if I confront him with the evidence, he'll deny it, tell me I'm the one with the problem, and refuse to touch me for a month.

Just Shoot Me Now

Are you dodging a challenge? In my work with leaders and their teams, I've discovered that a universal talent is the ability to avoid difficult conversations. "I take the high road" is often an excuse for not tackling the issue. It is far better to take the *direct* road. Granted, revealing painful truths—our own or others'—is tough. Upon contemplating a needed confrontation with an individual who, when challenged, had a history of becoming defensive, emotional, and irrational, one client said, "Just take me to the vet right now and have me put to sleep."

"I take the high road" is often an excuse for not tackling the issue.

If your stomach flips at the thought of confronting someone's behavior, you're in excellent company. It is far less threatening to talk about declining sales than to look straight into someone's baby blues and address her specific behavior that may be causing the decline. Instead, we talk with others over lunch and by the coffeepot about the person whose behavior is driving us mad.

James Newton shared a unique point of view on critiquing others behind their backs. He asked, "How do you housebreak a puppy? Put it in a crate. What's the one thing a dog won't do in its crate? Poop. I sure wish human beings were as smart." Complaining to anyone other than the person with whom you have a problem is like soiling your own crate. If you really want to resolve the issue, go directly to the source and confront the person's behavior one-to-one, in private.

Understandably, many of us fear confrontation because it hasn't gone well in the past. All attempts to date have failed miserably. We don't know how to make it better this time, and the stakes are fairly high. We sense that a monster is lurking in the bushes and today is not the day we are prepared to take him on. Or this is not the hill on which we're prepared to die. Our fears may include these:

- A confrontation could escalate the problem rather than resolve it.

- I could be rejected.

- I could lose the relationship.

- Confronting the behavior could force an outcome for which I am not prepared.

- I could incur retaliation.

- The cure could be worse than the disease.

- I could be met with irrationality or emotional outbursts.

- I might hurt his or her feelings.

- I could discover that I am part of the problem.

Yet, the results of not confronting a problem include these:

- The problem could escalate rather than be resolved.

- I could be rejected.

- I could lose the relationship.

- I could lose my job.

- Emotions could escalate until someone blows up.

You get the drift.

The very outcomes we fear if we confront someone's behavior are practically guaranteed to show up if we don't. It will just take longer, and the results will likely occur at the worst possible moment, when we are least expecting it, with a huge price tag attached.

Repositioning *Confront*

When people first hear the term *fierce conversation*, they often assume it is a conversation in which you tell others exactly what you think of them and the horse they rode in on. If this was your first impression, I hope that by now you've gained a different perspective.

Even so, when it comes to the topic of confrontation, many people picture angry faces, clenched teeth, roiling emotions because of their negative context for confrontation. For example, let's imagine you believe that dogs are dangerous. The door opens, and a dog walks in and heads toward you. You are afraid. The dog didn't scare you. Your belief scared you. "Projects like this are stressful." "My spouse always gets angry." Beliefs determine how you feel and therefore what you do.

My father doesn't have conversations. He has *versations*.

I'd like to recast the whole notion of confrontation.

Last fall, on a train from Salisbury to London, I was talking with a couple sitting opposite me. I mentioned that I was working on a chapter about confrontation and that it had occurred to me that the meaning of the Spanish word *con* is "with." Therefore, the word *confront* could mean "to be *with* someone, *in front* of something." The woman said, "And what about the word *conversation? My father doesn't have conversations. He has *versations*. Everybody in the family gave up trying to have conversations with him long ago."

I winced at this insight, wondering what her father would feel if he had heard her words. *Conversation* and *confrontation* both begin with the idea of *with*. The "fierce" version of confrontation is not firing at someone from across the room, but rather standing side by side, looking at the issue together.

Who owns the truth? Each of us owns a piece of it, and nobody owns all of it.

All confrontation is a search for the truth. Who owns the truth? Each of us owns a piece of it, and nobody owns all of it.

Let's keep in mind that a confrontation is a conversation. As with all fierce conversations, the four purposes of a confrontation are to:

- Interrogate reality

- Provoke learning

- Tackle tough challenges

- Enrich relationships

Think about these four purposes. When we are preparing to confront someone's behavior, our obligation is to describe our reality concerning the behavior and then invite our partner to describe reality from his or her point of view. When multiple realities are explored, learning is provoked, and most people are willing to take action once they have gained a new understanding. Such conversations enrich relationships.

Assignment

Think of that conversation out there with your name on it, the conversation that every subatomic particle in your body would prefer to avoid. Write it down.

PERSON   **TOPIC**

For example:

Boss: Our company lacks a clear, compelling vision.

Customer: Working with you is unpleasant and difficult. We may need to part company.

Work team: Our strategic plan looks good on paper, but it's not being implemented.

Manager: Your sacred cow is causing intolerable problems.

Employee: People on your team are having a hard time with you, and there have been some complaints about it.

Colleague: You have a pattern of withholding important information from team members.

Spouse: I love you, but I do not love our life together.

Spouse: Your commitment to work seems stronger than your commitment to our marriage.

Teenager: I suspect you may be sexually active.

Friend: I am concerned that you may have a drinking problem.

Sam and Jackie

Before I walk you through a model for successfully having this conversation and coming away from it with all your body parts intact, consider the case of Sam. This is not my brother, but a different Sam, the CEO of a software company, who had the following problem to solve.

Sam is a thoughtful leader and a truly good human being, who was beaming when I walked into his office for our monthly one-to-one. He reported that he had successfully recruited Jackie, known in the software industry as a miracle worker with a reputation for never missing a deadline. Jackie had agreed to head up Sam's software development team for the eight months Sam estimated it would take to move the latest version of their software from concept to reality. Sam and his competitors run neck and neck in their attempts to introduce the newest, slickest versions of their products to the marketplace, and Sam felt, "With Jackie heading up the team, we'll hit our target delivery date. Getting Jackie is a real coup. She had lots of options, including working with one of our competitors. But she chose us and she starts tomorrow. This is too good to be true!"

A mere thirty days later, Sam groaned when I asked, "What is the most important thing you and I should be talking about today?"

"If you ever hear me say that something is too good to be true, kick me."

"What's happened?"

"About a week after Jackie came on board, John [a member of the software development team] and I pulled into the parking lot at the same time, so I asked him how things were going. He said things were a little tense. I asked him what he meant, and he told me that the day before, he had been in Jackie's office asking her questions, and she had said, 'I don't have time for private tutoring sessions. Work this out on your own time.' John told me this seems to be typical of how Jackie deals with people. Of course, I was sure they'd get through this. After all, they're all adults, professionals in their fields. I assumed this was just a bump in the road."

Sam sighed deeply. I prompted, "More like a land mine . . ."

"Oh, yeah. A week later, Sarah passed me in the hall and said, 'Guess you heard about the meeting.' 'What meeting?' I asked. She told me that the software team had met, and at one point, they were all stumped. Seems there's a glitch in the software and nobody knows how to resolve it. So they were just sitting there, looking at a diagram Jackie had drawn on the flip chart, when suddenly Jackie ripped the page off the flip chart, crumpled it up, and pitched it over her shoulder. She said, 'I thought you guys were better than this. This team is not what I signed up for.' And she walked out the door. Left them all sitting there."

"Yikes."

"And you know what really frustrates me? I still didn't do anything."

"Sam, what were you . . ."

Sam smiled ruefully, as he finished my sentence: ". . . pretending not to know? Well, you know how much I hate conflict, so I clung to the fantasy that somehow this would all go away and they'd play nice."

"And the coup de grâce?"

"Delivered this morning by Peter [Sam's first employee, his alter ego, and the single individual besides Sam who most influences the culture of the company]. This morning he came into my office, closed the door, and said that something had happened that I needed to know about."

"Sounds ominous."

"Yeah, my thought was, 'What fresh hell is this? Embezzling, sexual harassment, industrial espionage?'"

"And the winner was . . ."

"Jackie. Peter admitted that he gets calls from headhunters from time to time but that he never takes those calls, never listens to the pitch. He told me that yesterday he got a call and this time he listened. He scheduled a meeting with the recruiter."

The look on my face mirrored Sam's.

Sam continued, "He told me that he had just canceled the meeting and that he doesn't want to leave. Of course, I asked him what was going on, and he said, 'The thought of working with Jackie for another seven months is not a good one. She's brilliant, no question. But she's got some seriously sharp edges, and people are getting hurt. I doubt I'm the only person wondering if I can endure the next seven months.'"

Sam sighed. "I've got to talk to her. Today."

Before I walk you through the model Sam and I used to prepare him for his talk with Jackie, imagine you are Sam. Let's assume you don't want to fire Jackie, at least not yet. Ideally, you'd like to save the relationship. What might you say or ask to open the conversation with her? Before you read on, take a moment to think about this. In a confrontation, the first sixty seconds are key. If you don't prepare your opening statement, but instead dive in, holding out hope that this time it will be different, you will probably make one of five common errors in confronting behavior.

Error 1: So, How's It Going?

When I tell workshop participants the story about Sam and ask how they would open the conversation with Jackie, someone always suggests that Sam should begin by asking, "So, Jackie, how are things going?"

Many of us have been a part of such confrontations: "How do you feel you're doing here in the company?" Or, "How would you rate your performance?"

Openings like this are disrespectful and dishonest. Plus, you're not fooling anyone. The minute you ask how someone thinks he or she is doing, the internal reaction is likely, "Well, apparently not as good as I'd hoped."

Imagine you are Jackie. The boss comes into your office, sits down, and asks, "So, Jackie, how are things going?" What do you instantly suspect? *Not well. Something's up.* After all, you already know things aren't going that smoothly. It's your team. You were there. You are also a person with darn good radar. You sense the boss has a hidden agenda.

Most of us can smell hidden agendas a mile away, and we don't like them. "How are things going?" is an age-old lead-in to bad news. So what do we do? Well, if you were Jackie, how might you have responded? Probably with something like, "Great! There's a little creative tension, but we're working through it." Sound familiar? Now where is the conversation? Nowhere useful, that's for sure.

> **"How are things going?" is an age-old lead-in to bad news.**

Most people determine to bluff their way through a veiled confrontation for as long as possible. Some are very good at it! Don't provide the opportunity. If what you really want to say is "Your job is on the line," then say that. Clearly, cleanly, and calmly.

Error 2: The Oreo Cookie

Well, how about the time-honored Oreo cookie approach? You know the Oreo cookie—two chocolate layers with cream filling. Many of us were advised at some point to begin a confrontation with a compliment, then slip in the real message—the cream filling—then tidy up with another compliment or some words of encouragement.

"You did a really good job on the Adams report." Then *splat,* the criticism, the negative feedback. "But you've come in late almost every day this week and you were out two days last week. Work is piling up and people are complaining." Ending with "I'm counting on you. You're a terrific person with much to offer."

Most of us have either done this or had it done to us. And we don't realize the downside of this approach, which is that people get downright paranoid as soon as someone in authority says, "You did a good job on . . ." We're **We're waiting for** waiting for "but," the equivalent of a face full **the sugarcoated** of cream filling, the sugarcoated spitball. The **spitball.** popularity of the Oreo cookie approach causes many people to break out in a sweat anytime they are paid a compliment, since it often signals an imminent kick in the backside. We say something nice and wonder why others seem to be waiting for us to throw a shoe.

People deserve better than this. Even if they haven't asked for it, each of us has an obligation to provide clear, straight messages. People deserve to know exactly what is required of them, how and on what criteria they will be judged (including attitude), and how they are doing. Praise is essential when deserved. And when you praise, keep that conversation separate, focused, and clear. Reserve your praise for specific behaviors and results deserving of celebration and congratulation. Do not use praise as a lead-in to a confrontation.

Error 3: Too Many Pillows

A third approach is to soften the message in order to lessen the impact and avoid hurting anyone's feelings. It's a good thing, part of human nature, to want to avoid inflicting pain. I remember wishing I could line the road with pillows when my **Sometimes we put** daughters were learning to ride their bi- **so many pillows** cycles. The trouble is, sometimes we put **around a message** so many pillows around a message that **that the message gets** the message gets lost altogether. We will **lost altogether.** have worked up a sweat and expended all of that emotional energy for nothing. Our employee, partner, or child may walk away thinking he or she has just had another casual chat with us.

The owner of the search firm of which I was vice president was the ideal boss for me. She came to my office monthly to meet with me, and I always enjoyed our conversations. But after the third or fourth meeting, I had an uneasy feeling, so I called her and said, "I enjoyed our time together today; however, I have the sense that there is something you want me to start doing or stop doing that I may have missed."

"Absolutely, Susan. I thought I made it clear that I want you to . . ."

I no longer recall the details, but it's clear I had managed not to hear her message. It reminded me of Peter Falk's line in the movie *Murder by Death:* "This can only mean one thing, and I don't have a clue what that is."

> **This can only mean one thing, and I don't have a clue what that is.**
>
> —PETER FALK
> IN *MURDER BY DEATH*

Fortunately, my employer and I could both laugh as I admitted, "I often miss subtleties and I'm downright lousy at interpreting. If there is something you want me to do, get out a two-by-four and hit me alongside the head. Just tell me."

Replace pillows with clear requests.

A secondary point here is that while we often tell ourselves we are softening the message so as not to hurt someone else's feelings, we are really trying to protect ourselves. We do not look forward to dealing with our own emotions, much less someone else's. So we

> **Would you prefer to continue limping, or are you ready to remove the stone from your shoe?**

wait for just the right moment when the other person is in the right mood. When we do this, it is often a long wait. Odds are, we may never have the conversation. One of the rules of fierce conversations is that you must go first. When? When you're tired of limping and decide to remove the stone from your shoe.

Error 4: Writing the Script

Many of us have a tendency to script in our minds what we think someone else will do or say if we bring up a certain topic. Certainly, if we have a history with someone at home or at work, it is natural to anticipate his or her reaction. It is also a problem.

If I play out like a movie in my mind what I will say and then what you will probably say, there is little possibility for improvisation. Little opportunity for new behaviors or responses on either side. I've got us both in a conversational box. An old one, well earned and understandable, but a box all the same. No hope for surprise.

When we script what others will say and do prior to a conversation, we can be so locked into the responses we're expecting that when someone responds differently, we do not notice.

She may not seem angry right now, but inside I bet she's seething. I know how she is.

Or we steel ourselves for the anticipated response, and, in so doing, our own words come out as metallic, cold, or menacing.

Our bodies manifest the pictures our minds send to them, so pay fierce attention to the negative scenario you are running in your mind. It just might come true. If what you intend instead is a frictionless debate, one that furthers the relationship, then hold that scenario as a possibility. That, too, just might come true.

Error 5: Machine Gun Nelly

Unfortunately we are all familiar with the person who confronts with heavy artillery. This individual is so terrorized by the notion of confrontation that he gets the adrenaline flowing, then runs into the room and hurls the message with vitriol or vengeance. He so fears the negative response he has scripted in his mind ahead of time that he skips anticipated defensive maneuvers and heads directly to the offensive.

This is the bully, who is, of course, terrified. So terrified that once the message is delivered, this person ducks and runs, without surveying the extent of the damage inflicted. Perhaps you are guilty of this yourself. If so, the model that follows will help you tremendously, and in chapter 6, you will gain additional skill and grace in the art of delivering a message without the load.

We've all had experience with these errors. It seems we're so uncomfortable with the whole notion of confrontation that we either build up a head of steam, burst through the door, hurl our words across the table, and then bolt, or we soften our message to the point that the other person leaves the conversation thinking we've just had a lovely chat. When we hurl and bolt, we damage the relationship. When we soften and protect, the message is lost and it's unlikely anything will change.

Delivering a difficult message clearly, cleanly, and succinctly is essential. In organizations where leaders have developed the courage and skills required to stay current and to communicate honestly with coworkers regarding behavior issues, there is far less stress and there are considerably fewer concerns about lawsuits.

Come straight at the issue. Get right to the point.

If you need to confront someone's behavior, do not begin by asking that person how things are going or by complimenting him or her. Don't surround your message with pillows. Come straight at the issue. Get right to the point. Say what you have to say in sixty seconds, then immediately extend an invitation to your partner to join the conversation.

Sixty seconds? That's not enough time to express all the angst that's been building up inside me. Not enough time to tell the long story I've told and retold myself. Not nearly enough time to unleash the emotional diatribe I've rehearsed in my mind.

But oh, how powerful. When your opening statement has been prepared and delivered with skill and grace, the invitation to your partner to participate wholeheartedly and thoughtfully in the conversation will be compelling. It's highly likely that the relationship will be enriched in the process. Remember, enriching relationships is one of the purposes of a fierce conversation.

Below is the model I use when I need to confront someone's behavior or coach someone else to do so. It's the model I used to prepare Sam for his conversation with Jackie. This model was inspired in part by Craig Weber, president of the Weber Consulting Group, who suggests that if you wish to craft conversations that moderate our worst conversational tendencies, you should:

- Advocate your position clearly and succinctly.

- Illustrate your position by sharing the thinking behind it.

- Publicly test your views and invite and encourage others to do so as well.

- Inquire into the views of others and actively explore their thinking.

I concur with Craig and have broken down potentially challenging conversations into three distinct parts: opening statement, interaction, and resolution. Let's look at the all-important opening statement phase of a confrontation. Later I will tell you what happened during Sam's interaction and resolution with Jackie. And what happened after that.

Opening Statement

Preparation of your opening statement is essential. Do your homework. Write down your opening statement and practice saying it. Out loud. If you just rehearse it in your head, when the curtain goes up you may be appalled at the words that actually come out of your mouth. There are seven components to an opening statement:

1. Name the issue.

2. Select a specific example that illustrates the behavior or situation you want to change.

3. Describe your emotions about this issue.

4. Clarify what is at stake.

5. Identify your contribution to this problem.

6. Indicate your wish to resolve the issue.

7. Invite your partner to respond.

You have sixty seconds to do it all. Let's take these components one at a time.

1. **Name the issue.** The problem named is the problem solved. Name the behavior that is causing the problem and the area the behavior is impacting. If you have multiple issues with someone, ask yourself what's at the core, what's the theme, the commonality of all or most of your issues with this individual. Do the thinking to name the central issue; otherwise, the conversation will lack essential focus and you'll both end up lost and frustrated. For example, after thinking about everything that had occurred, Sam began his opening statement with these words: "Jackie, I want to talk with you about the effect your leadership style is having on the team."

2. **Select a specific example that illustrates the behavior or situation you want to change.** Since you've got only sixty seconds in which to make your entire opening statement, this example must be succinct. No long stories. Besides, if you've ever been on the receiving end of someone who went on and on citing all the details about whatever you did that upset her,

at some point either your eyes glazed over, you shut down, or you began building your defense. By the time she came up for air, you were loaded for bear. So keep this short. Must you have an example? Absolutely. When someone is upset or disappointed with us but can't think of a specific example that illustrates what is irritating him, his case loses credibility and is easy to dismiss. Take the time to think of an example that hits the nail on the head. Let's stay with Sam. For example: "I learned that when John was asking questions, you told him you didn't have time for private tutoring sessions and that he should work it out on his own time. I also learned that during a meeting with the team, you tore a page off the flip chart, wadded it up, threw it on the floor, said that this wasn't the team you had signed up for, and left the room."

3. **Describe your emotions about this issue.** Why do this? Because emotions are deeply personal. Telling someone what emotion his or her behavior evokes in you is intimate and disarming. You are letting the person know that you are affected, that you are vulnerable. Contrary to popular opinion, I believe it actually has quite an impact to say, quietly, "I am angry," if anger is what you feel. It helps a lot if you aren't yelling and waving your arms. Perhaps you are concerned, worried, sad, frightened, or frustrated. Describe whatever emotion is true for you. If you are sad or afraid, say so. Such emotions are experienced both at work and at home, and it is appropriate to admit them. For example, Sam's words were brief yet personal: "I'm deeply concerned and I am fearful of the possible consequences."

4. **Clarify what is at stake.** In other words, why is this important? What do you feel is at stake for the individual whose behavior you are confronting? What is at stake for yourself, for others, for the customer, for the team, for the organization, or for the family? What is at stake for the relationship? Use the

words *at stake.* Those words have an emotional impact. Heads will raise and eyes will lock when you say, "This is what is at stake." Talk about this calmly and quietly. What you say during a confrontation should be delivered not in a threatening manner, but simply as a clarification of why this is important. For example, Sam said: "There is a great deal at stake. A long-term employee has considered leaving the company rather than work with you. I am not prepared to lose good people who I hope will be here long after you've gone on to your next assignment. Meeting our deadline is essential. Our reputation as a product leader is on the line, as well as our professional pride, pleasing our customers, and considerable financial gain. Perhaps there's little or nothing at stake for you, Jackie. If it doesn't work out and you leave us, you can undoubtedly get another job quickly, but for us the stakes are high."

5. **Identify your contribution to this problem.** This is your answer to the question, "How have I behaved in ways guaranteed to produce or influence the very results with which I am unhappy?" Before we confront another's behavior, it is essential that we first look at the ends of our own noses. No long confession is needed here. With sixty seconds, you couldn't do that if you wanted to. What is appropriate here is a brief acknowledgment that you recognize any role you may have played in creating the problem and that you intend to do something about it.

   I have often realized, to my chagrin, that my primary contribution is in not communicating clear expectations from the outset of a relationship or project. This may seem obvious, but the majority of problems I see in both professional and personal relationships are due to a lack of clear expectations of all parties, and the rest are due to a lack of accountability to appropriate expectations. As you think about behaviors you wish to confront, you may see that most are ones you could

have anticipated. By being clear up front regarding which behaviors and results are acceptable and which are not acceptable, you can avoid many problems, and you'll have a simpler
task if you need to go back and remind a coworker or family
member of the expectations he or she agreed to when the relationship began. For example, you might say: "I have contributed to this problem by not reviewing your priorities and
due dates with you. I will correct that." Or: "I've contributed
to this problem by not letting you know months ago how upset I was. Instead, I withdrew, and consequently, our relationship deteriorated even further. For that, I am sorry." If you
believe you did not contribute in any way to the problem,
leave this part out. Sam recognized that he should have dealt
with this sooner. He noted: "My role in creating a growing
rift between you and others is that I did not bring it to your
attention earlier."

6. **Indicate your wish to resolve the issue.** Use the word *resolve*.
It shows that there is no firing squad waiting outside the
door. This is not a termination or an ending. In fact, when
this model is used to confront a behavior or issue, more relationships are saved than ended. To say "This is what I want to
resolve" communicates good intent on your part. Additionally, you should restate the issue. That way you will have come
full circle, beginning and ending with absolute clarity about
the topic on the table. Sam said, for example: "This is what I
want to resolve with you, Jackie—the effect your leadership
style is having on the team."

7. **Invite your partner to respond.** When our own behavior has
been confronted, it may have felt as if a court had found us
guilty and we had simply been called in to learn the date and
manner of our execution. In this model, however, there has been
no attack. Instead, there has been an extraordinarily clear and

succinct statement describing the reality of this particular behavior or issue from one person's point of view. We have been
reassured that the intent is to resolve the issue. Now the invitation is offered for us to join the conversation. And the conversation has barely begun. For example: "I want to understand
what is happening from your perspective. Please talk to me
about what's going on with you and the team."

I imagine some of you are thinking, "This all sounds well and
good, but you don't know Ed (or Shirley or Mark or Elaine)! There's
a serious issue I need to discuss with him, but I can tell you right now,
he won't play fair or nice. How do I influence such a person to come
out from behind himself into the conversation and make it real?"

Ask him to. Ask her to. And make your part of it real. That's all
you can do.

*All conversations are with myself—and sometimes they involve other
people.*

This idea can be tough to come to terms with, yet it is essential
that you grapple with it; otherwise, while you may understand the importance of conversations, you may find yourself holding back, not
having them because of one of the
most common concerns I hear in my
workshops.

**All conversations
are with myself—and
sometimes they involve
other people.**

The most popular reason for not
engaging a particular individual in a
conversation is: "They can't handle it."
Other familiar versions go something like: "They'll get defensive."
"They'll be hurt." "They won't talk about it." "They'll get emotional,
irrational, angry, illogical." And sotto voce: "They'll get even!"

Countless corporate teams and families are held hostage by a single dysfunctional human being who has got the entire tribe cowed
into avoiding the topics that need addressing. Such a person teaches us:
*If you dare to bring up this topic or talk to me about things I'd rather not
face, you'll be sorry. It won't be pretty.* Even though we recognize that

we've got to address this issue, we still hear ourselves saying, "He can't handle it. He isn't ready."

It is critical to recognize that we ourselves can't handle it, aren't ready, lack the courage. Fierce conversations cannot be dependent on how others respond. If your life succeeds or fails one conversation at a time, and if the conversation is the relationship, ensuring that these conversations take place is up to you. In other words, if you know something must change, then know that it is *you* who must change it. Your job is to extend the invitation. What if the invitation is declined? Extend it again. And again. My experience is that when the invitation is extended with grace and skill, it will be accepted, even by those you have almost given up on.

If you know something must change, then know that it is *you* who must change it.

Give an impeccable opening statement and extend a sincere invitation. If there is someone in your life who has consistently refused to have the conversation that is desperately needed, you might preface your opening statement by saying something like "Nobody owns the entire truth about [the topic], including me. I would like for the two of us to interrogate reality, side by side, as if we are walking down some stairs, one at a time. If it gets scary, we can sit down on a step until we're ready to continue. Imagine that we both have flashlights to illuminate the issue. Both of us might see something new. Both of us may gain perspective. If we have this conversation in Rumi's field—out beyond ideas of rightdoing and wrongdoing—we may both learn something."

If someone came to you and spoke words like this, then used the model we've explored to address a problematic behavior or situation in which you are a key player, how would you respond? Yes, you might wonder if that someone has taken his or her meditation practice a little too far, but I bet it would get your attention. I have used these and similar words to prepare the way to address or help others address a highly charged issue. Use different words, if you like, but do find the words.

I often ask work teams, "On a scale of one to ten, at what level would you like to be confronted—ten being told straight, no holds barred, what someone thinks or feels about something you have said or done?"

Surprisingly, most team members say, "Nine or ten." Recently, a team member suggested, "I think I could handle ten on Mondays, nine on Tuesdays, eight on Wednesdays, seven on Thursdays, and six on Fridays. I don't want to go into a weekend stressed." When I then ask, "At what level do you feel you are currently being confronted?" the answer is usually, "About a three, maybe four." We profess to have more courage than our colleagues give us credit for.

We can have the conversations needed to create the results we say we want in our lives, or we can have all of our reasons why we can't have those conversations. But we can't have both. Reasons or results. We get to choose.

Which would you rather have?

Staying current regarding issues that are **Reasons or results.** troubling or perplexing us enriches and sim- **We get to choose.** plifies our relationships. Neither of us has to try to figure out what the other person really thinks and feels—an altogether exhausting and futile endeavor anyway.

Sam's opening statement took about forty-five minutes to prepare and practice. It covered all the bases, avoided common errors, and took about sixty seconds to say. When you put all the pieces together, Sam's opening statement went like this:

Jackie, I want to talk with you about the effect your leadership style is having on the team. I learned that when John asked you questions, you told him you didn't have time for private tutoring sessions. I learned that during a meeting with the team, you wadded up a page from the flip chart, threw it on the floor, said that this wasn't the team you had signed up for, and left the room. I'm deeply concerned and I am fearful of the possible consequences. There is a great deal at stake. A long-term employee has considered leaving the company rather than work with you. I am not prepared to lose good people who I hope will be here long after this project is completed and you've gone on to your next assignment. Meeting our deadline is essential. Our reputation as a product leader is on the line, as well as our professional pride, pleasing our customers, and considerable financial gain. Perhaps there's little or nothing at stake for you, Jackie. If it doesn't work out and you leave us, you can undoubtedly get another job quickly, but for us the stakes are high. My role in creating a growing rift between you and others is that I did not bring this to your attention earlier. This is what I want to resolve with you, Jackie, the effect your leadership style is having on the team. I want to understand what is happening from your perspective. Please talk to me about what's going on with you and the team.

If we were to simplify Sam's conversation with Jackie, essentially, the flow would go like this:

Several individuals on your team are having a difficult time with you. Let me give you some examples of what I've been hearing. This is what I'm feeling and what I believe is at stake. I recognize my contribution to this outcome. So that we can begin to resolve this issue, give me your take on the situation.

Let's return to the confrontation model and then learn what happened following Sam's opening statement.

Interaction

8. **Inquire into your partner's views.** Though there is only one step in the interaction part of a confrontation, it is here that the bulk of the conversation takes place. You have extended an invitation to your partner and now you are listening. This is where reality will most certainly be interrogated. If your partner says something with which you violently disagree, resist the temptation to build a stronger case. Simply listen

so that your own learning may be provoked. Ask questions. Dig for full understanding. Use paraphrasing and perception checks; don't be satisfied with what's on the surface. For example: "Please say more about this. I see it quite differently, so I'd like to understand your thinking, how you came to this conclusion." And/or: "May I tell you what I'm hearing? I want to make sure I've understood you."

We are often severely tested during the interaction phase. It is not easy to contain your emotions during an interaction with someone whose comments or behavior makes you want to leap over the desk or coffee table and strangle him or her. When we struggle to wrap our minds around a partner's alternative reality, it's helpful to recall that in all conversations, including confrontations, we are all interpreting what is said through our own highly individualized filters. Rather than jump back in and start talking as soon as your partner says something you feel is off base, focus on examining your partner's reality and his or her filters. It may help to give yourself the secret rule of Mineral Rights. Questions only.

Finally, when your partner knows that you fully understand and acknowledge his or her view of reality, move toward resolution, which includes an agreement about what is to happen next.

Resolution

Throughout the interaction phase of confrontation, reality is interrogated, learning is provoked, and relationships are enriched. Now it's time to come to an agreement about what happens next. After all, you said your intent was to resolve the issue, and the following questions will help you accomplish this:

9. What have we learned? Where are we now? Has anything been left unsaid that needs saying? What is needed for resolution? How can we move forward from here, given our new understanding?

How do you end the conversation?

10. Make an agreement and determine how you will hold each
    other responsible for keeping it.

Though I was not present during Sam's conversation with Jackie,
from his later account, it's clear that Sam did a number of things really
well. First, he kept in mind the four purposes of a fierce conversation:

1. Interrogate reality. *After his opening statement, Sam made it
   clear that he was genuinely interested in what reality looked like
   from where Jackie stood.*

2. Provoke learning. *There is no surer way to shut down a conversation than to come in to it with an entrenched position. Sam
   was open to learning, willing to be influenced by Jackie.*

3. Tackle tough challenges. *It was time.*

4. Enrich relationships. *Sam intended that, even if the relationship with Jackie ended, there would be no blood on the floor.*

Often when we let someone know that others have complained,
the person whose behavior we are confronting will attempt to justify
the behavior by going into details about who said what to whom.
Don't get trapped here. You wouldn't have decided it was time to
have this conversation if you knew of only one complaint or negative
result.

As soon as Sam extended the invitation to Jackie to offer her perspective, she responded, "If people were upset, it would have been
nice if they had come to me." Sam was prepared for such an attempt
at deflection, and he replied, "We're here to talk about the effect your
leadership style is having on the team, Jackie. What's going on from
where you sit?"

During the interaction part of the confrontation, Sam gave himself the rule to make no declarative statements until he couldn't stand

it anymore and then for a while longer. He pitched his tent on questions. Eventually two things happened. Jackie figured out that she was not going to be shot at dawn—at least not immediately. She also saw that there was no place to hide. Sam could not be seduced onto rabbit trails. Whenever Jackie headed off into the bushes, Sam brought her back. Sometimes he just quietly said, "Return to the topic, Jackie." And she came back.

In the course of their conversation, Jackie settled down and became thoughtful, less defensive, and Sam learned what his contribution to the problem had been. There was, indeed, a glitch in the software that no one, including Jackie, knew how to resolve. No one on the team had any experience with this particular problem. Jackie's concern was palpable. She had a reputation for never missing a deadline, and now she had a critical problem that no one knew how to resolve. Naturally, she feared this project might tarnish her reputation. Most of us have heard the phrase "Where there is anger, there is fear." Not that it made everything okay, but Sam began to understand the edge to most of Jackie's comments.

In moving toward resolution, Sam acknowledged, "I misdiagnosed the capabilities of the team. I thought we had all the talent needed on this project, and clearly we don't. Do you know anyone who has the experience we need?"

"Yes. I know exactly the person. I don't know if he's available, but he could help."

"Well, it blows the budget, but I'm willing to put the money in to get someone on board. Will you call and find out if he's available?"

"Yes, of course."

"Now tell what you are willing to do, Jackie."

Perhaps because their interaction had been productive and even pleasant, Jackie attempted to minimize her role in the problem. "Oh, we'll be fine. I'm sure the team will get used to me."

It was at this point that Sam's particular genius was revealed. I share this with you because there is a great lesson here.

Sam sat quietly for a moment, then said, "That isn't adequate,

Jackie. There must be some changes on your part. Tell me something. Have you ever received feedback like this anywhere else in your life?"

Jackie sat back in her chair. Her face reddened and she looked away. At last, she murmured, "As a matter of fact, yes, I have."

Sam waited a moment, then continued, "Jackie, you don't have to change your leadership style. You don't have to change, period. Nobody does. You'll need to make some changes to stay here, but if you aren't willing to do that you can leave, get another assignment, and get on with your life. And possibly get this same feedback down the road. If that's your decision, then so be it. I'll have another problem to solve, but I'll solve it. On the other hand, you could decide that this is as good a time and place as any to take yourself on. Because that's what we're talking about. Taking yourself on. Going inside with clippers and a soldering iron and doing some internal rewiring. That's a lot to ask of anyone, and you may not be willing or able to do that right now. I see this as an important choice point for you, so I'd like to meet with you at eight tomorrow morning and learn your decision. If you are willing to make some alterations in your leadership style, I'll help you, coach you. If you aren't, we'll part company, no hard feelings."

The next morning Jackie looked like something the cat had dragged in. She'd clearly had a bad night, but she said, "I made the call to the person I told you about and he's available. He's coming on board the day after tomorrow. And, Sam, I'd like to stay. I don't know how it will go, but I'd like to make it work. It's an exciting project, and the people on the team are good, and I sense this is where I need to be. For lots of reasons."

"That's wonderful, Jackie. I'm really glad. Okay, let's get to work. What's your next meeting? Who is it with and what is the purpose?"

Thus, Sam began coaching Jackie. He didn't attempt to change her essential nature. He just took it step-by-step, asking a lot of questions. The first was "What's the next thing you need to do?"

Jackie grimaced and said, "This is the part where you're going to suggest that I apologize to John and the others on the team. I hate this. I'm lousy at apologies."

They both laughed.

Seven months later, right on schedule, Jackie and the team rolled out a product that blew the competition out of the water. Following the big splash, there was a going-away party for Jackie, during which appreciation and congratulations were extended. "I learned a lot from you. It's been great working together." The team said these things. Jackie said these things. All were sincere. Before leaving, Jackie pulled Sam into his office.

When they returned, Sam pulled me aside and told me what had happened. His eyes were shining.

"Sam," Jackie had said, "there's something I want to tell you." She was clearly struggling with her emotions. "You know that conversation we had a while ago? You know the one I mean?"

"Yes, I think I do," Sam replied.

"Well, that conversation"—Jackie looked at Sam and her eyes filled with tears—"that conversation saved my marriage. So I owe you, Sam, big time. If you ever need me, please call me and I'll find a way to get here. That's a promise."

Sam and Jackie have since worked together on another project. It has been wonderful to see the pleasure they take in their professional relationship, and it has been a privilege to see a talented woman add compassion and considerable grace to her brilliance.

What was Sam's genius? Recognizing that when someone has a behavior at work that is causing a problem, it is inevitably showing up elsewhere in his or her life, causing similar problems. What we do at work that hurts people or alienates coworkers we also do at home, hurting and alienating those we love. Likewise, our behavior at home shows up in the workplace. Like the orange. When you squeeze it, you get orange juice, all over the place.

When we confront behavior with courage and skill, we are offering a gift. And, of course, it goes both ways. While it may be difficult to hear others' truths about ourselves, there is likely to be a vein of gold worth mining.

This behavior is hurtful. This is the result it is producing. This is what's at stake.

And sotto voce: *Where else is this behavior showing up in your life, and what results is it producing there?*

Michael and Joe

Michael, a friend and colleague, told me about his college-age son, Joe. Michael loved Joe deeply yet didn't currently feel connected to him, didn't feel that their conversations had heft or meaning. Michael decided that he needed to go down the conversational staircase with Joe no matter what they might discover in the basement, so he invited Joe to lunch and told him what he was feeling.

Joe asked, "How long have you felt this way—not connected?"

To his surprise, Michael heard himself answer, "Since you were in the third grade."

Joe gulped. "That's a long time, Dad."

Michael thought about that time, so long ago. "When you started third grade, you didn't want to go to school. So every morning I would play catch with you. I'd throw the ball toward school, and you'd run out to catch the ball, then throw it back. Each throw would take us closer to school. Finally, we'd be out front and I'd roll the ball through the door. You'd run in the door, pick up the ball, wave at me, and disappear."

As Michael shared this memory, both he and Joe were surprised by their emotions. Neither had known what he would find at the bottom of the stairs. But both were willing to go there.

It took a moment for Michael to continue. Finally, he said quietly, "What I just admitted to you and to myself makes me very sad."

Over the next hour, father and son found their way back to each other and created a plan to stay engaged. Following Michael's con-

versation with Joe, he realized there was
another person in his life from whom he
felt disconnected: his wife.

**When we
spend a lifetime
curbing our anger,
our sadness, or
our frustration
for fear of offending
others, in the process
we curb our joy.**

When we spend a lifetime curbing our
anger, our sadness, or our frustration for
fear of offending others, in the process we
curb our joy. We cannot find the words to
name what we love and why we love. We
lose the ability to express deep and gen-
uine appreciation. Healthy relationships require appreciation *and*
confrontation. Rather than tell someone "I value you, but I am angry
with you," replace it with the deeper truth of "I value you *and* I am
angry with you." Or "I love you *and* I feel disconnected from you."

Assignment

Think about the fierce conversations you identified on page 85. Your
first step is to write down the date by which you will have had this
conversation.

DATE:

Now choose one of these conversations and prepare your opening
statement by writing down exactly what you will say, covering steps 1
through 7.

1. Name the issue:

2. Select a specific example that illustrates the behavior or situation you want to change:

3. Describe your emotions about this issue:

4. Clarify what is at stake:

5. Identify your contribution to this problem:

6. Indicate your wish to resolve the issue:

7. Invite your partner to respond:

Once you're satisfied with a final draft, practice your opening statement until you own the words. Until the words come out straight, clean, and clear. Until you know and own the ground on which you stand. Have the conversation with the person you wish to address by the date you indicated.

With courage and practice, your discomfort in confronting difficult but important issues will lessen over time. The goal is for you to become and remain current with the important people in your life. No more recycled tears. No recurring anger.

❖ A Refresher . . .

- ❖ Burnout occurs because we have been trying to solve the same problem over and over.

- ❖ The problem named is the problem solved.

- ❖ All confrontation is a search for the truth.

- ❖ Healthy relationships include both confrontation and appreciation.

- ❖ A courageous, skillful confrontation is a gift, a vein of gold worth mining.

PRINCIPLE **5**

Obey Your Instincts

It is only with the heart that one can see rightly; what is essential is invisible to the eye.

—Antoine de Saint-Exupéry, *The Little Prince*

Y ou know before you know, of course. You are bending over the dryer, pulling out the still-warm sheets, and the knowledge walks up your backbone. You stare at the man you love and you are staring at nothing: he is gone before he is gone."

This is the opening paragraph of Elizabeth Berg's novel *Open House*.

Do you recall a moment when a realization walked up your backbone? It is not your imagination. Each of us is equipped with exquisite calibration that allows us to sense when there's a storm brewing, snow coming down, an unexpected blizzard. Thunder rolls across your mind. Lightning flickers. Static and noise. And the scent of rain. It's going to rain. Hard.

There is a point where fact-finding and research accomplish nothing. Sometimes we just have to ask ourselves, "Is it right or wrong, yes or no, right or left?" And we know. A businessperson takes a deep breath

Our radar works perfectly. It is the operator who is in question.

and commits funds to a vision. Lovers let go of the past and commit to the present, or recognize that they are fundamentally wrong for each other and say good-bye. Our radar works perfectly. It is the operator who is in question.

Kim Murphy, a reporter for the *Los Angeles Times,* wrote an article about the search for grizzly bears in the Bitterroot region of Montana. Murphy reported that "Brian Huntington, a researcher for the Great Grizzly Search who has spent most of the summers of his life in the woods . . . has learned to trust the hair on the back of his neck. He feels it rise when he's walking down a trail, and he stops. 'Don't think it's probably your imagination,' he says. 'It's probably not.'"

Things don't always make sense—they just are. There are things our gut knows long before our intellect catches on. Every day, all day, an intelligent agent is sending us messages.

There are things our gut knows long before our intellect catches on.

We hear them in our heads, feel them in our guts, discern them in our hearts. They come to us while we're sleeping. Albert Einstein had his best ideas in the morning while shaving.

Do not trust your instincts. *Obey* them. What is, is. And what is must be acted upon. This instinctual wisdom is readily available to all of us. Tune in. Pay attention.

I'm Trying to Concentrate!

How does an intelligent human being make poor decisions? When President Kennedy got the idea to invade Cuba, only one person, Arthur M. Schlesinger, Jr., questioned this decision; however, other advisers talked Schlesinger out of bringing up his concerns. The invasion was a disaster. The "team" got caught in the type of thinking best illustrated by a well-loved Winnie-the-Pooh story.

Winnie-the-Pooh and Piglet are walking together. They walk in a circle, heads down, examining the ground. All of a sudden Pooh says something like, "Look, Piglet. Tracks. Two other creatures were on this path not too long ago." They walk in a circle for a bit longer, and Pooh declares, "More tracks, Piglet. Where do you suppose everybody is going?" They continue walking in the circle and Pooh says, "Wow, look at this! There are so many paw prints, something exciting must be going on. We're definitely not alone."

Before we know it, we're off and running, heads down, following a well-trodden path. Perhaps if we looked up and around, we'd become acutely aware of a different reality, an alternate route that would take us someplace more valuable, someplace we've never been before.

Obeying your instincts requires that you listen to your own internal voice, acknowledge your internal reference point, rather than rush to embrace the myriad references and voices of others. Most of us allow ourselves to be influenced or persuaded that the voice within us is mistaken, flawed, at best a distraction. And if we are intent on gaining others' approval, we are quick to discard our insights, commanding the voice inside us, "Shut up and go to your room."

In fierce conversations there is neither a struggle for approval nor an attempt to persuade. There is, instead, an interchange of ideas and sentiments, during which you pay attention to and disclose your inner thoughts while actively inviting others to do the same.

Our thoughts, wonderings, unexplained memories, and yes, suspicions speak to our oldest neurons and synapses. We know things. We sense things. We don't know how or why we know things. We just do. For example, as you read this chapter, I encourage you to pay attention to the connections you're making in your mind between what I'm suggesting and your own life. Go beyond the words I've written and pay attention to what you're thinking and feeling as you read them.

This is what I want you to do in your conversations. Principle 5 asks you to obey your instincts. In this chapter, you will practice becoming intuitively aware of the thoughts and feelings of the most important people in your life. You will learn how to employ this phenomenon called *instinct*, often unexpected and inexplicable, to provide explosive insight, thus greatly enriching the quality and outcomes of your conversations. You will learn to obey your instincts while inviting others with differing views to challenge your thinking. You will continually check in with your inner reference point and disclose what you find there, with no concerns about approval or control, either yours or that of others.

Examine more than surface evidence. Resist automatically accepting what you see at face value.

If you have ever felt lost in a conversation—and who hasn't?—it may be because you were so focused on the literal words that you were ignoring the clues all around you. Examine more than surface evidence. Resist automatically accepting what you see at face value. There is value in paying fierce attention to our instincts, which are readily available to us 24/7.

But how do we tap into that terrific resource, our instincts? What can we do when we're in the middle of a conversation or a meeting, and we find ourselves distracted by our thoughts? After all, we've been advised to pay attention to the people we're with, so we attempt to cordon off those pesky insights we keep getting from somewhere north of the Pleiades. We consider them suspect and are careful not to disclose them, ending up like the central character in Steve Tesich's novel *Karoo*, who says, "My insights were many. I was full of penetrating insights. But they led to nothing except an ever-growing private collection."

How we enter our conversations is how we emerge from them.

How we enter our conversations is how we emerge from them. Holding back, not paying attention, disengaged, half-asleep. Or available, present, engaged, awake. If we're to be the latter, as you learned in chapter 4, we need to listen for more than content. We need to listen for emotion and intent, as well.

In *Crossing the Unknown Sea,* David Whyte writes, "In the surface conversation of our colleague we listen for the undercurrent; the persistent tug and ebb that tells us she is actually going in the opposite direction to her speech."

The Left-Hand Column

Take a moment and think back to your conversations during the last thirty days. Imagine yourself sitting with your coworkers, with your boss, with your customers, with your lover, with your child, with your friend. As you listened to each individual, what did you think but not say? What were your thoughts about these thoughts? What did you do with those thoughts? Did you think, "I need to say something here, but I don't know what it is." Or did you know you needed to say something, yet acted inconsistently with that impulse?

What did you think but not say?

In the interest of fierce conversations, what is really needed here is a reality check of some kind, a conversation about your conversation. Remember, the conversation *is* the relationship.

How is it possible to have a conversation about a conversation? We can do it only if we first carry on a private, internal conversation. This is how we find out what we are thinking.

Sometimes we don't know what we think until we hear ourselves say it aloud.

But how do we find out what we are thinking? This sounds obvious, but it isn't. Sometimes we don't know what we think until we hear ourselves say it aloud. Sometimes we believe that our internal conversation is in the way of our being present, so we try to push it

away. Being 100 percent present means being present for everything
that is occurring in that moment. It's like a split-screen TV:

PRIVATE THOUGHTS	PUBLIC THOUGHTS
What you think	*What you say*
Not visible/audible	*Visible/audible*
"You're crazy. We can't do that."	"Sure. No problem."
"People are scared to death of you. There's no way they will tell you the truth."	"What does your staff think?"
Belief: Don't show what you feel.	Behavior: The Corporate Nod

We filter our private conversations, making public only what we
assume will be heard, will not upset people, will get us what we want,
and so forth. When we keep important thoughts private, our ability
to learn and to make good decisions is reduced. But if we say what we
think, we are afraid it will make things worse by upsetting people or
making ourselves vulnerable.

Our dilemma is: Keep it private (in other words, be diplomatic)
and prevent ourselves and others from learning, or, say it, knowing
that we might upset someone or make ourselves vulnerable.

Yet unconsciously, most people are asking us to visit the "edge" or
frontier with them. To go there, we may need to change how we
think in the first place. What if we drilled down, hit oil, decided
what's the rich part and what's junk, refined it, and used it? To do
this, we need to value our instincts as a resource. In addition to paying attention to the person, we must also pay attention to and value
the messages we're receiving from ourselves. This approach, developed by Chris Argyris and Donald Schön, was first presented in their
book *Theory in Practice*. It has come to be known as the "left-hand
column."

Essentially, you can think of your brain as split into left-hand,
middle, and right-hand columns.

PRIVATE THOUGHTS	NEUTRAL ZONE	PUBLIC THOUGHTS
What you think and feel but don't say.	You are aware of what you think and feel without attachment.	What you see and hear. What is shared and known.
Assumptions and judgments. Your private view.	You don't claim it's right or special. It just is. And you want to share it to see if it brings insight to the conversation.	

There was a time in my life when I considered my left-hand column to be a royal pain. All those distracting private thoughts. All those crazy notions that derailed the conversation:

"Why is she talking about this? This isn't the real issue."

"I've lost the thread of this conversation. I'm completely disoriented."

"He says the plan's on track, but I sense an undercurrent of fear."

"He says everything is fine. I don't think he believes that."

In fact, attending to my left-hand column is, at times, like writing. In Patricia Hampl's essay "Memory and Imagination," she writes, "I sit before a yellow legal pad, and the long page of the preceding two paragraphs is a jumble of crossed-out lines, false starts, confused order. A mess. The mess of my mind trying to find out what it wants to say. This is a writer's frantic, grabby mind, not the poised mind of a reader ready to be edified or entertained."

Then years ago I read about Dr. Carl Simonton, whose clinic in California had an amazing cure rate for supposedly incurable cancer victims. He encouraged his patients to listen carefully to their personal insights about what they needed to do. Most important, he urged his patients to take action on those insights as soon as it was humanly possible. He said something like, "Those messages are from

If you ignore those messages, eventually you'll stop getting them.

you to you. They are from the part of you that knows what is needed to help you get better. If you ignore those messages, eventually you'll stop getting them. The part of you that offers insights will say, 'No use telling her. She doesn't listen.'"

This got my attention, and I resolved to get better at putting my instincts to work as the powerful tools that they are. I began to meditate, starting my day with a brief quiet time, which ends with the question "Is there a message?" A message often presents itself.

Several years ago, at a time when I was trying to make multiple things happen in my personal and professional life, I asked if there was a message and was startled at the vehemence with which the message arrived. Two words, loud and clear: BE STILL.

I recall my response. *What do you mean, be still?* And the immediate answer: *What part of BE STILL don't you understand?*

I got the message. For many months, "BE STILL" became a personal mantra, pulling me back from the brink of wrong action on numerous occasions.

Still, to this day, during my early morning quiet time, it takes a while for the stillness to arrive. Thoughts swarm.

"I need to call so-and-so. Repond to e-mails. Get to the bank. Write the job description. Call the accountant. Review the goals. Update the action plan."

I am reminded of Holly Hunter's character in the movie *Always*, who dreams grocery shopping lists. *Kitty litter, potato chips, milk.* Like many individuals running organizations and living full lives, I dream to-do lists. During my morning meditation, it is often all I can do not to rush from the chair and hurl myself into a flurry of activity. Yet, over and over, I have discovered that a rush to action can be counterproductive. When I am still, underlying truths surface, pointing me toward right action. Stillness has become a discipline.

What needs to be my focus for today? The theme for today's endeavors? Is there a message from me to me? And often there is. These conversations with myself, during which a nugget of gold is revealed amid the rubble, have become invaluable.

> **When I am still, underlying truths surface, pointing me toward right action.**

I remember a time when I faced a difficult decision. It involved leaving a particular corporate client whose president had an ongoing integrity outage that he refused to correct. Not surprisingly, he encountered the same problems over and over, yet insisted on pointing the finger elsewhere. In addition, I wondered if he had attention deficit disorder. His son had been diagnosed with this challenge, and I was aware that it was inherited. He declined to investigate this possibility, even as our conversations raced from one incomplete thought or issue to the next with no resolution, no clarity, no conclusions. Our conversations were maddeningly unfocused, circuitous, and confusing.

I became keenly aware that, despite my best efforts at helping him frame a topic for discussion and remain, at least for a while, within the boundaries of one topic at a time, and despite having confronted behavior that was at odds with the company's stated values, our work together was unsuccessful and deeply frustrating.

The voices inside my head urged, "You are not the right person to help this individual. You are only a phase on the way to someplace more useful for him. Get out of the way, so someone else can step in."

I realized that it was I who had an integrity outage. My emotional fatigue was understandable. I had not been present with or attentive to myself. One part of me was urging me to cease my work with this client, and the other part of me was countering, "Yes, but . . ." In disregarding my instincts, I essentially had been telling myself that I didn't exist 50 percent of the time.

I met with my client that day and told him what I'd been feeling. I spoke of the integrity outage that I could no longer look past, and also of my concern that he might have attention deficit disorder, which contributed to his inability to communicate effectively. I told him that, on the basis of results, I wasn't the right resource for him, and that I felt we should stop working together. He said, "I've been expecting this. I've been thinking about some of the things you've said. Maybe I do need to get tested for ADD." I noted that he didn't say anything about correcting the integrity outage, so I thanked him for having allowed me into his confidence, pointed him toward the resources we both felt could be useful, shook his hand, and left, feeling energized, grounded, and determined to pay fierce attention to that ongoing conversation we all have with ourselves.

And what of our conversations with others? We all have many thoughts as we listen to friends, colleagues, kids, spouses, customers. For some time now, as I have practiced Principle 3—be here, prepared to be nowhere else—I have attempted to capture and share elusive thoughts and emotions. During a fierce conversation, my role is not to say what is easy to say or what we all can say, but to say what we have been unable to say. I try to pay attention to things that may pass unobserved by others and bring them out into the open. The most valuable thing any of us can do is find a way to say the things that can't be said.

> **The most valuable thing any of us can do is find a way to say the things that can't be said.**

Trapping Furtive Truths

The left-hand column will assist you in this process. You will pull your thoughts from the dim corners where they would prefer to hide. You will bring them into the light, catch them in midflight.

This is how it's done.

Listen to both sides of your brain as if you were hearing two conversations at the same time. One conversation is the literal conversation that is visible, audible. The other conversation is the one going on inside your head—what you are thinking and feeling.

Bring some of your private thoughts and feelings into the neutral zone by noticing them without attachment. They aren't right or wrong. They just exist. Become interested in them as phenomena in the world, as if they were interesting shells you found on the beach. When you are ready you can bring these thoughts into the public conversation. If you like, you can use these words: "While you were speaking I had a thought that I would like to check out with you . . ."

This is called "perception checking." It lets your partner in on what you have been thinking and feeling, but it doesn't invite defensiveness because you didn't interject your thoughts as the capital-T Truth.

Another approach is to ask a question to open up a willingness on another person's part. For example, you might ask, "Would you like to hear something I'm feeling [or thinking or wondering] right now?" Then, assuming your partner is willing and interested, share your thought.

Here's an example of how the left-hand column works.

David and Ron

I was listening to a client named David talk about the disappearance of his twenty-year-old son, Ron. Ron had fallen in with a bad crowd and had been expelled from high school in his junior year. Ron refused to return to school and scorned all offers of counseling. He continued to live with his parents but had become increasingly abusive to his mother and, on one occasion, had threatened her physically. In addition, Ron got into numerous messes, fights, and predicaments, all the while remaining adamant that none of it was his fault.

David intervened to shield his wife from Ron's abuse, to bail him out of his latest problem and to influence him to change his ways. After yet another blowup between Ron and his parents, Ron packed up and headed out. No one had heard from him for several months.

David was disturbed by his feelings of relief. "Is it normal to feel this way?" he asked. "I mean, we've done everything we could, and at this point, frankly, Katie and I are glad to have our home back, our lives back. But shouldn't I feel more concern about Ron's whereabouts? Should I be doing more than I am to try to find my son?"

Throughout David's detailed description of all that he had endured at Ron's hands, and his admission of relief that his son was gone, I noticed that his voice was absolutely flat. Although David used emotional words, he didn't seem to be feeling emotion himself. He sat slumped in his chair, his face and body devoid of animation.

I tuned in to an impression that hinted at itself, then grew stronger the longer he talked.

While listening to David, I tuned in to an impression that hinted at itself, then grew stronger the longer he talked. The impression was of someone enveloped in a dense fog bank, to the point of near invisibility. Even to himself.

This impression persisted, so at a pause when David seemed to be thinking about all he had said, I offered my left-hand column to David for his consideration: "As I have been listening to you, I've had a sense of you inside a fog bank, as if you were invisible, perhaps even to yourself. Does that impression make any sense to you, or am I imagining it?"

He sat quietly and seemed to examine the space in front of him. Then he said, "You know, that is what it feels like. I can't see anything clearly right now. That's interesting. It's almost as if I'm running blind. I'm afraid I'm going to walk off a cliff."

I said, "As you've been telling me about Ron and Katie and all that the three of you have been through, you seem emotionally flat, as if you had been drugged and were unable to feel anything. Is there anything to this or am I off base?"

His response was instantaneous. "You're right. It's as if I've been anesthetized."

"How long have you felt this way?"

David thought awhile, then said, "I think it started coming on the year Ron was expelled, when we had one knock-down-drag-out after another. It was horrible. Katie and I had no time or energy for ourselves. Everything was about Ron. Trying to help him, clean up after him."

As our conversation continued, David realized that, like many who have been in a war zone for an extended time period, in order to survive he had desensitized himself to the awfulness of his situation. The trouble was, he had numbed himself to the point of narcolepsy. His work and his relationship with Katie were suffering as a result. David concluded that a useful step would be to seek the help of a professional therapist to work through how best to help his son, while staying alive and engaged in his own life.

It takes a certain fearlessness to make your private thoughts public. But if what you're thinking makes you squirm and wish to wriggle away, you are probably onto something. In David's case, it was rewarding that my internal musing helped him recognize what he was experiencing and what he might do to help himself.

Can Our Instincts Get Us in Trouble?

Our instincts are not always correct. There have certainly been times when I managed to possess an incorrect but fervent understanding of an issue. And sometimes I've found myself just plain lost. I have no idea what a conversation is even pretending to be about. At times like that, I have sometimes said, "I'm as confused as you appear to be. How do we dig out of here?"

It's not our thoughts or feelings that get us into trouble. It's not our disclosures that cause distress. It's our attachment to them, our belief that we are right. I want to emphasize the importance of releasing any attachment to our thoughts and interpretations as the *truth*. Even so, I would rather err on the side of checking out my instincts than passing them over for fear that I could be wrong or that I might offend someone. I have at times said to new clients, "I will tell you what I'm thinking, sensing, wondering. I will push you to make decisions or to take actions on important issues. I am on your side. I will go too far, and when I do, you must stop me."

We deservedly get into trouble when we ascribe motives or when we determine the "truth" thirty seconds into a conversation and inject our opinion, under the misapprehension that we are on track, that we know what is really going on. We are guaranteed to offend others when we present our impressions and interpretations as the truth.

I will go too far, and when I do, you must stop me.

Few people appreciate being told, "What you really mean is . . . ," followed by a motive or meaning that could not be further from the truth. That would feel like a violation, like trying to play tennis with someone who refused to stay on his or her side of the net. The left-hand column is about how to stay on your side of the net without violating someone else, but still playing a really great game of tennis.

We are guaranteed to offend others when we present our impressions and interpretations as the truth.

A friend recounted a conversation that marked the beginning of the end of her marriage, during which she told her husband, "You misinterpret me completely, consistently. I wear one face and you have given me another that is dark, malevolent. You ascribe to me thoughts, feelings, motives that are not mine. You miss me entirely."

I recall listening to someone recount a conversation we had both witnessed and wondering, "It's amazing that he interpreted it that way. After all, we were both at the scene of the 'crime.' Wonder where he got his story."

The fundamental outcome of most communication is *mis*understanding.

The fundamental outcome of most communication is *mis*understanding. We all just attended the same different meeting or participated in the same different conversation. No matter what a person says, we decide in the privacy of our minds what he or she really means by it and then operate as if our interpretation is true, without checking it out. He said this. You heard that. You intended one thing; however, the recipient of your message gave your words a meaning that never even crossed your mind. How many times have you said to someone, "I wish we had tape-recorded our conversation because it would prove that I never said . . ." or "that I *did* say . . ."? Each of you was convinced your interpretation was the right one.

Our context determines how we experience the content of our lives.

It is not so difficult to understand how misunderstandings and conversational fly-bys occur, given that each of us experiences life in a unique context—a filter consisting of our strongly held opinions, beliefs, and attitudes, which have been shaped and reinforced over a lifetime. Our context determines how we experience the content of our lives. Often our context takes the form of rules to live by. For example, ask yourself:

At what point is a room messy?

How many minutes make a person late?

Should dogs be allowed to sleep on the bed?

Which are preferable—plastic plants or live plants?

Each individual has his or her context and lives his or her life accordingly. It gets interesting when the content in our lives includes the meaning and intent of every conversation in which we participate. And therefore, the outcomes.

Remember, all conversations are with *myself,* and sometimes they involve other people.

This is true in the sense that we all unconsciously, automatically put our own interpretation or spin on the words of others. We are all constantly interpreting everything we hear others say. And constantly being interpreted in turn. If your conversations with a particular individual are always negative, is it possible that you hold a belief that guarantees your negative interpretation of and response to everything this person says?

During fierce conversations, people don't cling to their positions as the undeniable truth. Instead, they consider their views as hypotheses to be explored and tested against others. Joseph Pine, author of *The Experience Economy,* suggests, "The experience of being understood, versus interpreted, is so compelling you can charge admission." There is a universal longing to be known, to be understood. Unfortunately, the experience is rare.

There is a responsibility here: to be clear, to check for meaning, and, most important, to examine the context in which we experience our conversations. Cardinal Newman said, "We can believe what we choose. We are answerable for what we choose to believe."

We can believe what we choose. We are answerable for what we choose to believe.

—CARDINAL NEWMAN

When we look at how often our choices about what to believe can lead to misunderstanding, we are faced with a problem. On the one hand, spending time with those who insist on misinterpreting us in almost every conversation will cause relationships to stall or end. On the other hand, what about *our* possible misinterpretations? What should we do when our left-hand column sends a consistent message over and over again: "Something is not right here. Something is going on. Somehow, I sense that there is more to this than meets the eye."

You may feel awkward as you begin to experiment with your left-hand column, offering your private thoughts to others for their consideration. We often speak of "feeling our way." To let your feeling lead you is not a bad tactic during a conversation.

Trouble Paying Attention

Phillip and I had met monthly for a year, usually on Monday mornings. Phillip is sociable, shares my macabre sense of humor, laughs easily, and is wonderfully candid concerning his shortcomings as a leader. During the second year of our relationship, I couldn't help noticing the increasingly visible veins in Phillip's nose and cheeks. He often looked sleep-deprived, his eyes red-rimmed and puffy.

Occasionally, I ventured a comment. "You look a little ragged this morning."

"Yeah, party last night. Got to bed around two. Great time."

And so it went.

In subsequent meetings, I became more and more distracted by my concerns over Phillip's appearance. It was difficult for me to pay attention to his comments about the issues in his company when I found myself wondering if he was becoming an alcoholic. I was stuck. Should I bring it up? How could I bring it up? How do you ask someone, "Do you have a drinking problem?" That's not the kind of thing one brings up out of the blue. Or is it? And who am I to venture a guess? I don't know beans about alcoholism. And sotto voce, my left-hand column asked, "Susan, what are you pretending not to know?"

As I got into my car following another session with Phillip, I sat for a moment, confronted by my cowardice. *You say you care for this person. Do you really? If he is an alcoholic, it's not only affecting his health, it's affecting his marriage and his ability to be the great leader he aspires to be. You've got to say something. You've got to ask him about this.* I resolved to share my concern when it seemed appropriate. I didn't have to wait long.

As soon as I walked into Phillip's office for our next meeting, I knew it would be impossible to concentrate on anything he had to say. He looked decidedly hung over.

"Bad night?" I asked.

"What? Oh, yeah. I got together with some friends this weekend."

The moment of truth. I screwed my courage to the sticking place.

"Phillip, it's going to be difficult for me to focus on business issues today unless I share with you a growing concern of mine."

Phillip paused, smiling quizzically. "Okay, shoot."

"It's not that easy. I'm worried that you'll be put off by what I want to ask you, so I want you to know that I'm prepared to be dead wrong about this."

Phillip's smile faded.

"It's this, Phillip. We always meet on Monday mornings, after the weekend, and, well, frankly, you usually look like hell." Phillip frowned. I took a deep breath and continued, "A couple of times I've asked you about it, and you tell me about another party with your friends, staying up late. You always laugh it off."

By this time, neither of us was eager to hear the next words I would speak out loud. The brief silence between us was hard at work, and my heart was in my throat. I spoke as gently as I knew how. "I may be way off base, and I know you'll tell me if I am. It's just that I find myself wondering if the way you look on Monday mornings is about more than good times with your friends. I worry that perhaps you have a drinking problem, that perhaps you are an alcoholic."

Phillip had lost his sleepy look. His face flushed. He snorted. "I can't believe it! I tell you about my friends, a few parties, and you take it to this."

I barely resisted the impulse to apologize, withdraw my observation, discount my concern. Instead, I waited. Phillip pushed his chair away from his desk. I could virtually hear the tension in the room—an electric whine. I was in the electric chair and was about to become toast.

Phillip's words were measured, his jaw clenched. He looked me squarely in the face and said, "One. I do not have a drinking problem. Two. I will never mention my friends and our parties again." He took a long breath. "Now can we get on with our meeting? I have some things I want to run by you."

Again, I fought off the impulse to apologize and instead said, "Yes, okay, let's move on."

At a meeting with Phillip six months later, I began with the first question from Mineral Rights: "What is the most important thing you and I should be talking about today?"

Phillip sat quietly a moment, then said, "My drinking problem."

Finding Out What You Know

A careful conversation is a failed conversation. When we enter the conversation with a goal of being poised, clever, instructive, we are inhibited, and all possibilities of intimacy are held at bay.

A careful conversation is a failed conversation.

If we approach a conversation with the assumption that we know where it is going and what we need to say, we assume that logic is running the show. Things are not that simple. A fierce conversation is more original and varied in its choices. The heart, the guardian of intuition with its unsettling intentions, is the boss; its commands are ours to obey. At least, they are mine to obey.

I speak in order to find out what I know.

It still comes as a shock to realize that I don't speak about what I know. I speak in order to find out what I know. Often the real trouble is that the conversation hasn't been allowed to find its subject; it isn't yet about what it wants to be about. But everything shifts when we entertain private thoughts that drop clues like bread crumbs along the conversational path. After countless fierce conversations, I am still touched to realize that the person with whom I am talking wishes to be discovered by a reflective self who is listening carefully

Everything shifts when we entertain private thoughts that drop clues along the conversational path.

in order to understand and make sense of this maze of words con-
cealing the heart of the story.

Obeying our instincts and offering them up to a colleague or
loved one allows both of us to know things we could not know otherwise. Together, we begin to see what this conversation wants to be
about, and where it wants to go, and how to make it pulsingly real.
One disclosure, one offering from our left-hand column at a time.

We select something to bring into the public conversation. We
put something forth, then something else, and so on, to the conclusion of the conversation. What we select is not necessarily the truth,
not even *a* truth sometimes. However, the thoughts or questions we
dare to share may assist the conversation in going where it needs to
go. The function of our left-hand column is intensely personal and
surprisingly revelatory.

As you will learn in chapter 6, the conversation isn't over just
because the conversation is over. The conversation with Phillip, for
example, was continued over the course of many conversations . . .
each one memorable.

What Is Appropriate?

There are differences of opinion about what is appropriate territory
for conversations, given one's area of expertise. I am not a trained
therapist, so when I encounter things that are beyond my ken, I refer
people to a professional. However, none of us needs a license to be a
fellow human being or a friend. We don't need a degree to be present.
It was not my intent or goal to advise Phillip. That's not my job. If I
thought it was, I would be in trouble. My job is to take my expert hat
off, leave it out in the hall, and come into the conversation and just
be available.

We all know how easy it is to get into conversational hot water
when we shoot from the hip and say whatever comes to mind. It's a
very different experience to obey our instincts after having gained

skill and practice in interrogating reality, in showing up authentically, in giving others the purity of our attention, and in confronting issues with courage and compassion. Since the conversation is the relationship, there is now a broad and rich context in which to offer our thoughts for others' consideration.

Your confusion is an asset; in fact, your search for clarity may blaze a path for others.

And what if your instincts occasionally miss the target?

Consider this possibility: *Your confusion is an asset; in fact, your search for clarity may blaze a path for others.* In working to express what you do not understand—but long to understand—you invite the kind of conversations for which others are searching. If you begin to wonder what others will think of you, you won't be able to pursue original avenues. Look for the deepest issue that engages or troubles you. Familiarity with the unknown and with the fluidity of the world is essential. Don't swerve away from it. Speak your way toward it.

Assignment

During your conversations today, pay fierce attention to what you are thinking and feeling. Notice what interests you that is not being addressed; notice the questions you'd like to ask; notice the observations your inner voice is urging you to share. Remember that what you are thinking and feeling is not right or wrong. Your thoughts are simply your thoughts. From time to time, choose one to bring into the public conversation. Invite your partner to explore it with you. In doing so, you give the conversation an opportunity to go deeper. Be courageous in your conversations today.

❖ A Refresher . . .

❖ A careful conversation is a failed conversation.

❖ During each conversation, listen for more than content. Listen for emotion and intent as well.

❖ Act on your instincts rather than passing them over for fear that you could be wrong or that you might offend someone.

❖ Watch what happens to the conversation when you do this.

❖ Invite your partners to do the same.

CHAPTER SIX

PRINCIPLE **6**

Take Responsibility for Your Emotional Wake

There are people who take the heart out of you and there are people who put it back.

—Elizabeth David

For a leader, there is no trivial comment. Something you might not even remember saying may have had a devastating impact on someone looking to you for guidance and approval. By the same token, something you said years ago may have encouraged and inspired someone who is grateful to you to this day. Everything each of us says leaves an emotional wake. Positive or negative. Our individual wakes are larger than we know.

An emotional wake is what you remember after I'm gone. What you feel. The aftermath, aftertaste, or afterglow.

An emotional wake is what you remember after I'm gone. What you feel. The aftermath, aftertaste, or afterglow.

One of my friends frequently struggles to resolve fights with her husband. She never remembers what he says, just how she feels when he says it. Later, he is angry at her withdrawal. "This is stupid. I didn't say anything worth barricading yourself in here all day!"

"Yes, you did," she thinks, "but I can't tell you what it was. I just know that I got the message. What you said. How you said it. Tone of voice. Sarcasm, I think it was. The look on your face. The long-suffering husband. Your back was half-turned to me. Dismissal."

She feels this in her bones. Angry words crouch behind her teeth, ready and willing. He sees the flash in her eyes and knows to stop, then pretends later that this is silly. *Silly woman, upset for no reason.*

"He says I'm his tuning fork," she told me. "His image of grounded, intelligent energy. He values my intelligence, but he doesn't reach for me. Doesn't touch me."

When she tried to say these words to her husband, her fear and anger triggered both of them and they added another topic to their list of undiscussables.

After one of their fights, my friend called her husband on his cell phone, hoping for some hint of clarity or resolution. Their connection kept going in and out, and there was a lot of static on the line. My friend kept shouting, "Are you there? Can you hear me?" Later, she realized it was a perfect metaphor for their four-year inability to communicate about the topic of commitment to their relationship.

If you wish to drown yourself, do not torture yourself with shallow water.

Their constant sniping at each other reminded me of a Bulgarian proverb: "If you wish to drown yourself, do not torture yourself with shallow water."

This marriage failed. Slowly. Surely. What was needed was a series of fierce conversations, during which each of them took responsibility for his and her emotional wake.

After they separated, I ran into her husband, a man whose sense of humor I had always enjoyed. He said, "Every time I go back to the house, she has two more black trash bags filled with my stuff. The other day I saw a black trash bag in the backseat of a friend's car.

'Wife throwing you out?' I asked. And he said, 'Yes, how did you know?' Black trash bags. Dead giveaway."

Funny, and sad. *What were the messages these two people were unable to deliver that might have saved the marriage?*

James Newton describes his home at the foot of San Diego Bay, where all of the houses have docks. The speed limit in the bay is five knots. Once in a while, some cowboy rips through the area and rocks all of the boats, knocking them up against the docks. The person might not have done this on purpose. Perhaps he was just doing his own thing. However, if a boater is thoughtless and causes damage, he is responsible for it. The water cops will make sure he pays for any damage caused by his wake. Yes, the other boats should have bumpers, the right-sized bumpers; still, each boater is required to take responsibility for his own wake.

The question is not "Can he boat in those waters?" Of course he can. The question is "At what speed?"

There was a period in my life in which I was unconscious of my "speed" and of the wake I was leaving during my conversations with others. If this is true for you as well, you can appreciate how challenging it is to live up to the vow of becoming more conscious of the effect of our words on others.

In the face of this task, some people decide not to say anything at all to certain "sensitive types." Or some decide just to let the chips fall where they may, feeling that "if I'm too strong for some people, that's their problem."

In the end, the "problem" belongs to both parties; however, since you and I have little control over how others will react, the most effective position to take is to focus on our own actions. We can say to ourselves: "This is my problem. From this day forward, I will take responsibility for my emotional wake."

Your Stump Speech

If you are a leader, taking responsibility for your emotional wake requires that you have a stump speech—the speech you must be prepared to give anytime, anywhere, to anyone who asks or who looks the least bit confused. Your stump speech must be powerful, clear, and brief.

> *This is where we're going.*
>
> *This is why we're going there.*
>
> *This is who is going with us.*
>
> *This is how we're going to get there.*

Great leaders share their stump speeches with their teams and with their customers repeatedly, not only to convey a clear and compelling story but also to leave a positive emotional wake. A leader's long-term performance is profoundly affected by the long-term spin the organization puts on him or her. Our emotional wake determines the story that is told about each of us in the organization. It's the story that's told when we're not in the room. It's the story that will be told about us after we're gone. It can be a wonderful story that makes us smile or a painful story with a bad ending.

Our emotional wake determines the story that is told about each of us in the organization.

What is *your* story? How would you like to be interpreted? What is the legacy you want to leave? If the people in your organization could tell one story about you, what would you want it to be? What is the message you wish to deliver to *your* customers? What wake do you wish to leave following each conversation? The conversation *is* the relationship. In the workplace this translates to your ongoing dialogue with all those essential to success.

Many of the great leaders with whom I have worked sustain a love affair with their work and their lives. They place their attention at the service of deep, long-term concepts and convictions in the workplace and the home. They possess a groundedness that comes from having wrestled core problems to the ground and lived to tell about it. They have become sensitized to the effect they have on others. They have become increasingly aware of the wake caused by their words and actions. Their perspective and goals have shifted as they recognized that leadership must be for the world.

What do I want them to remember when I'm gone? I need to say that, and only that . . . clearly!

A CEO who was frustrated with the results of his attempts to communicate with his executives mused . . .

> What I *get* to say is not what I *want* to say,
>> is not what they *listen* to,
>>> is not what they *hear,*
>>>> is not what they *understand,*
>>>>> is not what they *remember* when I'm gone.
>>>>>> *What do I want them to remember when I'm gone?*
>>>>>> I need to say that, and only that . . . clearly!

What do you want them to remember when you're gone? Are you saying it . . . clearly?

Assignment

If you lead an organization or a team within an organization, write your corporate stump speech. Antoine de Saint-Exupéry wrote, "If you want to build a ship, don't gather your people and ask them to provide wood, prepare tools, assign tasks. Call them together and raise in their minds the longing for the endless sea."

- This is where we are going:

- This is why we are going there:

- This is who is going with us:

- This is how we're going to get there:

Andy and Roger

A negative emotional wake is not caused exclusively by thoughtless or unkind comments. It is created at times by a lack of appreciative comments. For example, my meetings with clients always end with the question "Given everything we've talked about, what's at the top of your to-do list for the next thirty days?" I follow up on that at the next meeting.

During a meeting with a client whose long and impressive history of successes was legendary, I got so caught up in the topic for the meeting that I forgot to ask him about his to-do list for the preceding thirty days. I began to wrap up the meeting, and he could see I was about to leave. He said, "Hey, wait a minute. Aren't you going to ask me what I got done in the last thirty days? I wanna brag."

I had forgotten that people at all levels in the corporate world, even those at the very top, deserve to be recognized for their good qualities and accomplishments.

Who deserves *your* praise? Who needs to know you care? Who needs to be told that you love him? How soon can you say it?

Andrew is a gentleman's gentleman, a consummate professional, and a world-class negotiator. Most who know Andy want to be just like him when they grow up.

I walked into Andrew's office for our monthly meeting to find him distraught. His first words were, "Roger resigned." Roger was Andy's heir apparent. Andy had great plans for Roger. He continued, "He took another job. It's a complete dead end for him."

"But why?" I asked.

Andy shook his head. "He saw me move other people around in the organization and assumed I didn't have a plan for him, assumed he was being passed over because I didn't think highly of him."

"But you had great plans for him. How could he not have known that?"

"I felt it was best not to promise him anything. You never know what's going to happen. I planned to promote him in time—soon, actually—but felt that it wouldn't be politically correct if I told him what I had in mind."

"Can you save him?"

"I tried, believe me, but his pride is involved. He won't budge. A year from now, he'll be miserable."

We sat quietly, Andy with his head in his hands. After a while, I ventured a question: "Maybe it's too soon to know, but what have you learned from this?"

Andy's eyes glistened. "I didn't tell him I loved him. I thought he knew."

Appreciation, praise. Unfiltered, unqualified. There is so little of it going around.

Appreciation, praise.
Unfiltered, unqualified.
There is so little of it going around.

While it might not have been appropriate for Andy to lay out the details of what he had in mind for Roger—after all, reality can and does shift—it was appalling to Andy to realize that Roger really did not know that Andy held him in high regard.

Tellmetellmetellmetellme

In the movie *Always,* there is a scene in which Richard Dreyfuss's character, Pete, a pilot who specializes in firefighting, has given Holly Hunter's character, Dorinda, a beautiful dress for her birthday. Very feminine and girly. Dorinda puts it on and makes a grand entrance down the stairs of a bar to the whistles of all the men, who line up for a chance to dance with her.

Later, alone with Pete, Dorinda pleads, "Tell me you love me. Tellmetellmetellmetellme. TELL ME!"

He doesn't, of course, until days later. As he is about to take off for an unexpected emergency, Dorinda cycles madly down the tarmac, climbs up onto the airplane, hugs him fiercely, then climbs down and starts pedaling away. In that moment, he is struck by his feelings and shouts toward her retreating back, "I love you!" She cannot hear him over the roar of the engines. He shrugs and taxis off. And dies moments later in an explosion.

That may seem a bit sappy, this notion of "you could die today, so who haven't you hugged?" Yet it's a real possibility. You could check out anytime with no advance notice. So could others in your life.

Who needs to hear from you? Who needs to know what you appreciate about him?

A taxi driver in San Francisco recently told me, "It's just never been in the cards for me to have a close, loving relationship with my parents in person. We got along from a distance but never when we were together. Things started getting better a few years ago. I visited and it went well; we had a good conversation, and I thought, 'Finally, it's possible.' I was planning another visit when my dad died. Now my mom is really sick. She's not going to last much longer."

Who needs to hear from you? Who needs to know what you appreciate about him? If there is any possibility that people don't know how much you value them, there's a conversation that needs to occur.

In the business world, confrontation, criticism, and even anger are more socially acceptable than expressions of appreciation. That's too bad, because appreciation is a truly value-creating activity. Sometimes the fiercest thing that needs saying is "Thank you. I admire how you handled that. You're important in my life."

And wouldn't it mean more if you named a specific quality, behavior, or physical trait that you appreciate in someone? For example,

"You're doing a good job" leaves a feeble wake compared with telling someone, "I overheard you handle that upset customer on the phone. It sounded like you were able to calm him down and really help him. I was impressed by your professionalism." Despite Dorinda's plea in *Always,* don't just tell people that you love them; tell them *why* you love them, what it is about them that you love. Specifically. You go first.

They Just Don't Understand

During a talk I gave in Orange County recently, one man said, "I am completely understood at work, but my wife doesn't understand anything about me. Not one single thing." His frustration was apparent to everyone.

I asked, "Do you understand your wife?"

It got really quiet.

It is possible that both individuals in this marriage are self-absorbed and strong-willed. I could envision a clash of wills at home that this man does not encounter at work, where he holds a leadership position. I wondered about his statement of being understood at work. I had the feeling that to him, a "fierce" conversation looked like him giving orders—"Bruce, you take that hill. Sally, you take this one"—or expressing his displeasure at marginal performance with a raised eyebrow and a tug at the cuffs of his exquisite Armani turtleneck. I wondered how his employees and his wife would answer the question "Does he understand you?"

The very next week at a workshop in San Francisco, following a practice session on Mineral Rights, a participant, Mike, protested, "But this isn't a conversation; it's an interview! I don't want to interview my employees. I want them to understand what I'm telling them!" Later in the workshop Mike talked about how frustrated he was with one of the people who reported to him. "This guy just doesn't understand me. He doesn't listen. I talk and I talk, and he just doesn't get it."

There's a theme here—this unfortunate context around the meaning of the word *conversation.* I see it all the time. Frequently, the context is: *I'll talk, you listen. We'll have had a good conversation when you finally understand me and admit that I'm right.*

Who is responsible for providing this *understanding* we all crave so much?

This definition of *conversation* will not serve you. In fact, it can be fatal to both professional and personal relationships.

We'd all like to be understood, yet very few feel understood. We talked about this in chapter 3. The question I want to revisit with you is "Who is responsible for providing this *understanding* we all crave so much?"

How about—me? How about you?

When the Relationship Is on the Line

Sometimes individuals in a relationship have created such a negative emotional wake that one or both participants are ready to pull the plug. Even at that stage, fierce conversations can turn things around—and it requires going back to basics.

Before any of us can answer the question "Do I want this relationship at work or at home?" we must accomplish two things.

First, our own lives must be working. In other words, we must have had the fierce conversations with ourselves that are necessary to sort out our own lives, to answer the big questions in chapter 2: *Where am I going? Why am I going there? Who is going with me? How am I going to get there?* And following these conversations, we need to step onto the path and remain on it for longer than a week or a month. Otherwise, when we are unhappy, we will have difficulty determining the source. It's easy to assume someone else is the source of our angst and that we'd be happier if that person were no longer in our lives; however, the problem may lie much closer to home.

Second, we must give to others what we most want to receive. Do you want to be with others who leave behind a positive emotional wake? Then leave one yourself. Do you long to be understood? Then focus on understanding others. Do you want to have a place at the corporate table where your ideas will be welcomed? Then welcome the ideas of the person who most confounds and irritates you. Do you want your life partner to listen to you the way he or she did when you were first falling in love? Then plan an evening during which you will focus entirely on listening to your loved one. Do you want to be able to discuss difficult issues without experiencing someone else's defensiveness and wrath, without unkind, thoughtless comments that leave you drowning in a negative emotional wake? Well, it's highly unlikely any of this will happen until you go first. And one day doesn't count. You must extend to others what you want to receive. It begins with you.

> **You must extend to others what you want to receive. It begins with you.**

People express and receive love in different ways. Read *The Five Love Languages,* by Gary Chapman. Find out what language your spouse understands. Is it quality time? Words of affirmation? Gifts? Thoughtful acts? Physical touch? Whatever the language is, learn it and speak it.

Make it important to learn the love language of your significant other and speak it to him or her every day. In difficult moments, ask, "What would love do?" And do it. Do not give up. Live what you are intent on learning.

Here's where the magic comes in. A funny thing happens between people when one of them is really asking and really listening, versus constantly interrupting with his or her own agenda and ascribing negative meanings to everything the other says. And when this person who is really listening operates from a well-built and well-stocked personal base camp—when what he or she lives is an authentic expression of who that person is or wishes to become—the invitation to come out from behind oneself into the conversation and make it real is often accepted. And once that happens, the armor begins to fall away, piece by piece, and we see, beneath the armor, a man's heart, a woman's heart, the heart of a child.

Very few hearts are rejected.
Very few hearts are rejected. It is the armor that seals us off from one another and causes us to move so awkwardly through life. We recognize armor, we hear it clanking from a mile off, and we ask ourselves: "Why is he so well defended? Anyone wearing that much armor must also be well armed. Is there something I should fear?"

When we remove the armor, when we come out from behind ourselves, vulnerable and without defense, there is an opportunity to understand and to be understood. When you start to hear your children, your life partner, and your coworker at a deeper level, you'll start getting far more information from them. The quality of your listening will allow your children to discover who they are and to start valuing themselves. They will know that you care about them, and they will eagerly commit themselves to their dreams.

Deliver the Message Without the Load

If we are capable of living our lives at times unconscious of what others are feeling, imagine how easy it is to toss off comments, blithely unaware of our emotional wake's effect on others. In the business world, there is a toll for such unconsciousness. Hallway comments can cause resentment, misunderstandings, plane wrecks. The wake of our comments is amplified when others put their personal spin on everything we say.

For example, we may have innocently asked Johnny how he was doing on such and such, only to learn that Johnny went directly to his colleagues and said, "I can't help you with this now. Other things are more important to the boss, so I've got to focus on them this week." Everyone sulks.

E-mail, as wonderful as it is, creates a huge opportunity for others to put a negative spin on our words. With no physical clues such as tone of voice and facial expression, the intent of our words can easily be misinterpreted. What should you do when you realize that words alone may be insufficient to convey your meaning and intent? Pick up the phone! The most powerful communications technology available to any of us is eye contact. In second position is the telephone. If you can't talk face-to-face, at least you can hear each other's voices. E-mail should be your last choice. Don't sacrifice results in favor of efficiency. Stop potentially leaving a negative emotional wake in favor of saving time.

Don't sacrifice results in favor of efficiency.

A negative emotional wake is expensive. Individuals, teams, customers, and family members pay the price. In order to leave a positive wake and lessen the opportunity for an inaccurate spin to be attached to your messages, learn to deliver the message *without the load.* This is a concept that was introduced to me by my colleague Pat Murray.

Loaded messages come in many guises. At times they arrive courtesy of a person who uses sugary sweet words yet who seems to have a malevolent undertone. Our radar picks up something else—some hidden agenda perhaps—embedded in the message, leaving us uneasy and reluctant to trust. It wasn't anything the person actu-

Learn to deliver the message *without the load.*

ally said, but rather something in the air around the message that didn't feel good. Our impeccable radar warns us to obey our instincts and be careful.

No matter how much sugar someone sprinkles throughout a loaded message, we read the underlying intent to do harm loud and clear. Consequently, we do not trust that person, we do not look forward to our next conversation, and we withhold ourselves from him or her in countless invisible ways.

Other loads are delivered straightforwardly, impossible to miss. An example is the parent who, no matter what the child has achieved, says, "That's really good, honey, yet next time why don't you do it this way . . ." The load attached to this message is "Nothing you do is good enough."

Likewise, many of us know people who trip all over their words and whose communication styles are inelegant, messy, or downright inappropriate, yet because there is no ulterior motive or hidden agenda attached to their messages, we are willing to listen to them and stay engaged in the conversations and in the relationships.

I often ask workshop participants to think of someone whose behavior they want to confront and imagine what they would say to that person. Then I ask each participant to identify his or her unique fingerprint—the load it would be tempting to attach to the message. Typical responses include such loads as . . .

- Blaming, my all-time favorite, the mother of all loads. *"This whole thing is your fault." "It's you, not me." "You really screwed this up."*

- Name calling, labeling. *"You're an insensitive narcissist." "You're a liar." "You're a failure."*

- Using sarcasm, black humor. *"Apparently, your life goal is to live on the cutting edge of mediocrity." "Seems you've hit bottom and have started to dig."*

- Attaching global weight to tip-of-the-iceberg stuff. This small thing happened and it means this HUGE thing! *"You don't love me and never did." "This ruins everything. We're finished."*

- Threatening, intimidating (always a winner!). *"Guess you don't value your job." "You'll never see your kids again." "You do this one more time and . . ." "Look, I don't want to pull rank, but . . ."*

- Exaggerating. *"You always do this." "Never once have you . . ." "This is the hundredth time . . ."*

- Pointing to someone else's failure to communicate, assuming a position of superiority; the other person is clearly inferior.

"You don't get it." "You can't handle it." "You aren't making any sense at all." "I can't get through to you."

- Saying, *"If I were you . . ."* That's a pretty loaded phrase. If I say that, then you'll feel I'm saying you should have done it my way, which is usually what I'm saying. An additional load embedded in the message is: *Why can't you be more like me?*

- Gunnysacking, bringing up a lot of old baggage. *"This is just like the time when you . . ."*

- Assassinating someone in public. This is sneaky and cowardly, and we usually try to get away with it by pretending it's funny. *"Oh, yeah, Janie thinks she's pretty hot stuff!"*

- Asking, *"Why did you do that?"* instead of *"What were you trying to do?"* I get a less defensive response with the second question.

- Making blatantly negative facial expressions. No matter what I say, if I am angry or disappointed, how I feel is written all over my face.

- Layering my interpretation on something someone has said or done; ascribing negative or false motives. *"What you really mean is . . ."* or *"What's really going on is . . ."*

- Being unresponsive, refusing to speak. Some would say this is the cruelest load you can attach. To others, it feels like a lack of caring, a lack of validation.

Assignment

Take a moment to recall one of your conversations at work or at home that did not go well. Forget about the other person's ineffective behavior. Focus on yourself. Revisit the conversation. Play it back in your head like a movie. See the expression on your face. What was your body language? Replay your words and listen to the tone with which they were spoken. View in your head the part of the conversation when your partner became upset or angry. What did you say or do that seemed to trigger your partner's response? Now review the list of load-attaching responses on pages 200–201 and answer the following questions about your conversation:

What load did you attach to your message?

Is that your typical, unique fingerprint?

What effect did it have on the conversation?

Messages with hidden agendas usually head south in a heartbeat. In fact, the nanosecond the underlying message is attached, whether verbal or nonverbal, one person becomes triggered and there is no longer a conversation. Instead of a one-to-one, we have a monologue, a diatribe. Or we have a fight. It's impossible to have a conversation when you've already moved the other person into defensiveness. The person feels: "I just want out of this, so I'll do whatever I have to do to gut this out, get the hell outta here (and get back at him/her later)." Or we get confusion: "What do you want?" Or hurt: "How could you say that to me?"

Attaching a load to a message leaves the relationship worse off than it was before you opened your mouth. Given that one of the four purposes of all fierce conversations is to enrich relationships, we need to acknowledge our load if we have one. But beware! Don't become one of those people who are so cautious that not only is there no load, there is no message.

A Crucible

If we can agree that our goal is to deliver the message without the load, what should we do when we're triggered? When our buttons get pushed? Unfortunately, for most of us, the instant our buttons are pushed, all our hard-won skills fly straight out the window.

We all have buttons. Mine invariably get pushed when I feel that I have been grossly misinterpreted. Or when what I have to say seems not to be valued. Whether or not someone intends this, those perceptions on my part invite instant triggering. When I'm triggered, I have two ingrained reactions, two automatic, hardwired responses. One is to exit the conversation by clamming up (the silent treatment) or walking out the door. The other is to make accusations and hurl blame. I'm not proud of this. It's just what every fiber of my body wants to do.

Of course, the instant I am triggered, my reaction triggers everyone else in the conversation. Then they do whatever they do when they're triggered, and we quickly arrive at endgame. It's over. Not pretty. We've all seen it happen. When we are triggered, it is essential to get ourselves untriggered and fight off the tendency to attach a load. The following story may be helpful.

Years ago, I went to Denver to meet Laura Mehmert, a dear friend from high school days, at the foundry where her eight-foot bronze of a cowboy carrying a calf was being poured. In a foundry, the crucible is what holds the molten metal, which is then poured from the crucible into molds to cool and harden so that it can become the work of art conceived months or years ago by the artist.

I was watching Laura's *Foreman* take shape as the molten bronze swirled, burbled, hissed, steamed. The question that intrigued me was "What the heck is the crucible made out of that it isn't melting?"

The foundry owner explained, "Most crucibles are made of either clay graphite or silicon carbides—fragile materials, essentially, some of the same ingredients in porcelain. If a crucible were dropped on a concrete floor, it would crack or shatter. When a new crucible arrives, I strike it to see if it will ring. If it has a sharp sound, it's okay. If it has a dull, thuddy sound, it's damaged."

The foundry owner warmed to the topic and continued, "The gold and silver used in computers are refined in crucibles. Your dentist has a crucible. You'll find castings in hospitals, cars, dams, wind generators, cemeteries. Crucibles have a role in forming castings that take people from birth to death."

As do our conversations.

Several weeks after visiting the foundry, I returned to Denver to see Laura's wonderful sculpture, which had been installed in a park near her home in Evergreen, Colorado. We arrived at the park in the early morning, long before anyone else. *The Foreman* was magnificent. His long coat blew out behind him, as if he were leaning into a storm. His head was lowered toward the calf, safe in his arms. The calf seemed vulnerable, yet its eyes were soft, not frightened. As I walked around *The Foreman,* touching it, marveling at its beauty, and recalled the crusty crucible in which it had begun to take shape, I had an epiphany, or as a young friend of mine would say, an apostrophe.

My "apostrophe" was this: What if *I* could become an utterly dependable crucible—a strong, resilient vessel in which profound change could safely take place—for my clients? for my family and friends? for *myself*?

What if *I* could become a crucible—a strong, resilient vessel in which profound change could safely take place?

In creating a work of art, the crucible has an important job—simply to *hold,* no matter what is poured into it, under extreme heat. I relate to the fragility of the crucible. If I get dropped, I could get hurt. I could crack or break. I am vulnerable. However, during important conversations, my job is to hold, so that we are able to discuss what needs discussing, no matter how challenging the topic and no matter how fragile and vulnerable I am feeling at the time.

The image of the crucible helps me reconcile being real and having all the emotion, including the occasional charge of anger (my own or that of others), while remaining a place where what needs to occur can occur. It reminds me that my job is simply to hold, so that whatever needs to be said, what needs to be heard, can safely be said and heard. It reminds me that works of art form as a result of fierce conversations. Those works of art are the enduring relationships essential to our happiness, success, and peace of mind.

Each of us is a place where conversations occur. You are a physical, emotional, spiritual, and intellectual place where conversations happen. You do not need a special weekend getaway to a romantic B&B in order to have that important conversation with your significant other. You do not need a title, a boardroom, or a fancy office to have the conversation needed to enrich your relationship with your boss, colleague, or customer. You do not need a diploma to be a human being, to be a friend. What is needed is *you*, willing and ready, available, clear, and clean.

Each of us is a place where conversations occur.

Fred Quiring, a fly fisherman, uses the metaphor of an alpine lake to describe himself. When still, the lake notices everything that is happening. Standing on the bank, Fred can see the tiniest mayfly light on the water; he can see the trout rise. It's as if the lake has soft eyes. Eyes that miss nothing. The lake knows its own depths, what life exists in the lake, while being still and paying attention to what is happening. Fred knows from experience, however, that when the lake is turbulent, you could drop the Empire State Building into it and the lake wouldn't notice.

If Fred becomes like that still, calm alpine lake during his conversations, others can put something difficult into the conversation and Fred can see it and respond. He can decide what to do.

In *The Amazing Adventures of Kavalier & Clay*, Michael Chabon writes, "Every universe, our own included, begins in conversation. Every golem in the history of the world . . . was summoned into existence through language, through murmuring, recital, and . . . was, literally, talked into life."

In Jewish legend, a golem is a creature made of clay and brought to life by magical incantations. It occurs to me that each of us has talked our own particular universe into existence. Every entrepreneur remembers talking his or her company into existence. And how did we get to this joyful or difficult place with our partner, with our children, with our sibling? We talked ourselves here.

The conversation is not about the relationship. The conversation *is* the relationship. All of the idols and ideas we use to defend ourselves have been talked into life. Our work, our relationships, and our lives succeed or fail, one conversation at a time. From birth to death.

What kind of conversational place do you want to be? Do you want to be described as a mentor or a tor-mentor? Assuming the former, what words come to mind? *Centered. Present.* You fill in the rest.

The conversation is not about the relationship. The conversation *is* the relationship.

Do you remember the African greeting exchange "I see you" and "I am here"? When I don't see you, I am unaware of what is going on for you. I am unaware of my effect on you. When I do see you, I am able to pay fierce attention not only to the words between us but to their effect as well. *I see you. I am here.* What a lovely way to begin a conversation.

Delivering Unmistakable Messages

Which is worse: not delivering the message at all or delivering a message with a load attached?

Can you imagine saying to someone, "I am not happy with you right now. In fact, I'm deeply angry and my intentions are less than noble, so how about having this conversation later." Or, "Last night I had a series of dreams in which bad things happened to you. They were fantastic dreams, in 3-D, surround sound, wide-screen, Technicolor. I enjoyed them. Guess that means we need to talk."

Wouldn't that at least alert the individual that this is going to be an important conversation and that, therefore, it would behoove him or her to pay attention and to show up for the event? Yes, the person might come to the conversation loaded for bear, but at least we will be fully engaged because we have been intentional about the message and its importance.

Unfortunately, what many people do with anger is bite their tongues. Fierce conversations fade and die because we don't confess, even to ourselves—much less admit to others—that we are not always operating from a base camp of love and harmony. There are occasionally dark instincts at play. Like jealousy, fear, revenge.

Being human is hard! I remember reading C. S. Lewis's *Surprised by Joy.* Looking inside himself, Lewis found "a zoo of lusts, a bedlam of ambitions, a nursery of fears, a harem of fondled hatreds." I felt elated and absolved. Was it possible that the people I admired—the good, wise people of the world—were at times like me?

The emotions to which C. S. Lewis admitted are natural and exquisitely useful feelings to have. And, as it turns out, to speak. *"I am angry." "I am jealous." "I wanted to see you fail."* Admittedly, it helps a lot if you are not screaming such words while pounding the table or pointing a bony finger at someone's nose, but it's human to be angry and it's okay to tell someone what you're feeling. Otherwise, if you serve up all your angst and fire boiled down to a pabulum, you may induce profound indifference.

> **If you serve up all your angst and fire boiled down to a pabulum, you may induce profound indifference.**

How can each of us reconcile being real, delivering the real message, while taking responsibility for our emotional wake? How do we reconcile feelings of anger with authenticity? How do we deliver the message clearly and cleanly, without the load? What is our responsibility to ourselves and to other human beings?

- Recognize that everything you say creates an emotional wake.

- Understand that you can create a wake without any emotion on your part. Check in frequently with others to see what kind of wake you are creating.

- Get in touch with your intent, be it noble or sinister. If your intent is sinister, now is not the time to speak. If your intent is good, it is possible to admit to anger and still leave a positive emotional wake.

- Accept the responsibility to be present, aware, authentic, appropriate, truthful, and clear.

Going into an important conversation with no intent at all is a risky proposition. After I suggested this to a client named George, he told me the following story:

When I was pitching for my college baseball team, the catcher would often walk out to the mound when I was in trouble and ask me if I had any idea about what I was doing. And what he was referring to is that behind my next pitch would be an idea, a purpose, a result that I wanted, which would then determine if I'd throw a fastball low and away, a fastball high and tight, a change-up, a slider, a curveball. So what looks like one man throwing a ball to another man with a big club in his hand is actually a well-thought-out strategy by both parties, because the batter also has an idea, a purpose, a strategy, a result that he's after. Trouble is, during too many of my conversations, I don't have a clue where I am going, what I am trying to do, what my purpose is. Everyone thinks I'm in the conversation. After all, my mouth is open or I'm nodding my head, but I'm just throwing a ball with no idea or purpose behind it. My only hope is for extra innings so I can buy a little time and come up with my idea.

Aim for the Chopping Block

It's the idea behind your words that matters. Learning to deliver the message without the load requires that you speak with clarity, conviction, compassion, and passion. You are not required to become a wimp. You do have certain rights, you know.

- You have the right to get your core needs met in a relationship or, at least, the right not to have them violated.

- You have the right to ask dumb questions.

- You have the right not to be a victim.

- You have the right to confront issues that are troubling you.

- You have the right to disagree.

- You have the right to say yes.

- You have the right to say no.

My best conversations result from obeying Annie Dillard's advice about writing. In *The Writing Life*, Dillard describes learning how to chop wood: Aiming for the top of the upended log resulted in splinters and chips. It was only when the thought came to her to *aim for the chopping block* that she cleaved a log cleanly in two.

My karate sensei gave me similar counsel when I lived in Japan. In karate, if you aim for the brick, you may break some bones and embarrass yourself. Aim for the space beneath the brick, beyond the brick. When the brick is merely an obstacle between you and your target, it will yield.

Aim past this conversation, past these words. Where do you want to go with your work? or this individual? or this marriage? or this life? What is your destination? That's your chopping block. Aim for that in every important conversation.

Sometimes we aim at the wrong thing or forget to aim at anything. *Blah, blah, blah*, we hear ourselves saying. *Darn, I'm doing it again. Okay, where was it I wanted to go with my life?* Might recalling that help us navigate a particular conversation? Well, it can't hurt.

What if your intended destination changes? I hope it does change as you get older, as you figure out what you are and what you aren't. Life is wonderfully curly, remember?

By the way, do not begin your comments with "Truthfully . . ." or "Frankly . . ." or "Honestly . . ." That always makes me

> **Do not begin your comments with "Truthfully . . ." or "Frankly . . ." or "Honestly . . ."**

wonder if someone wasn't speaking truthfully before. Just speak truthfully, frankly, and honestly, and get on with it.

Be Prepared

During workshops, I ask participants to think about a confrontation they need to have and to answer this question: "What do you need to do to have this conversation without attaching a load to your message?" Below are some terrific answers.

- Thinking about the wake of a boat before entering into a conversation would help me to imagine that the conversation has ended, and to visualize the wake left by my boat. What wake do I hope to see?

- I need to keep in mind that being in a relationship with the persons close to me is more important than being right all the time.

- I need to recognize that there are multiple truths.

- When my emotions are negative, the more I say increases the likelihood that there will be a negative wake, so I need to say less and listen more.

- Be intentional and choose words that are not loaded. Find words that accurately name or describe what I want to say, but navigate intentionally in my choice of words.

- Allow space for other interpretations.

- Don't use absolutes: "You NEVER . . ." "You ALWAYS . . ."

- If I expect a load from the other side, it may prevent me from initiating or participating in a conversation. If I don't expect a load from the other side and there is a load, it may push all my buttons and I could become instantly ineffective. I need to expect nothing and be ready for anything!

If you recognize that you often leave a negative emotional wake and now have a desire to correct that, the danger for you may be in going too far over to the other side. *Well, I'm just not going to say what I'm thinking. It will come out all wrong. It will harm the relationship. Every time I try to talk about this, I get in trouble.*

Withholding the message is as dangerous to the relationship as delivering a message with a load attached. For each of us, the challenge is to reconcile being real and doing no harm.

> **The challenge is to reconcile being real and doing no harm.**

When Saying No Is the Solution

Over the last several years, I have developed a meaningful relationship with the word *no.* I highly recommend it. If we do not learn to say no, there will be no space in our lives when a powerful yes appears. Each of us will say yes and no to people, to ideas, to belief systems, to invitations, to the myriad possibilities that present themselves over the course of our lives. It is impossible to say yes to everyone and everything.

> **Saying no is not the problem; in fact, it is often the solution.**

Saying no is not the problem; in fact, it is often the solution. It's the way you say no that gets you in trouble. It's the way you disagree that harms or enriches a relationship. For example, "You don't know what you're talking about" is guaranteed to prickle the person on the receiving end. "I have a different perspective" will likely go down smoother and keep the conversation going. The challenge is to say what we need to say, what is true and right for ourselves—one conversation at a time—and to say it in a way that does not leave boats crashing against the dock in our wake.

In *Repacking Your Bags,* Richard Leider shares his personal mantra: "I am in the right place, with the people I love, doing the right work, on purpose." I like this because it is short and simple, covers lots of important ground, and most decidedly provokes choices—about personal relationships, professional opportunities, lifestyles, and with whom and how Leider spends his time.

Sometimes people we count on fail us once too often. We come to grips with the fact that the financial value of a customer does not counterbalance the frustration of doing business with that person. We accept that an employee simply cannot succeed in this job. And, most painful of all, we can no longer deny that the marriage cannot be saved.

We know something needs to end.

Early in any significant relationship, pay attention to what someone does. Relationships go on far longer than makes any sense because we don't want to believe what we see, hear, feel, and sense in our gut. We don't want it to be true. When you find yourself frustrated by someone's behavior, remind yourself that our behavior—how we show up—comes directly from our capacity, both genetic and historic. When someone shows you who he is, believe him. Do not delude yourself that if you say just the right words, in just the right tone of voice, at just the right moment, with just the right music in the background, you will rewire genetics and transform history.

When someone shows you who he is, believe him.

Pay attention. We show one another who we are every minute of every day.

If the message you've been trying to deliver is that you want another human being to change at the core, reexamine your message.

Sit, Stay!

There is one requirement: *Complete the conversation.*

Hang in there. See your conversations through to completion. No fair starting a pebble rolling and then running when the landslide begins. No fair behaving in ways guaranteed to evoke anger or fear or sadness in any sensate human being, and then exiting the conversation, declaring, "I can't talk to you. You're too angry." That's cheating.

If you create a mess, either single-handedly or in partnership with someone, do not bolt when things get emotional. Some topics of conversation are dicey, at best. But if you started it or you caused it, stay to the finish, even if the finish isn't what you had envisioned ahead of time. You hoped for twittering bluebirds. You ended up with a seriously teed off condor. Sit. Stay. Complete.

Sometimes you just need a well-oiled reverse gear.

Sometimes you just need a well-oiled reverse gear. "I was wrong. I'm sorry." These are important words that too often remain lodged in our throats, even when we know they are desperately needed.

To whom do you owe an apology? Above all, admit it when you're wrong and, if it's appropriate, apologize. People who are never wrong are teetering on the edge of divinity. And likely teetering at the edge of the end of a relationship.

When Is It Okay to Lie?

I was tempted to invent an eighth principle: When all else fails, lie like a dog. I do it very seldom, but I have lied on occasion. Shocking, isn't it? I do it to avoid inflicting completely undeserved and unnecessary pain on others . . . and sometimes on myself.

Recently, for example, a friend named Sandy called to ask how she could tell an on-line dating candidate whose photo she had just seen that she was not interested in meeting him. His accompanying e-mail had read, "If you see the photo and change your mind, it's okay." Very sad. Heartbreaking.

What do you do when you encounter an individual who is used to rejection and whom you too intend to reject? This is where that old fallback—When in doubt, ask, "What would love do?"—comes in handy. It wouldn't have felt very loving and would have done no earthly good to give the honest reply, "I'm glad it's okay, because now that I know what you look like, I'm not interested." So Sandy lied. She e-mailed him that she had met someone else with whom she wanted to spend time before exploring other possibilities.

Yes, there were issues of guilt, feeling small and petty, thinking that she should be bigger than appearance. But the truth was, his physical appearance was not remotely attractive to Sandy. She would not have been able to get past it. Life is short. You have to pick the personal issues on which to work. This one wasn't at the very top of Sandy's list. So why be unkind?

Where we get into trouble is in taking the high road too often. It's easy to withhold important messages from others, supposedly for the sake of being kind, when in reality what we most need to do is come out from behind ourselves into the conversation and let someone know how we really feel.

I faced a real moment of truth with my mother many years ago. My spiritual practices had diverged from hers, and because I knew it would trouble her, I avoided the topic and said as little as possible when she brought it up. "Why bring her pain?" I reasoned. "Why cause her worry?" I certainly didn't want to try to persuade her to my beliefs. I just wanted to follow my own path and felt I could do that quietly, with no media alerts.

It had become apparent that my mother sensed my changing sensibilities, because her letters were increasingly sprinkled with quotes from pamphlets and books she was reading, and she seemed determined not to miss any opportunity to proselytize. It had gotten so bad that I hated to open her letters. My mother, my sister, and I were going to spend a week on Sanibel Island, Florida, and I was beginning to wonder if we'd end up in one long dance of avoidance.

It took me the better part of a day to compose a letter letting her know of my concern. I wrote and rewrote the letter. I wrote, "You have always valued truth, and so it is wrong for me to conceal my current beliefs or to withhold my concern about our upcoming vacation together. I want to enjoy every moment with you, and right now, I imagine at times trying to avoid you."

I waited an agonizing two weeks to hear from my mother. When I finally did, I cried tears of relief. She wrote, "Darling, I understand completely. Yes, I'm sad that you no longer go to my church, but don't worry. We'll have fun together in Sanibel. That's what I want too."

We had a wonderful time, shelling, swimming, eating out, just sitting quietly, talking. My mother created the same photo album for each of us. Since my disclosure, there has been no awkwardness in our conversations, no hidden agenda. We speak freely of our beliefs, with no desire to influence the other, only to understand and explore.

Today I hear grown women like me say, "I can't tell my mother." Or, "Don't tell my father." Or, "I can't tell my husband." All supposedly for fear of leaving a negative wake by disappointing or hurting someone. The reality is that the negative wake is left by the lack of those very conversations, as the list of appropriate topics dwindles to a pitiful few.

Assignment

Write down the name of someone at work or at home to whom you need to deliver a message. Craft your message, taking care not to attach a load to it. Practice saying it out loud. Go to the person and say it.

Ask yourself, "To whom do I need to deliver a message, and what is the message I wish to deliver?" Here are some ideas to get you started:

- My employee Carolyn. The message I want to deliver is: I'd like for you to step up to the plate on this project and become less dependent on me.

- My son, Allen. The message I want to deliver is: I'm very proud of you.

- My husband, John. The message I want to deliver is: I am frightened that our marriage is at risk. I'd like for us to find a way back to each other.

What is your idea behind this conversation? In other words, what do you want of this relationship? Remind yourself that you have a responsibility to come out from behind yourself into the conversation and make it real, while taking responsibility for your emotional wake.

A word of congratulations. You've come a long way since chapter 1. You've deepened your understanding of six principles of fierce conversations and developed your skills. You're having memorable conversations that interrogate reality, provoke learning, tackle tough issues, and enrich relationships.

You will be surprised by Principle 7. Practicing it will add the perfect grace note to your conversations yet to come.

❖ A Refresher . . .

- ❖ In any important relationship, there is no trivial comment.

- ❖ Give to others what you want to receive; live the principles you are intent on learning.

❖ To deliver the message without the load, clarify your intent; aim for the chopping block.

❖ When you get triggered, become a crucible—a strong, resilient vessel in which profound change can safely take place.

❖ Complete the conversation.

PRINCIPLE **7**

Let Silence Do the Heavy Lifting

Where in your life did you become uncomfortable with the sweet territory of silence?

—Native American saying

D o you know someone who will most likely die with his or her mouth open? Many CEOs could go on this list. That is not good. A dazzling way with words rarely proves to be enough to guarantee success as a leader. Joseph Conrad suggested, "To have the gift of words is no such great matter. A man furnished with a long-range weapon does not become a hunter or a warrior by the mere possession of a firearm; many other qualities of character and temperament are necessary to make him either one or the other."

The best leaders talk *with* people, not *at* them.

Many people attempt to forge relationships exclusively through words. Lots of words. However, the best leaders talk *with* people, not *at* them. Emerging entrepreneurs have special challenges. They can get so wrapped up in telling the story of their businesses, in order to attract employees, vendors, and investors, that they no longer have conversations. They have "versations," talking at people rather than with them.

Talking at people is a common affliction. In fact, on a purely practical note, did you know that eight out of ten sales proposals fail? And 50 percent of those eight fail because we spent too much time talking about ourselves or the features and benefits of our product, and not enough time talking about the customer and listening to the customer *before* we explained how wonderful doing business with us would be.

We all know people, intent on impressing us, who talk so much that they turn us off completely. Such people are often unconscious of the effect they are having on others, as they run on endlessly about their accomplishments and clever ideas.

They may be spectacularly brilliant. They may be kind and good-hearted, with a work ethic that would buckle John Calvin's knees. The trouble is, it wears us out to be with them. They talk incessantly, going from one story to the next, without taking a noticeable breath. Though their stories are at times entertaining and laced with insight, after a while we get the feeling that we are merely a spot on the wall to which they direct their comments.

In *Siddhartha,* Hermann Hesse writes, "Within you there is a stillness and sanctuary to which you can retreat at any time and be yourself." *The 7 Habits of Highly Effective People* by Stephen Covey begins, "I'm busy, really busy. But sometimes I wonder if what I'm doing will make any difference in the long run." Montaigne wrote, "If my mind could gain a firm footing I would not make essays. I would make decisions. But it is always in apprenticeship and on trial."

It is exceedingly difficult, almost impossible, to gain a firm footing in conversations filled with noise. At a party recently, several guests had paired off in conversation. But the noise of all the other guests interfered with their ability to discern the message and intent of the one person to whom they were trying to listen. Struggling to be heard, each speaker became louder and louder, but that only increased the total noise in the room, making it even more difficult to hear. Several individuals periodically shouted into cell phones.

What happened next? Most people gave up and settled for the traditional cocktail party chitchat.

There is a place for big, noisy gatherings. I enjoy the energy, the full sensory experience, of a room filled with high-spirited individuals: the family gatherings in my home during the Thanksgiving and Christmas holidays, the parties celebrating individual or organizational milestones. However, while there are remarkable conversations to be experienced in the crush of crowds, amid the din of voices and music, the need for spaciousness in our most important conversations inspires me to take work teams on retreat to places where we can build a fire, rather than to a traditional hotel. We have taken over a small lodge in Sun Valley. We have rented log homes on the Deschutes River in Bend, Oregon. We have boated in the San Juan Islands. We had time simply to hang out beside a crackling fire, perhaps cook dinner together, and talk about nothing, about something.

And when it was time to talk, we turned off our cell phones. In theaters an announcement is usually made before the curtain goes up. "Please turn off all cell phones, and if you have a piece of candy or a breath mint, please unwrap it now." This always inspires laughter. And gratitude. I wish important conversations began with similar instructions.

Bob

On the mahogany credenza in Bob Sloan's office sat an executive version of the lava lamp, an upright glass tube in which floated glass teardrops filled with colored oil. Next to it was a rose-colored blownglass shell. I worried for their safety, since Bob moved about his office as if he hadn't gotten the hang of steering his body. Like a helium balloon, he glanced off doorjambs and the corners of furniture.

Bob blew words like bubbles, lips puckered as if to make car sounds for the amusement of a child. His pout was so extreme that by the time the sound of a word made its way from his mouth to my ears, he had gone on to the next word. The effect was that of watching an out-of-sync movie.

He went from word to word to word. Endlessly. To make matters worse, he spoke in a monotone. Consequently, I often struggled to pay attention during his droning monologue.

During my third visit to his office, I determined to improve things, at least from my perspective. I mustered my resolve and began to talk on top of Bob's words. "Bob, you remind me of someone who had a style of lovemaking that did not require my presence."

Though Bob usually ignored my attempts to interrupt, this time he paused and asked, "What did you say?"

"Just that you remind me of someone. The point is that I don't think you've taken a breath in the last twenty minutes, and I haven't been able to get a word in edgewise."

He smiled sheepishly. "Yeah, my wife tells me the same thing." And he kept right on talking. About ten minutes later, I got up and walked to the door. Bob looked at me quizzically as I paused in the doorway.

"Don't stop," I said. "I'm going to take a little walk, maybe visit with some of your employees. You don't need me."

"Wait a second. This is what I pay you for," Bob said.

"I see it differently." I knew I had to be bold and clear to get my message across. "You did not buy my time or my posterior in a chair. You paid to have an interaction with me and you're not getting it. Consequently, I'm having trouble paying attention. Perhaps some fresh air will revive me."

I waited as the words sank in, and then continued. "There are times for each of us when what we need most is simply to talk to someone who is really listening. There is also value in dialogue. You and I haven't had the second experience. We don't have one-to-ones. We have 'ones.' Now, I've got a pretty strong personality. If I've given up trying to interject a comment into our conversations, I wonder where else this is going on in your life, and what price you might be paying."

Bob looked away, down at his desk, out the window. Finally I asked, "So where else is this going on?"

He answered immediately. "At home. My wife is unhappy." He stared at his hands. "Probably with some people here too."

"Who in the company is unhappy?" I asked.

"I don't know."

"Who would it be if you did know?"

Bob smiled faintly. "If I did know, it would be Jim, my director of engineering."

"Okay, can we talk about this? And about your marriage? And I suggest that we allow some silences as we talk, so that we can sit and think and feel and get as in touch with reality as possible." Bob nodded, I sat down again, and we began our first real conversation.

So Many Words, So Little Substance

In an article titled, "Language, Customs, and Other Cultural Tips for Job Interviews," Chinese job applicants are counseled: "The Chinese are more likely to accept or even to appreciate silent periods in conversation. American custom is not to allow long silence during conversations, especially during business meetings, including the interview. Silence makes many (but not all) Americans nervous." A Web site advises Finnish exchange students that an American characteristic is "general discomfort with silence in conversations, homes, working places."

> **An American characteristic is "general discomfort with silence in conversations, homes, working places."**

This strikes me as embarrassing but true. And it's no wonder. From the time most Americans are small children, we are taught to dislike silence. The punishment of being sent to one's bedroom for "quiet time" or "time out" causes children to plead for mercy and promise to be good. And what is this dreaded sentence they wish to avoid? Silence.

It is a phenomenon of our times that, for many people, silence is almost unendurable. Silence makes us nervous. So do innovation, change, and genius. As adults, we fear that silence may be interpreted as low self-esteem or questionable intelligence. We feel we're expected to interject witty comments and wise observations on the spot. Many feel silence is a form of nonparticipation, signaling lack of interest. We fear people will think we have nothing more to say. The worry may be "If I just sit here and think for a moment, somebody else will jump in and say the clever thing I would have liked to say."

> **Silence makes us nervous. So do innovation, change, and genius.**

At a workshop with executives of a global organization moving at the speed of light, we were discussing the question "What am I pretending not to know?" The house came down when one executive admitted, "My question ought to be 'What am I pretending to know?' I say the first thing that comes to mind and pray to God that it is accurate."

For fear of being thought clueless, have you dived into a conversation, throwing out opinions, arguing your point, defending your ideas throughout a debate, only to discern later, once you stopped to catch your breath, that there was another, wiser road you could have taken?

It is understandable that emerging leaders believe they need to be fast on their conversational feet, able to engage in clever repartee. That is what is admired and rewarded. The belief is that leaders always have answers at the ready. It's not okay to just sit there. You've got to say something.

Fierce conversations, however, *require* silence. In fact, the more emotionally loaded the subject, the more silence is required. And, of course, this carries over into our homes, into our personal relationships. Often we are simply trying to intuit something about ourselves, our companions, or the topics themselves. Sometimes we need silence in which to make a decision about the closeness we feel for our companions or the distance we feel from them.

The more emotionally loaded the subject, the more silence is required.

Once in a precious while, silence is merely abstinence from self-assertion. For many work teams and couples, however, it is easy to fall into a conversational pattern that contains so many words, so much white noise, that it leaves all parties deaf to any comments of substance that could have been interjected into the conversation. Our habitual ways of talking with (or *at*) each other prevent us from allowing silence to help us get in touch with what we really want to say.

Here are signs that indicate silence is needed. No doubt you have observed these in others, and perhaps you are guilty of some of them yourself.

- Interrupting by talking over someone else

- Formulating your own response while someone is talking

- Responding quickly with little or no thought

- Attempting to be clever, competent, impressive, charming, and so on

- Jumping in with advice before an issue has been clarified

- Using a silence or break in the conversation to create a distraction by changing topics

- Talking in circles, nothing new emerging

- Monopolizing the airspace

Slow Down

Sometimes a dramatic intervention is required to stop the words in order to start a conversation. There are issues that our colleagues and customers will ignore every time they come up. If we are not alert, we will walk with others right past the issue. We may sense that something is there, but the conversation is moving too fast. Or because we are so invested in playing the role of "expert," we fill the air with words, missing the real issue entirely.

When our ego is dialing 911, we wouldn't notice it if our own teeth were crumbling as we drone on and on. Often my role is to slow down a conversation, and silence is my greatest tool in this. As we talk with people, as we sit with them in silence, what is in the way—anger, numbness, impatience, manipulation, rigidity, blame, ego, cruelty, ambition, insensitivity, intimidation, pride—may fall away. It is in silence that such attributes, emotions, and behaviors reveal themselves as unnecessary.

I am friends with an elderly couple who held each other and cried when their Border terrier died. For twelve years the dog had slept at the foot of their bed, snoring quietly. Each night, when one of them said, "Well, I believe it's bedtime for me," the other person and the dog rose and trundled off to bed. Each took an assigned place. The three of them, breathing through the night; shifting positions carefully, so as not to disturb. And in the morning, when one got up, so did the other two. Good morning. Sitting quietly, sipping the coffee, reading the newspaper, exchanging plans for the day and dreams of the night before. When I visit them, we sit quietly and contentedly—once four of us, now three—in silence. Impossible to explain to others, great and easy friendships like this, nurtured in silence.

Have you lost a healthy, affectionate relationship with silence? Are you uncomfortable with even brief moments of silence? Do you turn on the TV, not to watch it but to be comforted by the background noise that you have come to require?

What if you turned off the TV? Turned off the radio? Do you know what the wind sounds like in the corn, in the hedgerows?

Do you know the sound of your own breathing?

When was the last time you listened to the sound of rain falling? Or frogs in the pond? Or cicadas in the pines? Do you know the sound of your own breathing?

Middle Beach Lodge

I recall a drive to Middle Beach Lodge in Tofino, British Columbia, where I was to talk with a group of CEOs and their spouses, early in the summer of 2001. The trip had required taking a floatplane from Seattle to Nanaimo. From the plane I glimpsed pods of orca whales. Striking swaths of ultramarine and emerald green currents stippled the water. The pilot had issued earplugs, which I welcome in small planes, not just for protection from the sound of the noisy engines but because wearing them is like being underwater. Hearing is turned acutely inward. Try it. Plug up your ears and listen. You can actually hear your heartbeat. Spending an hour or so listening to one's own heartbeat while watching orcas is, as Martha Stewart would say, a good thing.

Upon arriving in Nanaimo, I rented a car and began the drive to Middle Beach Lodge. The road winds through mountain gorges, along lakes, through tunnels. I had planned to find a good radio station and sing along, but in the mountains there was only static, so I turned it off and surrendered to the view.

Ahead of me were two and a half hours of simply looking, breathing, and using my own availability for focused thought. A topic, a complex issue that I had skillfully postponed addressing, presented itself unbidden. I didn't know when I was going to take it on—just not any time soon. However, driving to Tofino, with no agenda and no distraction, the conversation began, as circuitous as the road I was navigating. Fascinating scenery, inside and out. I arrived at the lodge in late afternoon, filled to the brim with the beauty of the physical terrain and having come to a helpful conclusion.

My hope is that, if for no other reason than to begin a practice that will enrich your conversations with yourself, you will begin to wean yourself from noise. Pull back your hand from the television or the radio. Sit silently for a few moments. Might this be uncomfortable? Yes; however, there are insights and emotions that can find you in no other way than through and within silence. This is true for our conversations with others as well.

> **There are insights and emotions that can find you in no other way than through and within silence.**

During his interview with Gabriel Byrne on *Inside the Actors Studio,* host James Lipton asked his traditional questions, including, "What is your favorite sound?" Byrne answered, "Silence." I have heard that this is true for Katharine Hepburn as well.

During my conversations with the people most important to me, silence has become my favorite sound, because that is when the work is being done. Of all the tools I use during conversations and all the principles I keep in mind, silence is the most powerful of all.

The Space Between Thoughts

In conversations, as in life, less is more. It is a good idea to breathe. Stillness is good. And walking. Breathing is best. Memorable conversations include breathing space—or just space, of any kind. My motto is: *Don't just rearrange the furniture. Toss it out. Become a minimalist.*

Deepak Chopra refers to the space between thoughts as the place where insight can make itself known. The trouble is, for most of us, there is no space between thoughts. This is true for me. To my delight, I discovered that fly-fishing is a remedy for my affliction, allowing me to flip the "off" switch in my head. When I have spent

half an hour or so entirely focused on placing a fly on a particular
glint of water, there begins to be spaciousness between my thoughts.
These days, I fly-fish because it gives me an opportunity to visit fish
in the beautiful places where they live, and because I need what it
does for me.

I also need what silence accomplishes during my conversations
with others. Thinking back, I see that my best and most memorable
conversations have been filled with silences.

Consider this: How can any of us successfully and authentically
interrogate reality, provoke learning, tackle tough challenges, and enrich relationships in a talkathon, where nary a breath is allowed?

Talking does not a conversation make. Words in the air are not
guaranteed to accomplish anything useful.

Never mistake *talking* for *conversation*. Mabel Newcomer, author of *A Century of Higher Education for American Women,* said, "Never mistake activity for achieve-
ment." I would add, "Never mistake *talking* for *conversation*." The
novelist Marjorie Kellogg wrote, "They had lived together for so
many years that they mistook their arguments for conversation." Or
worked together for so many years.

While the occasional stream of consciousness can be illustrative,
important conversations require moments of silence during which
we may reflect on what someone has said and consider our responses,
before opening our mouths. Otherwise, our knee-jerk responses may
not reflect our highest and best thoughts. How could they? We
haven't had a moment to consider what they might be.

The Rest Between Notes

Listen to almost any piece of classical music. As you listen to the conversations in your life, compare them with music performed by skilled
musicians.

My gardening companion is often my next-door neighbor Melinda

Wang, age seven. Melinda and I have wonderfully fierce conversations while we are weeding and digging. We discuss the pros and cons of certain insects' insistence on cohabiting with us. How difficult it is to like some people. What a crazy, mixed feeling of terror and glory it is to stand before an audience. (Melinda gives violin and piano recitals; I give keynote talks.)

When Melinda spots me unloading plants from my car, she knows where to find me for the next several hours. I've encouraged her to let herself in through the garden gate and join me. Often she finds me standing still, gazing at the garden, considering moving plants from here to there like furniture, to create a more pleasing outdoor "room." Melinda instinctively falls silent, and I am grateful. Otherwise, my mind's eye would strain to bring the master plan into focus.

Special treats are the backyard concerts we have when Melinda brings her violin. Mozart and melons. Schubert and sugar snap peas. Years ago, my own daughter, Jennifer, studied violin and often played for me in the garden. If you haven't planted Magic Carpet spirea to the tune of a Vivaldi violin concerto, you haven't lived, I tell you.

At seven, Melinda phrases the pieces she is learning with a growing sophistication. Unlike most young children who play a piece hellbent to the end, no stops, no pianissimos, in a race to the finish, Melinda has a maturing ear. She is noticing that it is in the rests between notes that the music is savored. It is in the silence trembling at the end of a gorgeous musical phrase that our hearts swell. It is in that moment that we believe all things are possible, that we can be good, that perhaps we can make a contribution to mankind.

> **Anyone can play the notes. The magic is in the intervals, in the phrasing.**

Anyone can play the notes. The magic is in the intervals, in the phrasing. That's where silence comes in. When we are completely engaged in talking, all of the possibilities for the conversation grow smaller.

How do we let silence do the heavy lifting? Provide it. Allow silence to fill in the greater meaning that needs to be there. Perhaps if I close my mouth, you'll open yours.

In *The Feast of Love,* Charles Baxter writes, "What does it mean, knowing how to keep silent? What kind of silence would this be? How does this particular silence contrast with being morosely mute? What is a knowledgeable silence? How would we know or for that matter recognize this knowledge?"

When you ask the opening question in Mineral Rights—*What is the most important thing you and I should talk about?*—keep silent. Wait quietly. The universe will not respond if we grow uncomfortable and impatient. Sometimes all that is needed is that we get out of the way, stop trying to help.

And what do you do when the conversation has lost its way? Sometimes the simplest thing you can say is "I'm sorry, I've lost the thread."

During company meetings, often the best responses, the most brilliant solutions, come from the person who has sat silently listening for a very long time while the rest of us filled the air with debate. Even when called upon, such an individual often appears reluctant to speak, sitting in reflective silence for agonizing moments while others click ballpoint pens and glance at their watches. Then he or she speaks, and everyone else in the room is compelled to shift to a broader, wiser perspective, with the result that elegant, complete answers begin to emerge.

Dangerous Silences

Since my work emphasizes the value of silence, it is important to acknowledge that not all silence is healthy. The silence I recommend is the restful kind, the kind that invites us to hear the quieter voices, the kind that allows us to hear the grass grow and the birds sing.

I do *not* mean the silence of nonparticipation, of passivity, of *I really don't care what you do or what you think*. I do *not* mean the cold war of silence fought by couples, the indifferent silence that chills their hearts when they are starving for conversation, close connection, time together. I do *not* mean the silence that merely denies topics that are uncomfortable.

Several months ago, in a workshop, a woman named Nora admitted that when another participant had given her feedback following an exercise, she had initially been angry. "I wanted to jump down your throat and rip it out." (It helped that Nora was smiling when she said it.)

I found this honesty appealing. In fact, the comment further endeared Nora to the others in the workshop, including the recipient of her comment. Yet later that day, a man pulled me aside, referred to Nora's comment, and said, "How'd you like to live with someone like that?" I responded, "I prefer honest, active aggression to covert passive aggression any day." Many of us have experienced hostile silences that are far more harmful than full disclosure.

Silence is a popular form of passive aggression, intended as punishment. *I don't like what you did or said, so I'm just not gonna play. I will withhold myself from you. See how you like that!* It can be an attempt to manipulate, to teach others that if they behave in certain ways, there will be consequences.

This backfires, of course. Silence over a period of time regarding an important issue or question ultimately equals a decision that will likely have negative consequences. Clamming up and refusing to talk about a particular subject at home or in the workplace reflects a decision to protect yourself at all costs, including taking the risk that someone important to you may eventually choose to leave the relationship if you refuse to address the issue.

I also do *not* mean a conspiracy of silence in an organization in which team members have taken the *omertà,* the Mafia vow of silence, not to tell who did it.

I worked with a large team within an international organization that had requested a customized software program. The company had spent millions to build it. All the end users had been involved in the shape and design and practicality of the program's functions. But now that it was available, very few were using it.

Forty people were assembled to address the issue. The conversation was messy, choppy, empty, full of more "huhs?" than answers. A key executive sat in the far left corner of the room. No one noticed his silence. I turned to him and asked, "Bill, why is the software not being used?" He frowned, then shrugged, opening his hands in a gesture of "How should I know?" I waited and saw his eyes rove around the room, exchanging a look of complicity with several of his team members. When I inquired about this—"Sally, Mike, Dan, as Bill looked at you and you smiled, what message were you exchanging? What is the feeling or thought shared between you?"—the three responded with absolute silence. I turned back to Bill. "Bill, I wonder if several of the people in this room could tell us what's really going on if they had your permission. Since you're their leader, the only wrong statement from you right now is silence."

He shifted, shot me a look, examined his fingernails. Then his shoulders slumped and he sighed. "I told them we don't have time for this right now. We've got other priorities." He stopped and waited for the rush of questions, waited to defend himself. No one said anything. The silence grew as we arrived at the center of what was happening.

He looked at the CEO. "I've been putting in eighteen-hour days for six months. Most everybody here has. This software may be great, and I know we asked for it, but if you want the deliverables you posted on every chart on every wall, we can't take time off to learn a new software program. At least, not right now. So I told my team to ignore your directives and just get the job done."

The silence continued as everyone considered what had been said, knowing it to be true. The CEO's face reflected both compassion and respect as he responded, "I hear you. I get it. Okay, what are we going to do?"

Checklist

Here is a sample list of common stories or rationalizations used to mask our fear and avoid reality. When we tell ourselves these stories, we become nonparticipants.

- "What do I know? She's the expert."

- "No use saying anything. He doesn't care what I think."

- "I have no idea what needs to happen here, so it's best to keep my mouth shut and pretend I'm tracking."

- "Nothing I say will make any difference. Why bother?"

- "She's just going through a hard time, just needs to talk."

- "I'm bored, fatigued, impatient with this person [and/or this topic]. I'll adopt an attitude of polite indifference and hope it's over soon."

These rationalizations cause our conversations and our relationships to slip, slide away. We are tuned out rather than tuned in. Reality is not interrogated, no learning is provoked, tough challenges are avoided, and the relationship is not enriched. Nothing memorable occurs.

In practicing Principle 7, you will experience the value of letting silence create spaciousness in your conversations, so that you and your partner can check inside and look for what is authentic and useful.

Thoughts on Silence

Silence offers us an opportunity to think and plan downboard. Each action step we decide upon will set other things in motion. None of us is behaving in a vacuum. Everything we do has consequences for the rest of the company (or the family). We need to think in terms of "If we do this, who and what will be impacted and how? What other steps may become necessary?" Sometimes teams need to sit quietly and think about these questions.

Silence allows us the space in which to focus on the cause, not the effect. Half the battle is identifying and resolving the real issues, as opposed to dwelling on symptoms illustrated with long stories. In work teams, when someone brings an issue to his or her colleagues for resolution, if we are fortunate, after an extended silence during which everyone reflects on what has been offered for discussion, someone will say, "I don't think that's the real issue. I think the real issue is . . ." And we're off and running, recognizing with relief that we are on track at last. The problem named is the problem solved. Silence allows us to reflect on and ultimately identify the problem, so that we may focus our limited time and resources on removing obstacles in the company's way.

Silence allows us to reflect on basic beliefs and paradigms regarding a particular issue before moving to options and strategy. It is imperative to give ourselves and our teams the challenge and the silence in which to ask ourselves, "What beliefs that we currently hold might be in the way of innovation and improvement?" This is almost impossible for anyone to do in a room or a house full of words.

Silence allows everyone in the room to participate fully. No matter what our areas of expertise, each of us has insights and ideas about other aspects of the organization. Silence assists individuals who usually take lots of airtime in listening more and talking less. Silence allows quieter individuals an opportunity to speak. Learning is provoked for everyone.

Silence is the best-kept secret for generating family dialogue. If you want your children to talk to you, make silence your primary skill. I used to interrogate my daughters lovingly each day on the way home from school. "What did you do at school today? Did you have fun? What did you learn?" If you're a parent, you may be smiling because you know from experience that such questions rarely elicit the lengthy responses we hoped for. Gradually I learned that the more I allowed silence following my questions, the more my daughters would willingly fill it with words like "Guess what my teacher said" or "Wanna hear something really weird?" When my daughters spoke, I could entice them to continue by simply saying, "Uh-huh," "Wow," "I see," "Really?" or even "No way!" Or I could simply nod and smile.

Silence allows us to scan our heads and hearts for ground truths. Silence allows us to examine the flotsam and jetsam in our lives and to determine its usefulness, affording us an opportunity to clear our personal and corporate windshields.

What is silence trying to teach us? *It is teaching us how to feel.* Silence encourages us to explore a more difficult peace.

Keeping Yourself Company

Awareness requires learning to keep yourself company. Years ago a client told me about his decision to go to Hawaii by himself for a few days. He had left Seattle stressed, overburdened, and obligated to make an important decision. Walking along the beach, he came across an inviting spot beneath a palm tree. He sat down and simply looked at the ocean and the beach. He explained:

Awareness requires learning to keep yourself company.

> *After a while, it seemed that my breathing matched the rhythm of the waves, and then it was as if I could see all my obligations sticking up through the sand. All the decisions I needed to make, the hundred things crying for my attention, the phone calls, the e-mails waiting for me when I got back, the meetings, all sticking up in the sand. But then it was as if a wind came up and steadily blew the sand away. And when the wind stopped, there were only two things remaining. And I knew exactly what those two things were, and I could see that*

if I moved those two things, everything else would fall into place, sort itself out. I tell you, from this point on, I'm advising anyone who's got some priorities to sort out to go to a beach or to the mountains or someplace where they can take a walk, where they can just sit quietly and breathe.

Do you remember those conversations with yourself that I have recommended? This is where it all begins.

There are phases to the silences in my life. Early mornings are best. I wake at four in the morning—"Oh-dark-hundred," a friend calls it. As the coffee brews, I step outside to breathe in the fragrance of the woods and pond behind the house. The scent of rain and rotting leaves. Daphne. The lingering scent of last night's applewood fire in the brazier. My Jack Russell terriers, Scout and Babe, are on alert. Crackling twigs beyond the fence signal a coyote or deer. We are amused by early spring frog passion. A few earnest individuals with unresolved issues. The air has weight; it slips through my fingers like a skein of silk. On clear mornings the stars take my breath away and I am made small, humbled. A good way to begin a day.

The dogs complete their fence patrol, and we go inside. I pour my coffee, light a fire, and sit in my favorite chair in the living room. I love it here in early mornings because, as dawn breaks, my view is of the feather grasses just outside the front windows, of the vine maple, birch, and pine trees. No early morning news, no stock market report. Not even music. Just morning light and the sound of Scout's quiet snores as he settles nearby for the first of his dozen naps for the day.

I sit there for an hour. At times it's all I can do not to spring out of the chair and rush upstairs to my office, as my head reels off the dozen things I need to do that day. "Wait," I advise myself. "Be still." And then phase two arrives. The chatter fades. I begin to learn what this conversation with myself wants to be about, the conversation that began while I was sleeping.

Before any of us can hope to engage others in wonderfully fierce conversations, we must engage ourselves in a dialogue so real, so sweet, so fierce, so filled with silences that we can hear our own heartbeat. Put your fingers up to your ears and plug your ears. Listen to your heartbeat. Look in a mirror. Look deep. What might you hear if you sat in silence and conversed with that person in the mirror? Perhaps he or she has much to tell you.

Samuel Johnson wrote, "That is the happiest conversation where there is no competition, no vanity, but a calm quiet interchange of sentiments." It is my goal that your colleagues at work and those closest to you at home will experience this during their conversations with you. This requires that you take a deep breath, ground yourself, and ask, "What is the most important thing you and I should be talking about today?" Then step with your partners into territory where there may be dragons, where you have plenty of questions and zero answers, where you leave your expert hat out in the hall, adopt a beginner's mind, and listen with every subatomic particle of your body. Where you screw your courage to the sticking-place and ask the question that expands the possibilities for everyone, including you. And then listen. And speak again.

All the conversations in the world cruise on a crest of silence.

All the conversations in the world cruise on a crest of silence. And sometimes the silence overshadows the rest. Let silence, like a Zen koan, be your riddle. Fill your conversations with silences during which reality may be interrogated, learning may be provoked, tough challenges may be tackled, and relationships may be enriched.

The risk?

I will be known.

I will be seen.

I will be changed.

Assignment

Over the next twenty-four hours during your conversations at work and at home, give yourself a private challenge:

I will allow spaciousness in my conversations, so that before I speak, I can reflect on what others have said. I will invite my partners to do the same. In doing so, I hope to get closer to what is authentic and valuable.

If you suspect that conversations filled with silence may feel strange or uncomfortable for you or others, it may help to say at some point, "I'd like a moment to reflect on what you've said." If your partners are going too fast or seem impatient with you, with the conversation, or with themselves, you might say, "I believe this is an important topic. Let's slow down a bit so we can both digest what we're saying and consider where we need to go from here."

Here, as in all the assignments throughout this book, you will gain skill and insight when you debrief yourself following a conversation. Reflect on your own participation in the conversation (good or bad) and what happened as a result. It helps to use the seven principles and four purposes of a fierce conversation as your checklist. For example, following this chapter's assignment, ask yourself, "Did I allow silence to do the heavy lifting during this conversation? Did silence help us interrogate reality, provoke learning, tackle a tough challenge, enrich our relationship?"

Include others in the debriefing. Following this chapter's assignment, for example, you might say, "Thank you for allowing spaciousness in our conversation. I found it helpful. Did you?"

Several of my clients have created their own checklists. They suggest you know you've had a fierce conversation when . . .

- you overheard yourself saying things you didn't know you knew

- you didn't take notes, yet you remember every word

- you listened with more than your ears

- you took yourself and your companion personally and seriously

- you left the conversation satisfied, satiated, awake, fully alive, and eager for more

Personal and corporate relationships have been enriched by taking and discussing the following survey.

Discussion Questions

Assess the degree to which fierce conversations occur in your organization and/or family. Explore your responses. Probe for full understanding of one another's views.

1 = entirely false   **10** = entirely true

There are no undiscussables in our company/family.
    1   2   3   4   5   6   7   8   9   10

There are no hidden agendas in our company/family.
    1   2   3   4   5   6   7   8   9   10

During meetings we say what we think, invite differing views, and explore one another's thinking.
    1   2   3   4   5   6   7   8   9   10

There is permission in our company/family for everyone to "show up."
    1   2   3   4   5   6   7   8   9   10

When lost in the complexity of a new situation, we pay close attention to new and unfamiliar aspects rather than take only those actions that will put things back on a track we already know.
    1   2   3   4   5   6   7   8   9   10

Talk about your ratings and what caused you to choose them.

Discuss what you would like your ratings to be.

Discuss what you can do to improve.

Discuss your perspectives on the following topics:

- The outcomes of the majority of the conversations in our organization/family

- How we avoid dealing with problems

- What is the most important thing we need to talk about?

❖ A Refresher . . .

❖ Talk *with* people, not *at* them.

❖ The more emotionally loaded the subject, the more silence is required.

❖ Use silence to slow down a conversation so that you can discover what the conversation really wants to be about.

❖ Allow silence to fill in the greater meaning that needs to be there.

❖ Allow silence to teach you how to feel.

Embracing the Principles

Let your
Intelligence begin to rule
Whenever you sit with others

Using this sane idea:

Leave all your cocked guns in a field
Far from us,

One of those damn things
Might go

Off.

—Hafiz, "This Sane Idea"

Some time ago I chose to live my life at the conversational cliff's edge, breathing my way through a whole series, a whole lifetime, of fierce conversations with friends, family, clients, colleagues, and, of course, myself.

While the principles of fierce conversations may be impossible to live up to every day in every conversation, they are certainly something to shoot for, for your organization's sake, for the sake of your personal relationships, and most important, for your own sake. Don't be hard on yourself if you stumble from time to time. Don't let a failed conversation keep you from trying again. Hang on and hang in. Take it one conversation at a time, one day at a time.

Rather than settle on a plateau of maturity, look around for people whose conversations are memorable, people who wake you up and provoke your learning—people who are real. Excellence rubs off. You will be better company for having kept the best company.

For me, an unforeseen reward for practicing the seven principles has been a sense of sinew growing throughout my body. I've lost weight. Gotten lean. Amazing. Maybe it has to do with being willing to be vulnerable, without defense. No protective mechanisms. No armor required. Perhaps it has to do with my effort to trim all that I say to the barest bone. How close to the bone can I get? How authentic? How accurate and clear? The result is that, these days, I travel light, agenda-free.

So where should you begin? By doing. Action teaches. Engaging in fierce conversations every day will reveal the value of saying what you need to say, what you long to say. Should you run out the door, collar the first poor bloke who catches your eye, and haul his sorry backside off for a fierce conversation? Not yet. Instead, begin by tuning in to yourself. Spend time alone, in silence.

When silence has performed its useful work, listen to music. Country, classical, blues, rock, opera, Celtic—whatever pleases you. Close the door, turn off the TV, let the answering machine kick in, put on music that you love, and let yourself feel.

Right now, I am listening to Kelly Joe Phelps's CD *Sky like a Broken Clock*. I am in love with his sound, a cross between Springsteen, Dock Boggs, and someone from somewhere on the banks of the Mississippi. The lyrics are lovely but secondary. It's simply what this music evokes in me. Unbidden. Dropping me into a funky, smooth, and groovy place where I want to pour a glass of red wine, light a fire, and reminisce. I remember evenings with friends, playing our guitars and singing by the Missouri River my freshman year of college. I can see Kelly Joe Phelps's music with my eyes. He's tapped into an artery somehow. You can't get that just anywhere.

Different gifts, memories, and emotions would be evoked by listening to Rostropovich playing Bach's cello suites or to Alasdair Fraser's Scottish fiddle. I pick my moods with my music. Gifts, all.

Listen to music that you love. It will allow you to feel what is there for you to feel, even if you have locked the door and wedged a chair under the knob. That's why we need music, seek it, sometimes avoid it. There are some songs I have to turn off. Just can't take it right now.

And read a book. Put down the newspaper, the magazine, the stock market report, the crumpled articles stuffed in your briefcase. Pick up a classic work of fiction, or a new one. Annie Proulx, Charles Baxter, Pat Conroy, Lorrie Moore, Wally Lamb, Charles Frazier, Richard Russo, Toni Morrison, Andre Dubus, Jane Smiley. Pick up Tolkien. Lose yourself with hobbits, orcs, and wizards. Lose yourself in hope of finding yourself.

If you want to meet someone who has had an extended fierce conversation with herself and offers that marvelously flawed self to any who care, read *Bird by Bird* or *Traveling Mercies* by Anne Lamott. Read *Pilgrim at Tinker Creek* by Annie Dillard. Or read *A Joseph Campbell Companion*. I fantasize what it would be like to have these people as neighbors. Oh, the conversations we could have! When there's a good book in the house, why turn on the TV?

Read poetry. Read good poetry, if possible. You'll know it's good when it evokes something for you . . . a memory, a vivid picture, an emotion, an insight, a trembling of tectonic plates. Read David Whyte's poems. Pick up *The Gift: Poems by Hafiz, the Great Sufi Master,* translated by Daniel Ladinsky. Here was a man happy to be in his own skin. You will smile, laugh. Out loud.

And take walks. There has been much talk of being on the

"path." Let the *way* itself arrive. For me, the way is an ongoing, robust conversation with all that life has to offer. During walks I converse with lavender roses beside the ocean, with quicksilver fishes in alpine lakes, with windsong and lapping water and the wide listening sky. I dream amid the blue-eyed grass and nodding campion by a laurel that has mated with a copper beech, conversing with my own essential nature. Back at home, the conversation continues with faithful friends and family. What matters is how quickly we do what our souls direct.

This past fall, after leading several workshops in London, I spent a day walking through the countryside of southern England with my friend Graham Thompson. In the late afternoon, as we returned to Graham and his wife Charlotte's home, I said, "Thank you for this glorious day."

He smiled and said, "Now you must pay. I've been asked to ring the church bells for a wedding this evening. It takes two people."

A few hours later, I followed Graham up a rickety staircase in an ancient country church atop a hill. Graham lifted a trapdoor, and we clambered through it into a tiny belfry. The ropes to eight bells above the wooden planks over our heads were attached to eight wooden levers. There was barely time to practice six variations, including the standard peal of the highest to the lowest note. Graham managed to unstick the lever connected to the smallest bell just as the guests and bridal party arrived. When the minister rapped on the trapdoor, Graham and I looked at each other and grinned, and I pulled the first lever.

Though our concentration was intense, our first efforts were not the joyful noise to which we aspired. But as our confidence grew and the bells responded to our touch and timing, I began to feel them in my chest—literally reverberating in my rib cage, thrilling the heart lodged within. I was not aware that we were laughing until the trapdoor lifted and someone called up to us, "They can hear you in the church."

Fierce conversations will allow you to feel. *Feel what?* Something.

Anything. What music evokes. Belly laughter. Your obligation to the planet. Bells in your bones.

In Elizabeth Berg's *Open House,* a character asks, "You know what a naked star is? . . . Stars with most of their gaseous atmospheres stripped away. And you know why they're revealed like that? Because of close encounters with other stars. I find something very human about that. Don't you?"

The risk is that in close encounters with others, you will be known. You will be revealed, changed. And why not? You've been strong for too many years. Try something different. Surrender.

Perhaps your daring disclosure will be a flop. There is nothing wrong with that. Some of us have to go too far if all of us are to move along.

Fierce conversations are not a form of showing off or parading a rich vocabulary. Erudite explanations numb listeners. *See what I mean!* They yawn and tune out, afterward wondering why—after all, she was "so well spoken." Fierce conversations are an effort to understand—first of all, for yourself—something that is worthy of your pondering. They are deeply probing explorations. Speak about the things you want to understand. Most people want to share journeys of this kind. Forget about being clever or impressive. What is called for now is quiet integrity.

I determined long ago that to change my persona or withhold a controversial view for fear of what others might think not only was dishonest and ineffective but would likely induce a contagious stupor, so I decided to show up authentically and consistently with everyone in my life. Might some people be put off by things I say? Certainly, and that is okay with me.

The secret is for you to show up—fully. You may be among people who don't support you. You may be among people who, loving or unloving, are simply not equipped to support the ambition of engaging in fierce conversations. This is not an unusual experience. The courage to show up is both simple and daunting. Once you show up, people can see you. They can judge and criticize and gossip.

Some safety and comfort are lost when an ambition or strongly felt emotion is expressed. Perhaps, if you have become impatient with the false identity you have created for yourself, life is inviting you into much larger worlds than you have imagined.

Intimacy is required in conversation now—at home and in the workplace. We must answer the big questions in our organizations. What are the questions that need posing? Philosophers, theologians, scientists, and great teachers have debated this for ages.

> *What is real?*
>
> *What is honest?*
>
> *What is quality?*
>
> *What has value?*

We effect change by engaging in robust conversations with ourselves, our colleagues, our customers, our family, the world. Whether you are governing a country, running an organization, or participating in a committed personal relationship, your ability to effect change will increase as you become more responsive to your world and to the individuals who are central to your happiness and success.

Fierce conversations' mission is: *Change the world—one conversation at a time.* Following the horrific attack on America on September 11, 2001, I was deeply moved as I listened to Mandy Patinkin sing Stephen Sondheim's "Children Will Listen." What are we saying to our children? The world will be well served if each of us makes a strong personal choice to pay fierce attention to every conversation that we have.

My vision is that world leaders, business leaders, couples, parents, and teenagers will embrace the principles of fierce conversations and engage in a level of dialogue rarely experienced in our history. It is not enough to be willing to speak. The time has come for you *to speak.* Be willing to face mutiny everywhere but in yourself. Your time of holding back, of guarding your private thoughts, is over. Your function in life is to make a declarative statement. Sit beside someone you care for and begin.

Good luck! Tell me how it goes for you!

susan@fierceinc.com

And if you would like to receive a monthly newsletter that will support you in your ongoing practice of Fierce principles, you may sign up at www.fierceinc.com.

Commitments and Thought Starters

- Today I will master the courage to interrogate reality. *What reality at home or at work most needs interrogating?*

- Today I will come out from behind myself into my conversations and make them real. I will speak of the things that are on my mind and in my heart, including those that seem risky. *Where and with whom am I failing to show up authentically?*

- Today I will be here, prepared to be nowhere else. *Who would benefit from my undivided attention? Perhaps it is myself.*

- Today I will tackle my toughest challenge. *What conversation am I dodging? What issue am I avoiding?*

- Today I will obey my instincts. I will take time to deliberate, and when the time to speak arrives, I will share what I am thinking. *What messages have been beckoning me?*

- Today I will take responsibility for my emotional wake. *To whom do I need to apologize? Who deserves my praise?*

- Today I will let silence do the heavy lifting. *What beneficial results might occur if I said less, listened more, and provided silence in which to think about what has (and has not) been said?*

MINERAL RIGHTS

One of the greatest gifts we can give another is the purity of our attention. To mine for greater clarity, improved understanding, and impetus for change, ask your partner to do the following and listen carefully to the responses.

Step 1: **Identify your most pressing issue.**

Step 2: **Clarify the issue.**

Step 3: **Determine the current impact.**

Step 4: **Determine the future implications.**

Step 5: **Examine your personal contribution to this issue.**

Step 6: **Describe the ideal outcome.**

Step 7: **Commit to action.**

QUESTIONS FOR ONE-TO-ONES

The following questions offer useful fuel for discussions with colleagues and direct reports.

1. What has become clear since last we met?

2. What is the area that, if you made an improvement, would give you and others the greatest return on time, energy, and dollars invested?

3. What is currently impossible to do that, if it were possible, would change everything?

4. What are you trying to make happen in the next three months?

5. What's the most important decision you're facing? What's keeping you from making it?

6. What topic are you hoping I won't bring up?

7. What area under your responsibility are you most satisfied with? least satisfied with?

8. What part of your responsibilities are you avoiding right now?

9. Who are your strongest employees? What are you doing to ensure that they're happy and motivated?

10. Who are your weakest employees? What is your plan for them?

11. What conversations are you avoiding right now?

12. What do you wish you had more time to do?

13. What things are you doing that you would like to stop doing or delegate to someone else?

14. If you were hired to consult with our company, what would you advise?

15. If you were competing against our company, what would you do?

16. What threatens your peace? What threatens the business? your health? your personal fulfillment?

THE DECISION TREE

The decision tree is a tool for delegation and professional development. You know employees are growing and developing when more and more of their decisions are moved to the leaf level.

Leaf Decisions: Make the decision. Act on it. Do not report the action you took.

Branch Decisions: Make the decision. Act on it. Report the action you took daily, weekly, or monthly.

Trunk Decisions: Make the decision. Report your decision before you take action.

Root Decisions: Make the decision jointly, with input from many people.

PREPARING AN ISSUE FOR DISCUSSION

Preparing your presentation of an issue helps prevent incoherent or incomplete explanations of the problem. Additionally, your team members appreciate good use of their time. At the top of the appreciation list is the accurate identification of the problem.

THE ISSUE IS:
Be concise. In one or two sentences, get to the heart of the problem. Is it a concern, challenge, opportunity, or recurring problem that is becoming more troublesome?

IT IS SIGNIFICANT BECAUSE:
What's at stake? How does this affect dollars, income, people, products, services, customers, family, timing, the future, or other relevant factors? What is the future impact if the issue is not resolved?

MY IDEAL OUTCOME IS:
What specific results do I want?

RELEVANT BACKGROUND INFORMATION:
Summarize with bulleted points: How, when, why, and where did the issue start? Who are the key players? Which forces are at work? What is the issue's current status?

WHAT I HAVE DONE UP TO THIS POINT:
What have I done so far? What options am I considering?

THE HELP I WANT FROM THE GROUP IS:
What result do I want from the group? For example, alternative solutions, confidence regarding the right decision, identification of consequences, where to find more information, critique of the current plan.

THE CONFRONTATION MODEL

This model allows us to confront tough issues with courage, compassion, and skill. Learning is provoked and relationships are enriched.

OPENING STATEMENT:

Write your opening statement and practice saying it out loud, in sixty seconds or less. Your opening statement should:

1. Name the issue.

2. Select a specific example that illustrates the behavior or situation you want to change.

3. Describe your emotions about this issue.

4. Clarify what is at stake.

5. Identify your contribution to this problem.

6. Indicate your wish to resolve the issue.

7. Invite your partner to respond.

INTERACTION:

8. Inquire into your partner's views. Use paraphrasing and a perception check. Dig for full understanding; don't be satisfied with the surface. Make sure your partner knows that you fully understand and acknowledge his or her position and interests.

RESOLUTION:

9. What have we learned? Where are we now? Has anything been left unsaid that needs saying? What is needed for resolution? How can we move forward from here, given our new understanding?

10. Make a new agreement and determine how you will hold each other responsible for keeping it.

Index

Fierce Tools and Assessments

Fierce Factor Organizational Tendencies

DIRECTIONS

Circle the number which most closely represents your organization's tendency
(1 = the description on the left is most accurate, 10 = the description on the right is most accurate)

Focus on activities. On reasons why it is not possible to reach individual or team goals. Stalled initiatives.	1 2 3 4 5 6 7 8 9 10	Focus on results. Deep-seated accountability. Initiatives executed.
Beating around the bush, dancing around the subject, skirting the issues. No one engages. Nothing changes.	1 2 3 4 5 6 7 8 9 10	An open culture which identifies and addresses issues truthfully and effectively. Generating the best decisions for the organization.
An "us versus them", "me versus you" culture. Politics, turf wars, competition for resources and attention.	1 2 3 4 5 6 7 8 9 10	High levels of alignment, collaboration, partnership at all levels throughout the organization, and the healthier financial performance that results from it.
Reacting to and recuperating from poorly thought-out conversations.	1 2 3 4 5 6 7 8 9 10	Engaging in effective, consequential conversations that resolve tough challenges.
Leaders micro-managing versus leading. No grass roots leadership development.	1 2 3 4 5 6 7 8 9 10	Effective coaching and delegation. Development of quality "bench" to fill future leadership positions.
A relationship with customers and employees based solely on price and salary. Difficulty maintaining margins.	1 2 3 4 5 6 7 8 9 10	Relationships with customers and employees that extend beyond price. Customers and employees are engaged on an emotional level.
Original thinking is happening elsewhere. Sleepwalking through the manual.	1 2 3 4 5 6 7 8 9 10	Shared enthusiasm for agility, continued learning and epiphanies; shared standard of performance.
A culture of terminal "niceness." Avoiding or working around problem employees. Tolerating mediocrity.	1 2 3 4 5 6 7 8 9 10	Effectively confronting attitudinal, performance or behavioral issues and creating impetus for change.

FIERCE FACTOR SCORE

Interpretation of Organizational Tendencies

8 - 10	Crisis – This organization is on an extremely dangerous trajectory. Immediate action is needed.
11 - 20	Serious attention is needed.
21 - 30	Organization is stifled.
31 - 40	This organization may be surviving, however, it's in no danger of thriving.
41 - 50	Organization is comfortable, and may lack any impetus to change.
51 - 60	Doing all right and plenty of room to improve.
61 - 70	Organization is performing close to its potential.
71 - 80	Is this organization on the "Best Places to Work" List?

Fierce Factor Personal Beliefs

DIRECTIONS

Circle the number which most closely represents your beliefs
(1 = the description on the left is most accurate, 10 = the description on the right is most accurate)

Disclosing my real thoughts and feelings is risky.	1 2 3 4 5 6 7 8 9 10	Disclosing what I really think and feel frees up energy and expands possibilities.
Most people can't handle the truth, so it's better not to say anything.	1 2 3 4 5 6 7 8 9 10	Though I have trouble handling the truth sometimes, I'll keep telling it and inviting it from others.
It's important that I convince others that my point of view is correct.	1 2 3 4 5 6 7 8 9 10	Exploring multiple points of view will lead to better decisions.
I will gain approval and promotions by exchanging my personal identity for my organization's identity.	1 2 3 4 5 6 7 8 9 10	My personal identity will be expanded as my colleagues and I exchange diverse points of view.
I will gain approval and promotions by exchanging my personal identity for my organization's identity.	1 2 3 4 5 6 7 8 9 10	Perhaps we can change reality with thoughtful conversations.
As an expert, my job is to dispense advice.	1 2 3 4 5 6 7 8 9 10	My job is to involve people in the problems and strategies affecting them.
I'll keep my mouth shut; this is a job for the experts.	1 2 3 4 5 6 7 8 9 10	My point of view is as valid as anyone else's
I need to ignore what I'm feeling in my gut; just put my head down and do my job.	1 2 3 4 5 6 7 8 9 10	I know what I know; and what I know, I need to act on.

FIERCE FACTOR SCORE [   ]

Interpretation of Personal Beliefs

8 - 10	Crisis – A culture of fear is deeply entrenched in this organization. Immediate action is needed.
11 - 20	Serious – Fear is a major dynamic, employees are discouraged and retention of high performers is likely to be a formidable problem.
21 - 30	Stifled – Helplessness is a present factor. Talent and energy are bleeding from the organization.
31 - 40	Tolerable (barely) – People show up physically but are apathetic mentally and emotionally.
41 - 50	Comfortable – People are nice, things get done, but there is little "spark" to take things to the next level.
51 - 60	Satisfactory – People are striving towards performance and occasional strokes of genius appear.
61 - 70	Great – People are engaged, energetic and innovative. This is fertile ground for exceptional results.
71 - 80	Excellent – Now just look out for headhunters because you've got a good thing going.

Principles I Will Focus on for the Next 30 Days

....

....

....

....

....

....

....

....

Commitments & Thought Starters

- Today I will master the courage to interrogate reality.
  What reality at home or at work most needs interrogating?

- Today I will come out from behind myself into my conversations
  and make them real. I will speak of the things that are on
  my mind and in my heart, including those that seem risky or
  unattractive. Where and with whom am I failing to show up
  authentically?

- Today I will be here, prepared to be nowhere else. Who would
  benefit from my undivided attention? Perhaps it is myself.

- Today I will tackle my toughest challenge.
  What conversation am I dodging? What issue am I avoiding?

- Today I will obey my instincts. I will take time to deliberate, and
  when the time to speak arrives, I will share what I am thinking.
  What messages have been beckoning me?

- Today I will take responsibility for my emotional wake.
  To whom do I need to apologize? Who deserves my praise?

- Today I will let silence do the heavy lifting. What beneficial results
  might occur if I said less, listened more, and provided silence in
  which to think about what has (and has not) been said?

Personal Action Plan (conversations I need to have)

NAME	TOPIC
....	....
	....
....	....
	....
....	....
	....
....	....
	....
....	....
	....
....	....
	....
....	....
	....
....	....
	....
....	....
	....
....	....
	....

Top 5 Goals

When your goals are clear, the necessary conversations also become clear. They may be the conversations you've been avoiding at home or at work, the topics that need to be addressed and resolved in order for you to move forward.

EXAMPLE

Goal 1 Clarify and re-vitalize my career trajectory

by when   90 days

conversation(s) Bob (my boss)

topic   My career ambitions, in particular my desire to prove myself a worthy candidate for the position of _____.

Goal 2 Wake up my marriage

by when   Immediately!!!

conversation(s) Jane (my wife)

topic   We're both so busy. We haven't spent much time together or had many laughs lately. I'm worried that our relationship is becoming stale. How do we resolve the challenges of our busy lives and create quality time together?

Goal 3 Decide whether Paul goes or stays

by when   30 days

conversation(s) Paul (my direct report)

topic   His performance has really slipped. I no longer feel I can rely on him to get things done. The stakes are high for him, for me, for our department. I'd like to resolve this.

Goal 4 Achieve our quarterly goals

by when   The end of the quarter

conversation(s) My team

topic   Progress is too slow regarding the initiative for which we're responsible. We need to openly discuss a sensitive, core challenge that we must resolve before everything else can fall into place. I want to schedule a "tank" so we can work through these issues together.

Goal 5 Become a better person

by when   Starting now!

conversation(s) Myself, then those close to me

topic   I'm not feeling so good about the emotional wake I've been leaving at work and at home. I intend to make it positive from now on. What do I need to know about what others need most from me going forward?

Now, it's your turn...

My Top 5 Goals

Write down your top 5 personal and professional goals for the next 30-90 days

....
Goal 1
       by when
  conversation(s)
        topic

....
Goal 2
       by when
  conversation(s)
        topic

....
Goal 3
       by when
  conversation(s)
        topic

....
Goal 4
       by when
  conversation(s)
        topic

....
Goal 5
       by when
  conversation(s)
        topic

10 Questions

As you answer these questions, what conversations do they suggest? With whom? When will you have them?

1. What one experience do I most want to have in my life?

Conversation with ....

Topic ....

By When ....

2. What do I most want to accomplish in my professional life?

Conversation with ....

Topic ....

By When ....

3. Who deserves praise or recognition from me?

Conversation with ....

Topic ....

By When ....

4. Who deserves an apology from me?

Conversation with ....

Topic ....

By When ....

5. If I could advise the CEO of my organization, what would I advise him/her?

Conversation with ....

Topic ....

By When ....

6. **What idea would I like to share with my boss and colleagues that could improve the way we get things done?**

    Conversation with ....

    Topic ....

    By When ....

7. **If I could improve one relationship at work, which one would I improve?**

    Conversation with ....

    Topic ....

    By When ....

8. **If I could improve one relationship in my personal life, which one would I improve?**

    Conversation with ....

    Topic ....

    By When ....

9. **If I could receive coaching from time to time, whom would I select as my coach?**

    Conversation with ....

    Topic ....

    By When ....

10. **What is the conversation that I have been putting off for days, weeks, months, years? What reasons have I given myself for not having it?**

    Conversation with ....

    Topic ....

    By When ....

Personal Integrity Scan

Clarify and write down your core values. Pay attention to each word you
consider. Maybe there's only one word or phrase that rings true for you. That's fine.
Write it down.

My Core Values

....

....

....

....

Now Run an Integrity Scan

Is my behavior out of alignment with my values in the workplace?
In a personal relationship? In my life? Are there integrity outages?
If so, where and what are they?

Integrity Outage in My Workplace

....
What must I do to clean it up?
....
When am I going to do this?
....

Integrity Outage in a Personal Relationship

....
What must I do to clean it up?
....
When am I going to do this?
....

Integrity Outage in My Life

....
What must I do to clean it up?
....
When am I going to do this?
....

Fierce Leadership Excerpt

Fierce Practice #3

From Holding People Accountable to Modeling Accountability and Holding People Able

It often happens that I wake up at night and begin to think about a serious problem and decide I must tell the Pope about it. Then I wake up completely and remember that I am the Pope.

- POPE JOHN XXIII

Out there in the real world, freedom means you have to admit authorship, even when your story turns out to be a stinker.

- STEVE TOLTZ, *A FRACTION OF THE WHOLE*

I recall hearing the true story of a pilot who landed just short of the runway in San Francisco. Luckily, no one was seriously injured, but the plane ended up partially in the water. When he was hauled to the official inquisition and asked how such a thing could have happened, he faced the battalion of lawyers and industry experts and said, "I messed up." End of statement.

Most of us would be stunned (and/or amused) to hear responses like that in business today. After all, when was the last time someone in your organization (maybe it was you) asked, "Who's accountable for this disaster?" and someone rushed forward, arms outstretched, shouting,"It was me! Hold ME accountable! I'm the one!"

Instead, we point the finger. *He, she, they, it did it! It wasn't me.* As Steve Toltz wrote in *A Fraction of the Whole*, "The great thing about blame is that she goes wherever you send her, no questions asked."

The words "I'm holding you accountable" are spoken thousands of times a day around the world during meetings, on the phone, in hallways to individuals, teams, and, yes, teenagers. And my thought is always *Good luck with that.*

Don't get me wrong. Accountability is a big deal, one of the rarest, most precious commodities to be found. Next to human connectivity, accountability is the single most powerful, most desired, yet least understood characteristic of a successful human being and a successful environment. The long-term benefits of personal accountability have enormous implications for the quality of our lives, and there is certainly a direct correlation between a company's health and well-being and the degree of accountability displayed by its employees.

Why, then, in a study by the Table Group, did 80 percent of 132 executive teams score "red," or poor, on accountability? And why are our efforts to improve the level of accountability in organizations so ineffective?

It's because we're so busy trying to find out who is accountable that we forget to check the one place we should be looking: in the mirror.

Common wisdom tells us that powerful partnerships require that we ...

1. understand needs;
2. clarify expectations;
3. collaborate on solutions; and
4. meet commitments.

Let's acknowledge that few of us are good at all of these steps, particularly the last one, and our efforts are further complicated because we don't understand what accountability really is, how it differs from responsibility, why it shows up, why it disappears, and what it really requires.

The purpose of this chapter is to address these issues and to provide a game plan for creating a performance culture that values initiative, problem solving, agility, risk taking, and a bias toward action. A company filled to the brim with individuals who, instead of laying blame, willingly and gladly accept accountability for everything that's got their name on it. Given challenges, they ask themselves, what am I going to do? The answer isn't" duck and cover." They step up to the task and hold others able to do the same,

Before we dive in, to get you thinking, write down your answers to the following questions:

What is an example of an issue confronting you or your team that is made worse by a failure of accountability?

_____

_____

_____

What results is this causing?

_____

_____

_____

What about an example in your personal life?

_____

_____

_____

What results is this causing?

_____

_____

_____

Who's Accountable?

Though you may be clear with others regarding due dates for deliverables, there are inevitably going to be problems, snags, bumps, obstacles, delays. People get busy, waylaid, a colleague doesn't do his or her part, a vendor is late with a shipment, a personal emergency (a sick child, toxic mold in the house, an injury to the family dog) derails a key member of the team.

And, too often, we give people more work than they can handle effectively, hold them accountable for getting it all done, and express frustration when they present us with a list of very good reasons for their failure to deliver. Maybe the package was mistakenly shipped to Ankora, when it was supposed to go to Anchorage. (As we speak,

Fierce Leadership Excerpt

someone in the Niger inner delta region is trying to figure out what to do with six pallets of advanced therapy moisture lotion,)

As we speak, someone in the Niger inner delta region is trying to figure out what to do with six pallets of advanced therapy moisture lotion.

The point is, when something like this happens, our knee-jerk response is often "I want to know who's accountable for this!" And the automatic reply? "Not me!"

I remember working with a team of high potentials at a global shoe manufacturer. At one point, the founder of the company, a tall, imposing figure, walked into the room and sat in the back. I had just begun to explore the notion of accountability with the team when he stood and thundered, "What I want to know is, if we take a successful store manager and move him into a territory that's struggling, and nothing improves, who's accountable- the manager or the person who moved him?"

In other words, who will receive my wrath? At which point, forty intelligent people-the future leaders of his company-did their best to shrink their subatomic particles and vanish from his radar .

Why? Because most of us associate accountability with blame, culpability, being responsible, being wrong, maybe even being fired. In fact, we'd likely define accountability as "clarity about whose head will roll when things go wrong." Given that *accountability* conjures the image of a firing squad without benefit of blindfold or last meal of Frito-Lays and Milk Duds (*I admit to strange and powerful cravings*), no wonder we don't eagerly raise our hands when we hear the question, "Who is accountable?" Instead, we insist that he, she, it, they did it to us!

And it's no wonder. Deflecting blame seems to be in our DNA!

A marvelous example is Koko, one of the world's most famous gorillas, known for mastering more than one thousand words in American Sign Language and, in doing so, helping to overturn preconceptions about the limits of animal intelligence. One day Koko broke one of her toys (the act was captured on video), The next day one of her trainers came in, picked up the broken toy, and asked, "Koko, what happened to your toy?"

Koko promptly pointed to the assistant trainer. True story!

Non Est Mea Culpa

Humans, including those in high places, often employ a slightly more sophisticated version of pointing. Take a statement from Attorney General Alberto Gonzales's attempt to exonerate himself from any accountability regarding the firing of U.S. attorneys: "I acknowledge that mistakes were made here."

With those words, Attorney General Alberto Gonzales was using a technique often thought to be a politician's best friend: the passive voice. Why is this technique so popular? Because the passive voice takes accountability out of the picture. Think about it. "Mistakes were made." There is no actor in this sentence. Why won't those pesky mistakes quit making themselves!

Passive voice has so cheapened the concept of a mea culpa that various officials in government hearings and press conferences actually seem to be proud of themselves when they acknowledge that "mistakes were made."

Wouldn't it be refreshing to hear an official say, "I blew it"? After fainting from shock, most people would admire that candor and maybe trust that the same mistake would not be made again. Think about how President Obama's candid admissions of error early in his administration bolstered his popularity, rather than harmed it. YouTube features a clip titled "Obama on Daschle: I Made a Mistake," and several other clips in which President Obama models the kind of personal accountability and candor we crave in our leaders today. But let's not hold our breath that everyone will embrace this behavior, wedded as so many are to the passive voice. A duck and dodge if ever there was one.

What we want to know is what mistakes were made and who made them? Please don't give us the generic *they*—as in "They didn't handle this correctly." Which actual human beings had their hands all over this? Give us a name. Was it you? And what exactly is going to be done to correct this and ensure it doesn't happen again?

In one 9 *Chickweed Lane* comic strip (rendered by Brooke McEldowney, my favorite cartoonist) the character Thorax, who sells strange goods and services from roadside stands when he isn't ruminating on his alien origins or dusting off the quantum anomaly in the tractor shed, sits at a roadside stand with a sign reading: REPUDIATIONS R US. He explains to Edda, another character:

> Being as it is election season, I have started up a denial consultancy. While the candidates and the news media uncork their relentless gush of allegations and accusations, I stand ready to provide custom tailored denials for every occasion. I have a new spring line of stout denials, categorical denials, unwavering denials, firm denials, swift denials, flat denials, emphatic denials, steadfast denials, outraged denials and, as summer approaches, a few angry denunciations with matching counter-accusations.

Funny and sad and true.

Of course, failings in accountability happen everywhere, not just in politics. Personally, I'd like someone to explain why Hollywood produces so many lousy movies, why I'm put on hold while a recorded message assures me that my call is important, why hosts of quilting shows sound like they're talking to three year-olds, why I can only use my hard-earned frequent-flier miles to go to places I don't want to visit at the most inconvenient times imaginable while sitting in the last coach seat next to the toilets, why doctors with whom I have appointments think nothing of making me wait for hours, and why there still isn't a cure for the common cold. A real cure. Whom can I hold accountable for all of THAT?

> I have a new spring line of stout denials, categorical denials, unwavering denials, firm denials, swift denials, flat denials, emphatic denials, steadfast denials, outraged denials and, as summer approaches, a few angry denunciations with matching counter-accusations.
> – Brooke McEldowney, 9 *Chickweed Lane*

And while I'm at it, to my knowledge, no individual or group has claimed culpability for the collapse of investment banks, the escalating price of gas, the failure to alert residents of Myanmar of the approaching cyclone that took the lives of one hundred thousand people, or the CIA's destruction of ninety-two interrogation videos. And will someone please tell me why Bernie Madoff did not receive swifter justice, once it was known that he had put thousands of people who trusted him in serious financial straits?

The point is: Are failures of accountability happening in your organization, in *your* life—perhaps including how you've handled or mishandled your own financial matters? (Bernie is a rat, in my opinion, but what might you have done differently?)

Before we identify the "tells" and talk about what to do, consider two competing ideas:

The progress of my organization depends on my leaders, colleagues, and customers.

or . . .

In a very real sense, the progress of my organization depends on my progress as an individual now.

To which of these beliefs do you subscribe?

One of the reasons so many of us fail to "succeed," by whatever definition we may choose, is that we believe in the first idea. In other words, we believe someone else is running the show, that our progress depends on our bosses and how they treat us, on our colleagues and how talented and helpful they are or aren't, on corporate politics, on customers and whether they have the capacity to understand why they require our products or services, on our spouses or life partners and the degree to which we do or do not feel appreciated and supported by them. And despite whatever therapy we may have endured, we still lay accountability for our progress, or the lack thereof, on our parents' doorsteps, on the degree to which our parents equipped us with all good things throughout our childhoods or messed us up forever.

This attitude certainly makes for a well-protected ego with built-in excuses for just about every eventuality. It allows us to take credit for the good stuff, but when results aren't so good, well, in that case it's not about us; it's about him, her, them, or it. We're merely

We're doing the best we can, but really, one can hardly expect us to overcome the pull of the moon.

well-intentioned jellyfish, buffeted by things beyond our control, carried this way and that by the waves, the tides, the politics, the marketplace, the economy, the budget. We're doing the best we can, but really, one can hardly expect us to overcome the pull of the moon.

On the other hand, if someone asked if we considered ourselves a victim, we'd say, "No way! I'm a powerful person, and for your information, my organization recognizes me as a high potential!"

Well, hang in there for a minute or two. Have you ever said any of the following things? Or thought them?

- My department is struggling because the strategy is flawed.

- I'm behind because so-and-so (or such-and-such) is a bottleneck.

- Our industry is suffering because the margins are tight, our unions are threatening to strike, our competition has forced us into a price war, and our customers have unreasonable expectations.

- Our problem? The price of oil! The board of directors, et cetera.

- We can't get this done without the right technology.

- I haven't been able to focus on this project because I have ADD. (*Have you noticed that some people aren't complaining when they tell you they have ADD? They're bragging!*)

I often speak at functions focused on women in leadership, offering my thoughts about what needs to happen for women to step into and remain in senior leadership roles: In 2005, when I read the Catalyst Census of Women Corporate Officers and Top Earners of the Fortune 500, I was appalled. Apparently, according to the women surveyed, the three significant barriers they face that men rarely do are

1. gender-based stereotyping;
2. exclusion from informal networks; and
3. lack of role models.

This was not the appalling part. It was the solution offered: Not that women should work to defy gender stereotypes, or make efforts to include themselves in informal networks, or strive to be better role models for their peers and for future generations of women. No, it was that companies should mandate diversity and inclusion, because clearly companies are to blame for the barriers facing women. Where's the accountability here?

I'm not suggesting that these barriers don't exist. The glass ceiling is still very real in many industries, and sadly, gender discrimination in the workplace still exists. But what appalled me was how quick the women surveyed were to deny any accountability for the struggles they face. After all, no doubt all three of those conditions existed for Madeleine Albright when she began her stint in the White House as a secretary. Lots of people wondered how "Maddie" went from secretary to secretary of state. Albright's answer: *"By doing whatever I was asked to do, including making a pot of coffee, to the best of my ability. I made the best coffee to be found!"*

Still, many women play the victim, blaming their flatlined careers on the company, society, the world. And then they wonder why things aren't improving. Accountability has to start from within.

For example, I agree with the female director of data management in a financial firm who suggests that where many women fail is in not being specific about their career aspirations with the people who are in a position to point them in the right direction. Not taking the time to reflect or network to understand what's out there for which they might have exactly what is needed. Not actively seeking candid feedback to learn what qualities and capabilities would make them a viable candidate for a new role. And not taking the steps to work on those qualities and demonstrate their considerable talents, abilities, and willingness to learn.

So I confess that I'm not sympathetic when I hear women say things like, "Me, well, the truth is, I don't have a real shot at the top because:

. . . relationships are formed on the golf course, and I'm not a golfer."
. . . I have young kids at home and can't put in the eighty-hour workweeks it takes to get ahead around here."
. . . so-and-so is plotting and scheming for the position I want, and I just won't play those games."

   ... frankly, why would I want a so-called promotion! Those guys
     in the C suite are miserable. I want to enjoy my weekends."

   ... people don't listen to me because I'm a woman."

I hear this last one from women a lot, and I suspect the reason nobody listens to them is that they say things like that! In my view, the best
reasons are really just the worst excuses.

Years ago, a woman who reported to me complained frequently
that she hadn't closed any sales because customers weren't returning
her calls. I finally said, "Then make yourself the kind of person whose
phone calls get returned!" She was shocked, hurt, angry. But starting
the next day, her phone calls got returned, and she soon became our top
salesperson. In other words, she did something differently. She changed,
not the customers.

I see victim tells all the time. For example, at some point during
every *Fierce Conversations* training, someone will say something like, "I
would love to have amazing conversations like this in my company. It
would be fantastic. But our leadership and our culture wouldn't support
this level of candor."

This statement, this belief is a huge tell. Among other things, it indicates that we don't have a leader here. We may have a potential leader
and very likely a delightful person, just not a leader. We have a victim.
Someone who tells him- or herself and others, *"I can't be myself here,"*
when actually, a more honest statement would be *"Right now, I'm choosing not to muster the courage, will, skill, energy, focus...whatever...needed
to do or say what needs doing or saying."*

So if I'm in the room when someone says they can't have fierce conversations because their culture won't support it, I usually say, "Where
is this so-called culture with which you're unhappy? Is it out there
somewhere? Or is every person in your orga-
nization, including you, a walking hologram
of the culture? As I look at you right now, I
am looking at the culture!" The point is, the
culture is not some nebulous and mysterious force out there somewhere. *You* are the culture. *I* am the culture. And each of us shapes

You are the culture. **I** am the culture.

that culture each time we walk into a room, pick up the phone, send an e-mail.

Fierce leaders know that they influence the culture one conversation at a time, responding honestly or guardedly when asked what they think. Since you are the culture, you go first! And don't point your finger at leadership-unless you ARE the leadership.

My visual for this:

WHO CAN FIX THE PROBLEMS?
(in the world. in a company. in a family)

x

ATTACH SMALL MIRROR HERE

Revisiting the two competing ideas, remember that in a very real sense, the progress of your organization depends on your progress as an individual now.

So what about the *now* part?

My thought used to be something on the order of *Look, here's the thing. I'm shoehorned into my calendar, got a to-do list that feels impossible! So how 'bout if I focus on some personal development next quarter, next year, when I have a little time?*

That was me not getting it. And then I remembered something a friend said: "Unconsciously, we're always choosing deep growth or slow death. And sometimes sudden death." A bit dramatic, but I got it. *I* was choosing excuses, practicing victim.

So I'm reminding myself and you, the reader, that *now* is where it happens. Great stories, great changes, great results—those fatal moments, events, choices, conversations that put in place something irreversible—turn on *now*.

End of Excerpt.

our foundational workshop

What gets talked about in an organization and how it gets talked about determines what will happen.

Or won't.

Based on the principles of Susan Scott's best-seller, *"Fierce Conversations: Achieving Success at Work & in Life, One Conversation at a Time"* this foundational, hands-on workshop will introduce you to transformational ideas and principles that will shift your basic understanding of conversations and the power they hold in leadership, relationships and results.

You'll learn to master team conversations, coaching conversations, delegation conversations and confrontation conversations—all essential to your individual and collective success.

To learn more about Fierce Conversations' and our other programs, go to www.fierceinc.com

Buy Susan's bestseller,
Fierce Leadership,
at amazon.com, bn.com
or borders.com

any conversation can.
www.fierceinc.com

our other programs

fierce LEADERSHIP®

We call them "best" practices, but are they? In this workshop, participants will gain the skill set needed to identify their worst "best" practices, learn a model to effectively communicate the need for change, and create an actionable plan that ensures all practices are aligned with organizational success.

fierce ACCOUNTABILITY®

At Fierce, we believe that our context (beliefs, attitudes, opinions, "truths") determines how we experience the content of our lives. In this workshop, participants recognize the cost of blaming, protecting, defending and playing it safe and develop a new context about accountability, one in which they welcome responsibility.

fierce NEGOTIATIONS®

Fierce negotiators learn how to enrich the relationship while steering the negotiations to a successful outcome as opposed to the compromises that are often the result of traditional "win-win" negotiations. Participants will also gain hands-on experience and explore traditional practices of negotiating so they are properly equipped to identify and respond to common tactics.

fierce GENERATIONS®

The stakes are higher than ever to better manage, motivate, recruit, and retain a diverse, multi-generational workforce. This workshop cracks the inter-generational code. Understanding what each generation thinks, values and desires is critical for a collaborative and successful work environment.

About Fierce, Inc.

Fierce, Inc. is a leadership development and training company that develops conversation as a skill to drive measurable results for business and education. Our award-winning training has helped clients worldwide achieve higher levels of alignment, engagement, collaboration, partnership and accountability throughout their organizations. In addition, Fierce principles and methods are:

Results-Oriented. Experiential training that leads to measurable ROI, improved engagement and successful outcomes.

Flexible. Leadership development and training tailored to your organization, available in instructor-led and online delivery methods.

Universal. Principles and methods that translate across the globe, throughout your organization, from the frontline to boardroom.

Immediate. Practical, easy-to-learn skills that can be applied immediately.

Fierce, Inc. is home to multiple training offerings including Fierce Conversations®, Fierce Leadership®, Fierce Accountability®, Fierce Negotiations®, and Fierce Generations®. Its founder, Susan Scott, is the author of two national bestsellers: *Fierce Conversations – Achieving Success at Work & in Life, One Conversation at a Time* and *Fierce Leadership – A Bold Alternative to the Worst "Best" Practices of Business Today.* For inquiries about keynote talks, online delivery methods and our services, please visit our website: **www.fierceinc.com**.